Strategic Management and Organizational Decision Making

Strategic Management and Organizational Decision Making

Alan Walter Steiss
Virginia Polytechnic Institute
and State University

Lexington Books
D.C. Heath and Company/Lexington, Massachusetts/Toronto

Library of Congress Cataloging in Publication Data
Steiss, Alan Walter.
  Strategic management and organizational decision making.

  Includes index.
  1. Corporate planning. 2. Decision-making. I. Title.
HD30.28.S728   1985   658.4'012   85-40319
ISBN 0-669-10965-7 (alk. paper)

Published simultaneously in Canada
Printed in the United States of America on acid-free paper
International Standard Book Number: 0-669-10965-7
Library of Congress Catalog Card Number: 85-40319

Contents

Figures

Tables

Preface

The concept of strategic management is being applied with increasing frequency in both the private and public sectors. However, much of the literature in the field is either limited to corporate applications or builds on the more traditional process of comprehensive public planning. This book seeks common denominators among these areas of application, while attempting to identify generic principles that may be useful in any complex organization.

Strategic management involves the process whereby goals and objectives are identified, policies are formulated, and strategies are selected in order to achieve the overall purposes or mission of an organization. In this presentation, strategic management is viewed in systemic terms, consisting of three component processes: strategic planning, resource management, and control and evaluation.

This book is designed to address the needs of managers and planners at several levels within any complex organization. Top management should find the chapters on decision making, strategic planning, financial planning and cost analysis, and information systems particularly useful. Middle management personnel should draw important insights from the chapters on resource management, budgeting procedures, management control, and managerial accounting. Anyone seeking to develop more effective management processes that are responsive to changing conditions in our complex society should find this book a most useful addition in their understanding of these processes.

1
Strategic Management

S trategic management is the process by which policies are formulated and strategies are selected in an effort to achieve the goals and objectives of an organization. In this process, attention must be given to both *external strategy* and *internal capability*. An interface is provided between the performance capacity of an organization and the opportunities and challenges it must face in the broader environment. Strategic management offers a framework by which an organization can adapt to the vagaries of an unpredictable environment and an uncertain future. It seeks to determine a long-range direction and is concerned with relating organizational resources to opportunities in the larger environment. Strategic management includes all the activities that lead to the definition of goals, objectives, and strategies, and to the development of plans, actions, and policies to accomplish these strategic objectives for the total organization.

The Scientification of Management

Various analytical approaches have come and gone in recent years, leaving behind fragmented sets of techniques that have found selective applications—and in some cases, misapplications—in the management of complex organizations. Meanwhile, practitioners and academics have refined these techniques, often rendering them either innocuous and hence more palatable to administrators, or so elaborate and esoteric that they are useful only in the context of full-blown academic research. As Bruce H. De Woolfson has observed: "At different times and in different places, different management systems are in vogue. Some of these systems represent real innovations; more often someone 'reinvents the wheel.' "[1] A brief review of some of these more systematic approaches should provide a better perspective to the conceptual framework of strategic management.

Systems Analysis: Panacea or Pearly Pachyderm?

During the late 1950s and early 1960s, systems analysis was offered as a cure-all to a wide array of organizational problems. Systems analysis often is associated with such people as Robert McNamara and Charles Hitch and with organizations such as the Rand Corporation. Emerging from the highly technical field of systems engineering, the concept of systems analysis often evokes images of high-speed computers, large-scale mathematical models, multidisciplinary teams of military strategists, and elaborate cost-benefit analyses.

None of these factors, however, is essential for successful systems analysis. *Systems analysis* has evolved as a generic term that can be applied to any explicit, theoretical, or deductive approach to problem solving. Thus, in some cases a good systems analysis can be performed by a single individual doing some elementary calculations on a scratch pad, without once mentioning costs or benefits. Such an individual, of course, would have to apply some criteria for the evaluation of alternative solutions to the problem at hand. Herein lies the key to systems analysis, the systematic identification and evaluation of feasible alternatives designed to accomplish organizational goals and objectives.

Equally important is the *information base* that may lead to the design of additional alternatives. A thorough and imaginative analysis may result in major modifications to the initial objectives. Thus, systems analysis is a dynamic process; as the problem unfolds through analysis, the desired solution or *objective function* may undergo a number of redefinitions based on the new information brought to light by the analysis. The systematic evaluation of alternatives is also a major focus of strategic management.

Systems analysis is concerned with the future—often the more distant future. As a consequence, the environment is often one of uncertainty. This is an important facet of the problem that should be recognized and treated explicitly from the outset. Quantitative methods often must be supplemented by qualitative analysis. The importance of good qualitative work in systems analysis and the use of appropriate combinations of quantitative and qualitative methods cannot be overemphasized.

Two additional elements are worth noting in applications of systems analysis to real-world problems. The first—which should perhaps head the entire list—is the need to address the right problem in the first place. The second is the need to interpret results in terms of the real-world decision environment.

The precepts of systems analysis force attention on raising the right questions rather than merely finding the right answers. As Drucker has observed, "The important and difficult job is never to find the right answers, it is to find the right questions. For there are few things as useless, if not as dangerous, as the right answer to the wrong question."[2] Short-circuiting this stage of analysis usually means that more time will have to be spent later in identifying the real problem. Emotional bias, habitual or traditional behavior, or a tendency to seek the path of least resistance may lead to a superficial analysis, resulting in a statement of the apparent instead of the real problem. Even an excellent solution to an apparent, but nonexistent, problem will not work in practice.

Applications of systems analysis in business and industry, the military, and, more recently, government have been dominated by an efficiency orientation. In such applications, analysis follows a fairly mathematical pattern, involving relatively simple *operational* or *optimization* problems.[3] Such problems typically involve efforts to increase efficiency in situations where it is clear what "more efficient" means.

In many decision situations, however, such analytical techniques can only assist in solving elemental components of larger, more complex problems. Such problems usually involve more than merely the efficient allocation of resources among some clearly defined set of alternatives. These problems are not solvable in the same sense as those in which some "pay-off" function can be maximized in a clear expression of what is to be accomplished.

In these more complex situations, many factors may elude quantification, and it may not be totally clear what "more efficient" means. The difficulty often lies, therefore, in determining what ought to be done (planning), as well as in how to do it (management).

Critics assert that, at base, systems analysis is little more than a rather obvious, explicit, commonsense approach to problem solving. They suggest that systems analysis has been given an undue scientific aura through the use of mathematical models processed on high-speed computers. Critics argue that, all too often, the form of the analysis rather than the problem becomes the center of attention. In their rush to embrace more sophisticated techniques, both analysts and clients may lose sight of the main purpose of the analysis.

Even the best systems analysis, properly applied, has its limitations. Bad analysis, improperly applied, can be worse than useless. It is all too easy for the analyst to begin to believe his or her own assumptions, even if they are drawn out of thin air. Undue significance may be attached to analytical results especially if some sophisticated mathematics and much hard work are involved. Clients also may be too easily impressed by analyses, particularly if the results come out of computers and are agreeable or plausible and are impressively presented. Other clients may be skeptical for the wrong reasons—because the results contradict their own biases rather than because of questionable features of the analysis.

The analyst and the client must both accept responsibility for the interpretation and continuous testing of analytical results in terms of real-world problems. The explicit nature of systems analysis can expose deficiencies that might otherwise go unnoticed. Systems analysis can become a "white elephant," however, when analysts and clients expect more than it can provide, when they assume it to be a panacea or cure-all to complex organizational problems. Systems analysis cannot guarantee against the possibility of addressing the wrong problem or of approaching it in terms of the wrong objectives, alternative systems, measures of costs, or criterion of choice. Nor does the methods ensure that the results will be interpreted correctly.

Management Science

Management science is a generic term, encompassing various forms of systematic analysis and a variety of management practices designed to provide a more rational basis for organizational decision making. It involves the application of mathematical and related systems approaches to the solution of relatively large-scale management problems. Management science includes techniques for examining complex problems of choice under uncertainty. As such, management science has had extensive application and utility in dealing with critical issues in complex organizations.

Critics, however, are quick to point to limitations in the capacity of management science to incorporate intangibles into its mathematical orientation, that is, political, institutional, nonrational (but real), and other nonquantifiable and/or value-laden factors.[4] Both critics and supporters of management science agree that these techniques are applied most effectively where problem parameters and constraints can be identified with relative specificity and where objective functions are clearly defined.

Thus the road to rational decision making in complex organizations still has many potholes that must be repaired before the journey can be smooth. Unfortunately, the rational model often is oversold, and advocates may offer somewhat idealized definitions of rationality that leave them vulnerable to criticism.

Lindblom and others have pointed out that decision makers rarely face the clear-cut problem situations suggested by the rational model. Moreover, information about organizational problems often is scarce and therefore, expensive. Decisions makers seldom are willing or able to incur the high cost of data collection for the sake of complete rationality in their decisions.

Lindblom offers the concept of *disjointed incrementalism* as the basis for a countertheory to the rational model.[5] He argues that the only decision alternatives considered are those for which the consequences are known incrementally—those that vary only slightly from the status quo. Human ability to foresee the consequences of organizational decisions is so limited that objectives must be approached in small, manageable steps. Since the problems confronting the decision maker are continually redefined, incrementalism allows for countless ends-means and means-ends adjustments. And thus, problems are made more manageable. Most organizational decisions, therefore, are simply marginal adjustments to existing programs. The question of the ultimate desirability of most programs arises only occasionally.

The concept of disjointed incrementalism has a certain pragmatic appeal. It has been embraced by academics and practitioners in both the public and private sectors. Decisions under the incremental approach can be carried on with the knowledge that relatively few problems have to be solved once and for all. Since there is no one right solution to any given problem, the test of a good decision is that various analysts agree on it, without necessarily agreeing that the decision is the most appropriate (optimal) means to achieve an identified objective.[6]

Incremental decision making, however, is essentially remedial, geared more to the amelioration of present imperfections than to the promotion of long-range goals. Many problems brought before decision makers have no precedents. And therefore, such problems cannot be examined solely in terms of their incremental differences. More innovative solutions are required since incremental adjustments may only postpone the inevitable or may even exacerbate the problem. Unlike day-to-day operational decisions which can be corrected if the incremental approach proves wrong, more fundamental problems require strategic decisions, arrived at through a more rational approach. This is the decision environment that management science has sought to influence.

Policy Science: Supradiscipline or Collection of
Partial Theories?

The limitations of management science have led some scholars and practitioners to assert that it is inadequate for effective application to many of the complex issues confronting modern organizations. What is needed, they conclude, is something beyond management science, something that might be called "policy science."

Charles Rothwell suggests that policy "is a body of principles to guide action. The application of policy is a calculated choice—a decision to pursue specific goals by doing specific things."[7] According to Rothwell, the formulation and execution of policy usually involves four steps: (1) clarification of goals, (2) an exhaustive evaluation of the situation(s) to be met, (3) selection of a course of action by weighing the probable consequences of various alternatives, and (4) the determination of optimum means for carrying out the action decided upon. He concludes that, "since the situation to be met is normally not static but involves a complex of moving forces, policy and action are, in effect, a design to shape the future by exerting influence upon trends that flow from the past into the future."[8]

Systematic interpretations of policy often emphasize that analysis and evaluation are merely tools for augmenting professional judgment. E.S. Quade, for instance, maintains that the analysis of policy "implies the use of intuition and judgment and encompasses not only the examination of policy by decomposition into its components but also the design and synthesis of new alternatives."[9]

What are the foundations of policy science that set it apart from other related disciplines? Harold Lasswell asserts that, "The emphasis on *decision process* underlines the difference between policy science and other forms of intellectual activity. By focusing on the making and execution of policy, one identifies a relatively unique frame of reference, and utilizes many traditional contributions to political science, jurisprudence, and related disciplines."[10]

Many are skeptical about the future of policy science. As Horowitz and Katz observe, "Lasswell's idea of a 'science of policy making' has largely given way to a *de facto* operational view that because of the fragmentation of power the social scientist is primarily concerned with facts, while the policy makers are concerned primarily with the strategies necessary to implement desired legislation rather than social goals as a whole."[11] If the twain shall never meet, is there any real hope that policy science will emerge above the level of a collection of interesting partial theories?

The types of problems and issues that form the focus of policy are those which emerge from the *open system* characteristics of policy making in complex organizations. *Systems engineering* uses sets of fairly complex mathematical equations to describe the functioning of systems. Its applications, however, have been limited, for the most part, to closed physical systems. Proponents of policy science have concluded, therefore, that systems engineering as a field of study is fundamentally irrelevant to the further development of policy science.

In the early years, operations research was heralded as the fundamental and final solution to management decision-making requirements. Attempts were made to optimize large systems, and operations researchers were welcomed in the inner circles of top-level decision and policy making. Over time, however, the focus of operations research has shifted to more narrowly defined problems that are more amenable to its mathematical orientation and techniques. "Operations research analysts . . . backed down to those small and middle-sized problems that provided them with the relatively easier opportunities for demonstration of quick, measurable results—the 'gold-plucking' period."[12] More recently, however, operations researchers have again turned their attention to the problems of large, complex systems. Michael Radnor suggests that, "Policy science today speaks much like operations research of yesterday. One cannot help but suspect that unless its advocates are willing to learn from the experience of operations research, policy science will suffer a similar fate."[13]

The success of policy science in application, as contrasted to theory, will depend in large measure on how well its operational techniques and method-

ologies can serve the decision needs of top-level officials in our modern organizations. The general models of systems analysis and operations research
may provide a point of departure. However, the identification and measurement of certain key variables, especially those related to criteria for success
(objective functions), will constitute, prima facie, the most difficult obstacles
for the policy scientist.

In seeking to identify these key decision variables, more extensive and
creative search procedures must be adopted, going beyond the comparison of
easily recognized alternatives. It must be acknowledged that "the organization consists of a cybernetic system in which, therefore, not only do strategy
decisions determine structure, but also structure influences strategy and activities create structure."[14] Such recognition leads logically to a rejection of a
"top-down" model of organizational decision making. Rather, what is
required is an interactive model that deals explicitly with the contributions of
operational levels of management in policy making. Such an interactive
model is the framework for strategic management.

Organizational Strategy

The word *strategy* is derived from the Greek *strategos,* meaning "general." In
a military sense, strategy involves the planning and directing of battles or
campaigns on a broad scale, that is, the responsibility of the general. In this
context, strategy is distinguished from *tactics,* which involve the initiation of
actions to achieve more immediate objectives. In the business world, however, the term *strategy* often is used to refer to specific actions taken by a
manager to offset actual or potential actions of competitors. In a more general sense, an organizational strategy is any course of action used to achieve
major goals and objectives. Strategic decisions involve a determination of
broad directions and the development of comprehensive plans to attain those
directions. Richard Vancil has defined the concept of strategy as follows:

> The strategy of an organization . . . is a conceptualization expressed or
> implied by the organization's leader, of (1) the long-term objectives or pur-
> poses of the organization, (2) the broad constraints and policies . . . that cur-
> rently restrict the scope of the organization's activities, and (3) the current set
> of plans near-term goals that have been adopted in the expectation of con-
> tributing to the achievement of the organization's objectives.[15]

Strategy as a Field of Study

A number of significant advances made in the past decade in the theory of
strategy include (1) the comprehensive work in paradigm development by
Hofer and Schendel, (2) the identification of various levels of planning and

their interactions provided by Vancil and Lorange, and (3) the studies on "strategic issue management" and response strategies by Ansoff.[16] The ongoing research of Mintzberg related to the processes of strategy formulation[17] and the efforts of Schoeffler and others in the development and refinement of the Profit Impact of Market Strategies (PIMS) model[18] also are of importance. Developments in practice are more difficult to document, but articles from *Business Week, Fortune,* and other periodicals suggest that a variety of businesses and industries are now broadly applying the tools and techniques of strategic management.

Bourgeois has observed that "the strategy concept has its main value, for both profit-seeking and non-profit organizations, in determining how an organization defines its relationship to its environment in the pursuit of its objectives."[19] Most treatises on strategic management, however, focus on its application in a corporate setting. Few authors have extended the concept of strategy to more general applications in an organizational context, whether in the public or private sector. Summer's focus on strategic behavior in both government and business represents a pioneering effort in this regard.[20] Glueck provides a short section on strategy for nonprofit institutions.[21] However, most books on corporate strategy are largely silent regarding such applications. Selected case studies drawn from government, education, health care, and so forth, may be included in these books, but generally, the nonprofit sector represents a new and virtually untapped area for research in strategic management.

Planning, Management, and Control

Decision making is one of the most pervasive functions of management, whether in business or in government. If an organization is to achieve its objectives, decisions must be made, and action programs arising from these decisions must be implemented. Organizational decisions can be arrayed on a continuum, with *strategic decisions* at one end and *tactical decisions* at the other. The goals and objectives of an organization are established through strategic decisions. Decisions are made at the strategic level as to what kinds of products or services the organization will provide, who the beneficiaries will be, and what major capital and operating expenditures will be required to produce these products or services. Tactical decisions deal with matters of more immediate concern. Such short-term decisions, however, frequently have important long-term implications, which, if overlooked or ignored, may have serious repercussions for the organization and its client groups.

A primary objective of strategic management is to broaden the bases on which to make decisions that fall along this continuum. Strategic managers must attempt to (1) identify the long-range needs of the organization, (2) explore the ramifications of policies and programs designed to meet these needs, and (3) formulate strategies that maximize the positive aspects and minimize the negative aspects for the foreseeable future. Strategic management is concerned with deciding in advance what an organization should do in the future (planning), determining who will do it and how it will be done (resource management), and monitoring and enhancing ongoing activities and operations (control and evaluation).

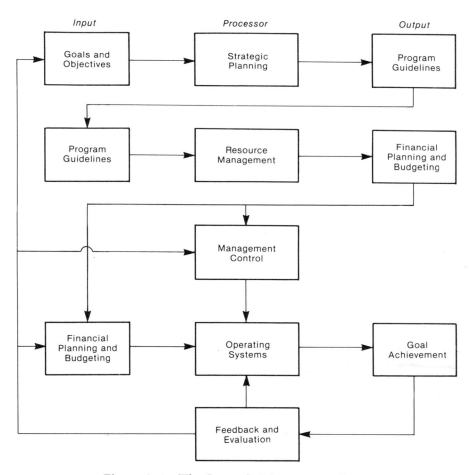

Figure 1–1. The Strategic Management Process

Strategic management involves the combined effect of these three basic components in meeting the goals and objectives of an organization (figure 1–1). *Planning* identifies the specific actions required to carry out a given strategy. *Resource management* involves a determination of the particular configuration of resources to be employed and the allocation of resources to those units within the organization that will carry out the plan. Organization structure and resource allocation provide the means through which proposed strategies are implemented.[22] *Control and evaluation* focus on the internal requirements for the implementation of selected strategies. Through various control mechanisms, performance is measured and feedback from these evaluations is used to determine necessary modifications in resource allocations and organization structure to meet environmental demands and to ensure the success of a strategy.

Rowe, Mason, and Dickel offer a four-factor model to illustrate the relationships between planning, management, and control (figure 1–2). According to this model, environmental demands are met through a strategic planning process, involving the formulation of missions, goals, and objectives.

> Strategic management can thus be seen as a "total" system perspective and not merely as the process of choosing from among alternative long-range plans. It reflects the organization's "strategic capability" to balance the demands imposed by external and internal forces and to integrate the overall functioning of the organization so as to allocate resources in a manner best designed to meet goals and objectives.[23]

Performance evaluation ties the output of the organization to the requirements of the internal environment. An assessment of the overall capability of the organization, as well as certain political considerations, help to relate the organization to the demands of the external and internal environment.

Donald Harvey offers a somewhat more elaborate, ten-stage model which encompasses many of the same components as suggested by Rowe, Mason, and Dickel. Harvey suggests that "strategic management encompasses all the decisions and actions leading to the attainment of long-range objectives."[24] He also emphasizes the need for an open systems perspective: "Without this systems perspective, managers tend to see problems in isolation, often failing to recognize the dynamic interrelationships among subsystems of the organization and with other external systems."[25]

Today's manager is faced with an accelerating rate of change in technical, social, political, and economic forces. Through all of these changes, the organization must be directed to meet unprecedented challenges. In the past, organizations often were relatively small and were focused on one major product or service. Today, tremendous changes have taken place in the size

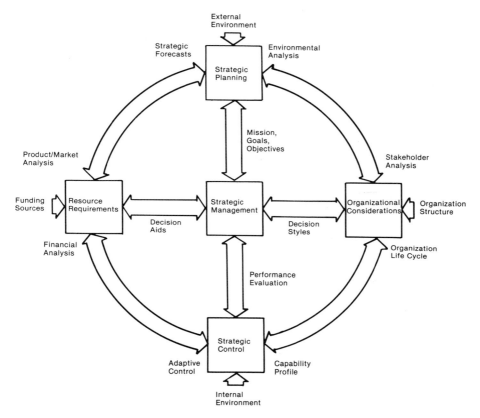

Source: Alan J. Rowe, Richard O. Mason, and Karl E. Dickel, *Strategic Management and Business Policy: A Methodological Approach* (Reading, Mass.: Addison-Wesley Publishing Co., 1982), p. 3, figure 1.1. Reprinted with permission.

Figure 1–2. Strategic Four-Factor Diagram

and complexity of organizational operations. As a result of these changing forces, the management process has become more difficult, requiring greater skills in planning, analysis, and control. These skills, aimed at guiding the future course of an organization in a changing and uncertain world, are the essence of strategic management.

Levels of Strategy Making

Vancil and Lorange, in their book *Strategic Planning Systems,* have identified three levels of strategy making: corporate, business, and functional.[26] *Corpo-*

rate strategy involves (1) the determination of a company's goal and objectives, including decisions as to which lines of business to pursue; (2) acquisition of the resources required to attain those objectives; and (3) allocation of resources among different corporate units (divisions) to ensure that the objectives are achieved. *Business strategy* focuses on the determination of the scope of a division's activities that will satisfy a broad consumer need, including decisions as to the objectives in the division's defined areas of operations and policies to be adopted to attain those objectives. *Functional strategy* involves the development of a set of feasible action programs to implement the division strategy. Goals and objectives are selected for each functional area (marketing, production, finance, research, and so on), and a determination is made as to the nature and sequence of actions to be taken by each area to achieve its goals and objectives.

This layering of strategy provides a useful starting point for the construction of a strategic management system. However, certain modifications are necessary, particularly in adapting this approach to a broader organizational setting.

Most complex organizations must deal with six strategic elements (see table 1–1).[27] Decisions along these six dimensions provide overall direction to all subsequent decision making and program activities within the organization. These variables also act as constraints on future decisions. Thus, the

Table 1–1
Strategic Decision Elements

Basic mission	Basic purposes of the organization and its guiding principles for behavior
Target groups	Clientele or benefactors of program activities of the organization
Goals and Objectives	What the organization seeks to accomplish through its programs Generally (goals) Specifically (objectives)
Program/ service mix	Types of programs and administrative activities offered in order to accomplish the goals and objectives
Geographic service area	Physical boundaries of the programs of the organization
Comparative advantages	Differential advantage sought over other organizations engaged in similar program activities

strategic decision elements (1) relate the total organization to its environment and (2) provide unity and direction to all organizational activities—two fundamental purposes of strategy making.

Organizational Strategy

First and foremost, strategic decisions must be formulated for the organization as a whole. In this sense, such strategy is analogous to the corporate strategy level in the Vancil and Lorange model. The six strategic decision elements, in turn, must be addressed under organizational strategy.

Basic Mission. Every organization first must determine its fundamental purposes and guiding principles for program activities. Specific decision issues to be addressed include:

1. major constituencies of the organization and the nature of the obligations to each,
2. relative emphasis placed on the various program activities that could be undertaken,
3. the role of the organization within its broader environment,
4. any particular priorities that will shape the nature of the organization,
5. other decisions that represent broad commitments and directions for the development of the organization as a whole.

While focusing on broad purposes, this mission statement must also convey specific decisions about the priority given to various programs or services, the basic character of the organization as a whole, and the expectations of support by participants in the organization. These guiding principles set the tone and direction for the organization as a whole.

Target Groups. Specific decisions must be made about the target groups to be served by the organization within the context of its mission statement. These clientele should be described in terms of their needs and demographic characteristics. The term *stakeholders* frequently is used in connection with corporate strategic planning and management procedures. Stakeholders are claimants on the organization. They depend on the organization for the realization of some of their goals and thereby have a stake in its activities. The organization, in turn, depends on these individuals and groups for the full realization of its purpose. The principal stakeholders of many organization are members who have made various tangible commitments to the programs of the organization. In other situations, the organization's customers are members of a broader public who avail themselves of the services of the organization on an "as needed" basis. The roles played by various institutions and agencies that may support and/or regulate the organization (for example, governments, foundations, and industrial sponsors) also must be identified. For most organizations, these external entities (organizations in themselves) continue to increase in importance. It is useful for strategic management purposes to define the needs and characteristics of these entities along with the more traditional client groups.

Goals and Objectives. Goals represent the end results that the organization seeks to achieve in order to fulfill its mission and to meet the needs of its clientele-stakeholders. In general, it is useful to identify three categories of goals:

1. goals for the clientele/stakeholders—outcomes which will facilitate the development of target groups—economic, social, political, physical, emotional, intellectual, moral, and so forth;
2. goals for societal development—the results sought in terms of the contributions of the organization to its broader environment;
3. goals for organizational development—the resource-related ends sought in order to facilitate goal attainment in the other two areas.

Decisions made in each of these categories help to further identify the unifying themes of a complex organization.

Program/Service Mix. The next step is to define the programs and services to be offered by the organization in order to accomplish its goals and objectives and thereby serve the needs of its clientele and fulfill its mission. In this context, three strategic decision issues are:

1. the programs or services to be offered,
2. relative emphasis (priorities) to be placed on the programs,
3. targets for new program development over an extended time horizon.

Many organizations typically have focused only on the first of these issues. The changing nature of the environment for most organizational activities, however, requires that increasing attention be given to the second and third decision issues as well.

Geographic Service Area. The fifth strategic decision element involves an identification of the geographic areas served by the various programs of the organization. Depending on the program, an organization may participate in varying degrees in local, state, regional, or national markets. All of the strategic decision elements are highly interdependent, of course, but the issue of geography is particularly tied to the target groups or clientele identified by the organization.

Verhältnismäßig

Comparative Advantage. Finally, an organization must seek to identify how it will gain a competitive edge or differential advantage over other organizations offering similar programs to similar target groups/markets. The key decision here involves the basis on which the organization will strive to differentiate itself from competitors. The basis for differentiation may well be in one or more of the other strategic decision areas, for example the particular types of programs emphasized by the organization or the uniqueness of its particular goals and objectives. On the other hand, the basis for differentiation may be nonstrategic in nature, for instance the sense of exclusiveness that membership in the organization may suggest.

At the organizational level, decision making along these six strategic dimensions is highly interactive. Much revision and change is likely to occur across all areas before final decisions are achieved along any single dimension. In this connection, note that the decisions on goals and objectives are not formulated as a separate, first step. The goals and objectives established for any complex organization are contingent upon the types of clientele being served, the nature of the programs (services or products) to be offered, and the basic mission. This is tantamount to saying that the types of objectives that can be established may be severely constrained by the nature of the organization. This point often is overlooked by those who assert that goal setting is the first step in strategy formulation.

Thus, the strategic decision elements are interdependent. Where one "enters the circle" for strategic evaluation often is dictated by the needs and circumstances of the organization in question. In the case of a long-established organization, for example, it may well be that the nature of the target groups traditionally served will determine the specific goals and objectives to be pursued, rather than the reverse being true. It simply may not be feasible to consider changing the definition of the target market in order to put a new set of goals and objectives into place.

Functional Strategies at the Organizational Level

Organizational strategies constitute the first-order, formative decisions. These strategies identify what the organization is and what it intends to do in a collective sense. The next set of strategies begins to address in a systematic way the "how" questions for the total organization. At this level, *functional strategies* serve as the initial steps toward the implementation of an overall strategic plan for the organization. Functional strategies address critical issues related to finance, membership size and recruitment, organizational structure, human resource development, and facilities.

Stanford University provides an excellent example of a very complex organization which has developed sophisticated functional strategy models to assist in achieving its goals and objectives. In particular, Stanford has become known as a leader in financial planning through (1) its long-range financial forecast; (2) its dynamic budget equilibrium model, whereby sustainable budget levels and growth rates are identified; and (3) its transition-to-equilibrium model which develops a plan for converting budget deficits into positive, long-run budget balances. It must be emphasized that these various financial models are used at Stanford as tools for the implementation of the overall organizational strategy related to mission, goals, clientele, and so forth. In other words, organizational strategies should *drive* decision making on finances, facilities, and the like, rather than the other way around.

This formulation suggests that functional strategies exist at the organizational (corporate) level as well as at the program (business) level. Furthermore, these functional strategies should be formulated *in advance of* program-level strategies. This sequence is necessary to ensure that program strategies are guided by an internally consistent set of parameters. For example, any strategy formulated in support of a particular program must take cognizance not only of the decisions made as a part of the total organizational strategy, but also the overall financial outlook of the organization, availability of personnel and facilities, and other contextual variables.

Program Strategies

At the program level, each subunit of the organization should formulate competitive strategies that encompass the same dimensions included at the organizational level (for example, basic mission, target groups, and goals and objectives). The strategic plans for individual subunits should also include statements of resource requirements in order to facilitate the review process by higher levels of management.

Program-level decisions on basic mission, target groups, and the like are constrained not only by organizational strategy but also by the functional strategies that permeate all parts of the enterprise. In this sense, the programs identified as planning units correspond closely to the concept of strategic business units (SBU), suggested by Vancil and Lorange.[28] The identification of these planning units, however, should occur in organizational strategy making, when decisions related to program offerings and priorities are made for the organization as a whole.

Program-Level Functional Strategies

The final level of strategy includes those actions that each planning unit intends to implement in order to effect its overall strategy. What kinds of recruitment strategies should be developed to attract the identified target groups? What program changes are necessary in order to serve the needs of newly identified target markets? Will it be necessary to hire a new personnel in order to give leadership to new programs? What financial strategies must be employed in order to increase external support for programs? Given a new statement of program priorities, is there a need to reevaluate the present distribution of funds among the subunits responsible for program implementation? These and other implementation strategies at the program level are analogous to the functional strategies of production, marketing, engineering, and so on that one would find within a division of any diversified firm.

Appropriate Methodologies

Strategic management is both a *conceptual framework* for orchestrating the basic decision-making processes of any organization and a collection of *analytical tools* designed to facilitate the making of decisions. Linking appropriate methodologies to the various stages in the decision process is a key responsibility of the strategic manager. Various analytical approaches are presented in some detail in subsequent chapters. Some of these methods and their linkages to the three basic components of the strategic management system, as envisioned in this presentation, are shown in table 1–2.

Strategic Planning

The concepts of strategic planning and strategic management have often been used interchangeably by various writers. However, as used here, strategic planning is the component of the strategic management system designed to (1) clarify goals and objectives, (2) select policies for the acquisition and distribution of resources, and (3) establish a basis for translating policies and decisions into specific action commitments. Strategic planners must attempt to identify the long-range needs of the organization, to explore the ramifications and implications of policies and programs designed to meet these needs, and to formulate strategies that maximize the positive aspects and minimize the negative aspects of the foreseeable future.

The interdependency with clientele or stakeholders requires that strategic planners carefully analyze their needs as well as those of the organization. Techniques such as environmental scanning, mixed scanning, as described by Etizoni,[29] and performance matrix analysis can assist the planner in this process. Churchman, in *The Systems Approach and Its Enemies,* identifies four historical impediments or "enemies" to rational thinking: politics, morality, aesthetics, and religion.[30] He argues that a planner should stop and listen to the "voices" of these enemies whenever a strategic plan is being developed. This *enemies check* is a heuristic test to see whether the nonrational forces of politics, morality, aesthetics, and religion are potentially working for or against the strategic plan.

Table 1–2
Analytical Tools for Strategic Management

Component of Strategic Management	Methodology
Control and Evaluation	Simple feedback mechanisms
	Use of heuristics Network analysis (CPM and PERT) Account scheduling
	Responsibility accounting Cost accounting Managerial accounting
	Management information systems Decision-support systems
	Linear and nonlinear programming Queuing theory Dynamic programming
	Financial ratio analysis Strategic funds programming Computer-assisted financial planning Allocation models
Resource Management	Cost-utility analysis Cost-benefit analysis Cost-effectiveness analysis
	Probability functions Cost sensitivity analysis Payoff matrices and decision trees
	Performance budgeting Service level analysis Program budgeting
	Simulation and gaming Decision theory
	Effectiveness measures Program analysis and evaluation Objectives matrices Multiple-policy matrices
Strategic Planning	Cybernetics General systems theory

Resource Management

Resource management involves (1) programming organizational goals and objectives into specific program, projects, and activities; (2) designing organizational units to carry out approved programs and plans; and (3) staffing these units and procuring the necessary resources to carry out the plans and programs. Effective resource management—sometimes labeled "organization and methods research"—requires a continuous search for more productive ways to operate the organization and to evaluate its ability to meet changing environmental conditions. Resource management is the link between goals, objectives, and the strategic plans and the actual performance of organizational activities. As such, a major tool of resource management is the *budget process*.

Leadership and decision styles link the strategic management to the organization. Often these linkages determine the effectiveness of strategic alternatives and their acceptance by organizational constituents. WOTS-UP analysis, a technique developed by Rowe, Mason, and Dickel, examines the weaknesses, opportunities, threats, and strengths of the organization in an effort to determine its ability to deal with its environment.[31] This analytical approach, like the concept of *systems readiness,* is designed to aid in finding the best match between environmental trends and internal capabilities.

The linkage between the resource requirements of an organization and strategic management includes the application of analytical models for the allocation of scarce resources and the evaluation of alternative strategies at the program level. Analytical techniques drawn from program budgeting and service level analysis are applicable in this context. The basic objective of service level analysis is to justify budget requests "from the bottom up" in terms of client service needs and program objectives. Various levels of funding both above and below current expenditure levels (the established budget base) can be assigned to component levels of service to determine the potential impacts of such changes.[32]

Other techniques applicable to resource management include cost-benefit and cost-effectiveness analyses, cash flow analysis, and simulation models. A computer-based interactive simulation is a powerful means for examining the impact of alternative strategies. Tools such as decision trees, the Pareto Law, and multiattribute decision making are receiving increasing use by strategic managers.

Control and Evaluation

Early definition of management control tend to emphasize the importance of initiation corrective action when deviations occur from some predetermined course of events (that is, a plan or program). In one of the better-known definitions, Henri Fayol suggests that: "Control consists of verifying whether everything occurs in conformity with the plan adopted, the instructions issued, and principles established. It has for an object to point out weaknesses and errors in order to rectify and prevent recurrence."[33] Mockler has suggested that greater emphasis should be placed on positive (instead of negative) control action. His definition of management control is as follows:

a systematic effort to set performance standards consistent with planning objectives, to design information feedback systems, to compare actual performance with these predetermined standards, to determine whether there are any deviations and to measure their significance, and to take any action required to assure that all corporate resources are being used in the most effective and efficient way possible in achieving corporate objectives.[34]

The effective control and evaluation of any organization requires relevant *management information*. Timely information is essential in understanding the circumstances surrounding any problem and in evaluating alternative courses of action to resolve such problems. In this sense, information is incremental knowledge that reduces uncertainty in particular situations. Although vast amounts of facts, numbers, and other data may be processed in any organization, what constitutes management information depends on the problem at hand and the particular frame of reference of the manager. Traditional accounting data, for example, can provide information when arrayed appropriately in balance sheets and financial statements. Accounting data, however elaborately processed, may be relatively meaningless if the problem is related to an evaluation of the effectiveness of a new program. Thus, to achieve better decisions, the information available to management must be both timely and pertinent.

In addition to (or as a consequence of) a well-organized management information system (MIS), the processes of control and evaluation can be assisted by such work programming techniques as work-breakdown scheduling (WBS) and Gantt and milestone charts, and by network analysis techniques such as the Program Evaluation and Review Technique (PERT), the Critical Path Method (CPM), and heuristic programming. Productivity improvement and performance evaluation techniques have become commonplace in the corporate manager's tool kit and are gradually finding broad application in other organizations, both in the public and private sectors.

Summary

Effective management must be a dynamic process, involving the blending and directing of available human, physical, and fiscal resources in order to achieve the agreed-upon objectives of the organization. A basic purpose of management should be to provide focus and consistency to the action programs of the organization. The effectiveness of such an approach must be measured by the results achieved and by the people served, that is, in terms of performance.

The Scope of Strategic Management

The concept of performance suggests a melding of the basic management objectives of efficiency and effectiveness. In this context, efficiency can be equated with doing things right, whereas effectiveness involves doing the right things. Moreover, effectiveness must be measured in terms of the response time required to make strategic adjustments when things go wrong. As a consequence, a more systematic and responsive approach to management is required, one which combines traditional administrative procedures with more contemporary techniques of systems analysis and comprehensive planning and budgeting. The objective is to achieve a coordinative process capable of yielding more rational decisions for any organization that chooses to apply these techniques.

The following procedural definition identifies the intended scope of strategic management:

1. establish overall strategic goals and objectives; select appropriate policies for the acquisition and distribution of resources; provide a basis for translating policies and decisions into specific action commitments (strategic planning);
2. determine requirements to meet identified goals and objectives; determine the available resources (fiscal, personnel, materials, equipment, and time) required for organizational programs; establish the organizational units, procedures, operations, and activities necessary to carry out the strategic plan; and judiciously allocate the resources of the organization in accordance with some system of priorities (resource management);
3. schedule programs from the point of commitment to completion; exercise control by reacting to (and anticipating) deviations between predicted and actual performance; monitor activities to determine whether or not reasonable, feasible, and efficient plans and programs are being executed and if not, why not (control and evaluation).

Many of the tasks identified in this procedural definition are presently assigned to various sectors in a complex organization. Planners plan, financial analysts prepare budgets, program personnel schedule and control resources for specific activities, and administrators monitor and evaluate. Some of these tasks are undertaken on a grand scale, while others are fairly routine. With the increasing complexity of organizational operations, however, the division of labor established to deal with complexity may well become the major impediment to effective policy formulation and implementation. Unless a more comprehensive framework is created to provide guidance and coordination, the sum of the management parts may be far less than an integrated whole.

Objective Methods and Subjective Ability

In general, it is the responsibility of the strategic manager to reduce uncertainty and to bring risk within tolerable bounds. An objective of strategic management is to strike a balance between the polar pressures for methodological sophistication and the ease of utilization. An effort is made to apply a mixed bag of analytical techniques and methods applicable to the variety of decision situations encountered in complex organizations. In these various applications, the primary focus of strategic management remains the integration of planning, analysis, and management in productive harmony. In short, the functions of strategic management must necessarily be carried out as a balanced blend of objective methods and subjective ability.

At least three categories of organizational decisions are reflected in the procedural definition of strategic management: (1) decisions relating to problem recognition, classification, and appraisal; (2) decisions required to convert the intentions of a strategic plan into more specific programs and projects; and (3) decisions that assess the performance of ongoing programs and provide additional inputs in subsequent cycles of the process. The conceptual framework of strategic management draws heavily on both existing and emergent theories of systems analysis, strategic planning, and program budgeting. Strategic management also borrows from the concepts and techniques of policy analysis and evaluation as it seeks to provide a possible stepping stone to the eventual development of a policy science. It attempts to amplify these concepts to find a coordinative mechanism that will build on their strengths while circumventing some of their shortcomings.

Notes

1. Bruce H. De Woolfson, Jr., "Public Sector MBO and PPB: Cross Fertilization in Management Systems," *Public Administration Review* 36 (July-August 1975): 387.

2. Peter F. Drucker, *The Practice of Management* (New York: Harper, 1954), p. 353.

3. Note the distinction between these types of problems and what have been identified as planning problems in Kenneth Kraemer, *Policy Analysis in Local Government* (Washington, D.C.: International City Management Association, 1973), pp. 24–27.

4. Michael Radnor, Michael J. White, and David A. Tansik, *Management and Policy Science in American Government* (Lexington, Mass.: Lexington Books, 1975), pp. 6–7.

5. See Charles E. Lindblom, *The Intelligence of Democracy* (New York: Free Press, 1965).

6. James E. Anderson, *Public Policy-Making* (New York: Praeger, 1975), p. 10.

7. C. Easton Rothwell, foreword to *The Policy Sciences: Recent Developments in Scope and Method,* edited by Daniel Lerner and Harold D. Lasswell (Stanford: Stanford University Press, 1951), p. ix.

8. Ibid., p. x.

9. E.S. Quade, *Analysis for Public Decisions* (New York: American Elsevier, 1975), p. 4.

10. Harold D. Lasswell, *A Pre-View of Policy Sciences* (New York: American Elsevier, 1971), p. 1.

11. Irving L. Horowitz and James E. Katz, *Social Science and Public Policy in the United States* (New York: Praeger, 1975), pp. 3–4.

12. Michael Radnor, "Management Science and Policy Science: Transition or Integration?" in *Management and Policy Science in American Government,* edited by Radnor, White, and Tansik, p. 302.

13. Ibid., p. 303.

14. Ibid., p. 304.

15. Richard F. Vancil, "Strategy Formulation in Complex Organizations," in *Strategic Planning Systems,* edited by Peter Lorange and Richard F. Vancil (Englewood Cliffs, N.J.: Prentice-Hall, 1977), p. 4.

16. Charles W. Hofer and Dan E. Schendel, *Strategy Formulation: Analytical Concepts* (St. Paul, Minn.: West, 1978); Richard F. Vancil and Peter Lorange, "Strategic Planning in Diversified Companies," *Harvard Business Review* (January-February 1975); H. Igor Ansoff, *Strategic Management* (New York: John Wiley & Sons, 1979).

17. H. Mintzberg, "Patterns in Strategy Formation," *Management Science* (May 1978); "Strategy-making in Three Modes, *California Management Review* (Winter 1973).

18. S. Schoeffler, R.D. Buzzell, and D.F. Heany, "The Impact of Strategic Planning on Profit Performance," *Harvard Business Review* (March-April 1974).

19. L.J. Bourgeois, "Strategy and Environment: A Conceptual Integration," *Academy of Management Review* (January 1980).

20. C.E. Summer, *Strategic Behavior in Business and Government* (Boston: Little, Brown, 1980).

21. W.F. Glueck, *Strategic Management and Business Policy* (New York: McGraw-Hill, 1980).

22. Alan J. Rowe, Richard O. Mason, and Karl E. Dickel, *Strategic Management and Business Policy: A Methodological Approach* (Reading, Mass.: Addison-Wesley, 1982), p. 2.

23. Ibid., p. 2.

24. Donald F. Harvey, *Business Policy and Strategic Management* (Columbus, Ohio: Charles E. Merrill, 1982), p. 19.

25. Ibid., p. 19.

26. Vancil and Lorange, *Strategic Planning Systems,* pp. 23–25.

27. Robert C. Shirley, *Strategic Planning in the Higher-Education Setting* (Boulder, Colo.: National Center for Higher Education Management Systems, 1980).

28. Vancil and Lorange, *Strategic Planning Systems,* pp. 139–151.

29. Amitai Etzoni, "Mixed Scanning: A Third Approach to Decision Making," *Public Administration Review* 27 (December 1967), pp. 309–390.

30. C. West Churchman, *The Systems Approach and Its Enemies* (New York: Basic Books, 1979), p. 173.

31. Rowe, Mason, and Dickel, *Strategic Management and Business Policy,* pp. 19–24.

32. Alan Walter Steiss, *Management Control in Government* (Lexington, Mass.: Lexington Books, 1982), p. 242.

33. Henri Fayol, *General and Industrial Management* (New York: Pitman Corp., 1949), p. 107.

34. Robert J. Mockler, *The Management Control Process* (New York: Appleton-Century-Crofts, 1972), p. 2.

2
General Systems Theory

N ew analytical techniques and related problem-solving tools emerged as by-products of World War II and have found widespread application in business, industry, and the military. These techniques formed the basis for the overlapping and complementary fields of systems engineering, operations research, management science, systems analysis, communications engineering, computer science, cybernetics, and information technology. Fundamental to all of these disciplines is still another field—*general systems theory*. General systems theory has particular application in understanding the operations and processes of complex organizations and serves as the basis for the strategic management model presented herein.

The Systemic Perspective

General systems theory is not so much a rigorous explanatory theory as it is a way of isolating certain important aspects of reality. It is a shorthand way of looking at the world, providing a framework within which apparently distinct sets of phenomena can be united. As a cognitive window on reality, general systems theory focuses not only on root causes but also on the complex interrelationships that may constrain the development of effective solutions. Such a systemic perspective is a necessary, although not sufficient, condition of strategic management.

A Holistic Approach

Ancient Greek philosophers attempted to take the widest possible view—to see things as an organic whole. At the same time, they sought uniformity in the phenomena they observed. Their efforts to derive a more comprehensive theory also led to guesswork, and often to a neglect of fact. "Philosophers tried to explain nature while shutting their eyes. And yet in shutting their eyes they kept something else wide open, namely their minds, and although the eye-shutting retarded the growth of science, the mind-opening led to things perhaps equally important, metaphysics and math."[1]

Until recently, modern science seemed to be preoccupied with the particular, with the subdividing of complex problems, and with thinking in relatively narrow categories. New subdisciplines were continually spawned from established disciplines. Science has attempted to explain complex phenomena by reducing them to "an interplay of elementary units investigatable independently of each other."[2] Thus, one might observe that, while modern scientists opened their eyes to the investigation of particulars, they closed their minds to the equally important task, the synthesis of the systematic whole.

In his call for a general theory of systems, von Bertalanffy suggested that:

> Modern science is characterized by its ever-increasing specialization, necessitated by the enormous amount of data, the complexity of techniques and of theoretical structures within every field. This, however, has led to a breakdown of science as an integrated realm: The physicist, the biologist, the psychologist and the social scientist are, so to speak, encapsulated in a private universe, and it is difficult to get word from one cocoon to the other.[3]

What is required, von Bertalanffy concluded, is a holistic approach that would stress similarities among the theoretical constructs of the sciences rather than their unique properties. It is important to study the organizing relations that result from the dynamic interaction among isolated parts and processes. Thus, von Bertalanffy asserted that:

> There exist models, principles, and laws that apply to generalized systems or their subclasses, irrespective of their particular kind, the nature of their component elements, and the relations of "forces" between them. It seems legitimate to ask for a theory, not of systems of a more or less special kind, but of universal principles applying to systems in general.[4]

General systems theory "can be viewed as an effort to fuse the mechanistic and the organismic approaches so as to utilize the advantages of each."[5] In a sense, general systems theory attempts to put the proverbial trees in a generalized perspective so as to make possible a clearer view of the whole forest.

The Basic Components of a System

General systems theory is built on the assumption that any system can be viewed as consisting of a *conversion mechanism* whereby certain inputs are transposed or converted into outputs. As used in this connection, the term *system* may be defined as a combination or aggregation of related elements in the real world, united by some form of regular interaction or interdependence. Thus we commonly speak of a political system or a social system as being made up of people who interact according to certain rules of conduct in order to accomplish certain objectives. By the same token, it is possible to think of a manufacturing firm as a system, made up of workers and management, investors, and customers, all focusing on the production of certain goods and/or services.

Quite obviously, any organization can be described in systematic terms. It is possible to illustrate the basic concepts of the general systems model in very schematic terms, as in figure 2–1. Certain functions are carried out within a given structure, while a conversion mechanism operates through a definable process or set of procedures (the dynamic aspects of a system). The structure of an organization describes how these processes operate, both in a formal, hierarchical sense and in an informal sense.

In order to study an organization in general systems terms, it is first necessary to set it apart from the broader environment of which it is a component element (or subsystem). In the case of a manufacturing firm, for example, the broader environment may be viewed as a larger system of economic linkages. By making this distinction, it is possible to look at the raw materials, including processed goods from other companies, that the firm must acquire as inputs and its finished products as outputs. The actual manufacturing process, then, constitutes the conversion mechanism.

Initially, inputs are governed by the availability of certain resources—money, technology, personnel, information, and so forth. Processes within

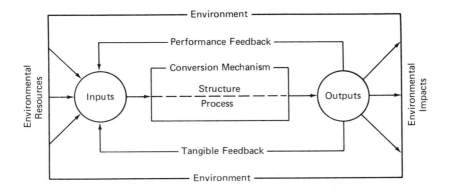

Source: Alan Walter Steiss and Gregory A. Daneke, *Performance Administration* (Lexington, Mass.: Lexington Books, 1980), p. 87. Reprinted by permission.

Figure 2–1. Fundamental Components of a System

the conversion mechanism act on the resources to produce a set of outputs. These outputs, in turn, are related to the goals and objectives of the system—what the organization is designed to accomplish. Moreover, outputs may have significant impacts on other systems in the broader environment.

Outputs can take two forms: (1) tangible products (goods and services) and (2) a level of performance. Both aspects have feedback in the system as a whole and provide new inputs in subsequent cycles. Tangible outputs determine, in part, the availability of resources for the next cycle. Performance level (how well the system has functioned) provides some indication of the need for adjustments in processes or structure in order to enhance performance (that is, to achieve objectives).

The concept of feedback is central to general system theory. In its simplest form, feedback is the kind of communication an actor receives from a live audience. If the audience is enthusiastic, the performer will react with similar enthusiasm. There is, in a sense, a closed circuit of communication between the performer and the audience, which provides a continuous interchange of information.

With perfect feedback, the desired output is attained by self-regulation. The input to the conversion mechanism is adjusted automatically by the output. Feedback may be either negative or positive. The classic example of the application of negative feedback is found in James Watt's governor for steam engines, usually regarded as the first man-made, deliberately contrived feedback mechanism. Positive feedback takes place when the function of the control mechanism is to amplify a measured deviation, as, for example, in the principle of power steering or power brakes.

Positive feedback is potentially dangerous and must always be under some form of control. If positive feedback gets out of control, it leads to the phenomenon known as "runaway," either toward zero or toward some maximum. Stanley-Jones has observed that a system that is running away under the influence of positive feedback has broken free from the monitoring or stabilizing influences of negative feedback and cannot be restored to normal except by active external intervention.[6]

Essential to feedback is the notion that information flow has reciprocating effects on behavior. Thus, the term *loop* frequently is used in association with the concept of feedback. This circular pattern involves the flow of information to some point of action, a flow back to a point of decision with information about the action, and then a return to the point of action with new information and perhaps instructions for the modification of the action.

Although initially separated from its broader environment, it must be recognized that no system (organization) functions in isolation. The *environment* establishes both the potential for system development and improvement, as well as the limitations. The environment can be described in such physical terms as climate, topography, temperature, visual attributes. In a nonphysical sense, the environment can be described in such relative terms as values, goals, aspirations, ideas, attitudes, and beliefs. Since there are many kinds of environment—none inherently mutually exclusive of others—often a total environment must be described in both physical and nonphysical terms.

In summary, complex organizations may be assumed to possess systemic characteristics. Among these are:

1. an established order or arrangement of component parts (a structural configuration), reflecting a set of relationships among elements and subsystems;
2. a set of processes, often difficult to perceive or understand from outside the organization;
3. a series of inputs that pass through the organization or are operated upon it to produce outputs;
4. a relationship to the basic functions for which the organization was established to serve (that is, goal-directedness or teleos, involving a monitoring of performance through some sort of feedback mechanism).

Each organization also operates within a larger environment, that is, the society.

Open and Closed Systems

Complex organizations do not merely survive or have static continuity. Rather, in surviving, organizations create conditions that permit them to attain new structural and functional configurations (that is, to survive at a new level). In recognition of this characteristic of complex organizations, early system theorists introduced the notion of a "moving" or "dynamic" equilibrium. Bateson defined *dynamic equilibrium* as "a state of affairs in a functional system, such that although no change is apparent, we are compelled to believe that small changes are continually occurring and counteracting each other."[7] This definition suggests that, while a system as a whole may appear to be in equilibrium, individual components within the system may be undergoing constant flux.

Dynamic equilibrium is somewhat analogous to the principle of *homeostasis* in biology, performing a similar function for organizational analysis. In this context, homeostasis is defined as the tendency of an organism to maintain within itself relatively stable conditions by means of regulatory mechanisms, while at the same time, incorporating those changes necessary to maintain a healthy state.

Until recently, approaches employed in the natural sciences have focused on parts and processes operating in *closed systems,* that is, systems studied in isolation from their larger environment. A closed system is more easily defined in mathematical terms. The state of such a system can be described by clearly perceived variables, and an equation connecting these variables constitutes a static theory of that system. This closed systems approach is also evident in many analyses of complex organizations based on mathematical models.

A static theory, however, says very little about how a system will respond if its equilibrium is disrupted. It merely posits equilibrium as a juncture of key variables. A dynamic theory, on the other hand, must be able to deal with successive states of the system.

Living organisms and their organizations survive in a continuous inflow and outflow with their environment in which various components are built up and broken down. Such systems never exist in a state of equilibrium, in the chemical or thermodynamic sense, but are maintained in a so-called steady state. Such systems seek stability rather than equilibrium. A system that receives inputs from the environment and/or acts on the environment through outputs is called an *open system*.

Equifinality and Verifinality

Recognition of the distinction between open and closed systems has led to two important concepts. The first is the principle of *equifinality,* introduced by von Bertalanffy.[8] In any closed system, the final state is unequivocally determined by the initial conditions. If either the initial conditions or the process is altered, the final state will also change.

This is not the case in open systems. Here, the same final state may be reached from different initial conditions and in different ways—such systems evidence equifinality. The corollary of this open system characteristic is *varifinality,* that is, where different end states can be reached from the same initial conditions.

The concepts of equifinality and varifinality have important applications in the modification of older mechanistic theories formulated to deal with closed systems. In the mechanistic view, derived from classic Newtonian physics of the nineteenth century, the inexorable laws of causality produced all phenomena in the world—inanimate, living, and even mental. There was no room for notions of directiveness, order, or teleos. Correspondingly, causality was essentially one way; processes could not be reversed once they were initiated.

The mechanistic view of causality has proven insufficient for explaining most organizational phenomena. One cannot begin to understand living organisms, much less complex organizations in modern society, without taking into account what rather loosely has been called "adaptive behavior," "goal seeking," and the like. Goal-directed behavior no longer can be avoided or assumed away by causal theories. The analytical focus cannot be limited to simple cause-and-effect relationships. Rather, careful attention must be given to the parameters of the system within which change can take place and the regulative mechanisms that can be organized to ward off disturbances that may challenge the system.

Entropy and Negentropy

A second important concept to be derived from the distinction between open and closed systems relates to what was once thought to be a violent contradiction between Kelvin's principle of degradation and Darwin's theories of evolution. According to the second law of thermodynamics, the general trends of physical events is toward states of maximum disorder and the leveling down of differences among component elements. At this final state, all energy is degraded into even distributed heat of low temperature (maximum entropy), and the world process comes to a stop—the so-called heat depth of the universe.

Around the turn of the century, Clerk Maxwell, an English physicist, suggested a very clever way to overcome the second law of thermodynamics. Maxwell envisioned a small, but very intelligent creature—a demon—who could see molecules and could serve as a "gatekeeper" between two containers of gas at equal temperature and pressure. By carefully opening and closing the gate, the demon could permit faster-moving molecules to pass into one container, while slower molecules moved to the other. Over time, one container would get hotter and the other cooler and, thus, the available energy in the system, as measured by the temperature differential between the two containers, would be increased without adding any new energy to the system (other than Maxwell's smart demon). Thus the second law of thermodynamics would be circumvented.

Maxwell's demon, of course, is an allegory for anything that contributes order to a disorganized or chaotic situation. Contemporary systems theory suggests that, in open systems, the process of entropy can be reversed and order can be restored to random arrangements of elements. The counterforces thus developed are referred to as *negentropy,* defined as "a measure of order or organization."[9]

Two points concerned the concept of negentropy are noteworthy. First, although negentropy can be evidenced as matter and/or energy, it is primarily considered to be synonymous with information. Second, there is a general tendency in open systems to create a continuous surplus of negentropy to "live on borrowed time during periods of crisis" and, where possible, to "develop toward states of increased order and organization."[10] Thus, living systems, maintaining themselves in a steady state, can avoid the continual increase of disorder, and in the process, may even develop toward states of higher order, heterogeneity, and organization.

Polystable Systems

A fundamental concept in general systems theory is that of difference, either that two things are recognizably different or that one thing has changed with time. In the first instance, difference refers to those characteristics or parameters which set apart one system (or subsystem) from another. In the second case, the differences are internal to the system, occurring over time. When such changes take place, it is said that the system has moved from one state to another. A *state* is any well-defined condition or property that can be recognized if it occurs again. Any system, of course, can have many possible states.

While any complex organization may exist in a variety of states, for purposes of analysis, contemporary organizations may be conceived as operating in three main sets of states:

1. states which merely sustain the organization,
2. states which result in growth and adaptation,
3. states of crisis of one kind or another.

As shown in figure 2–2, there is more than one state of equilibrium or stability in each of these sets, and some cycling will occur. Therefore, any organization can be viewed as a *polystable system,* that is, having stability in more than one set of states.

As long as the cycling is kept within reasonable bounds, no harm is done. Furthermore, some alteration between the growth mode and sustaining activities may be beneficial, as when an organization attempts to consolidate the gains achieved through technological progress. Some states are near the boundaries of crisis, however. If proper care is not exercised in responding to pressures at these boundaries, the organization can end up in a trapped state of crisis, where every attempt to get out leads straight back in.

In a polystable system, the interaction of *error-actuated feedback* at every level determines the dominant behavior characteristics. This phenomenon is somewhat analogous to the "pendulum effect" which can be observed in contemporary society—a swing too far to the left is countered by a swing to the far right. In a closed system, a pendulum will oscillate in decreasing arcs until a point of equilibrium is achieved. In an open system, however, forces may act on the motion of the pendulum such that equilibrium is never achieved. In fact, these forces may result in an amplification of the pendulum's arc. In such cases, it is difficult to predict outcomes or to intervene in the system to predictable ends. Thus, a complex organization may become entrapped in a potential state of crisis.

If the organization is to survive, some kind of *regulatory mechanism* must be introduced to realign the states of the system. It no longer is possible to simply yield to pressures in the trapped state. Thus, to remain viable, an organization must develop some avenues for strategic management.

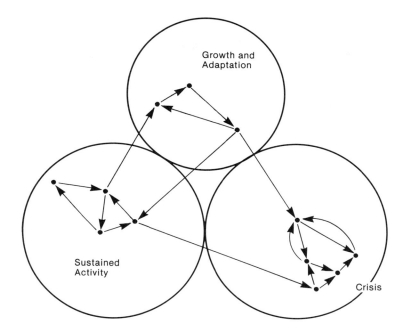

Figure 2–2. A Polystable System

What are the appropriate targets for strategic management? The objective is to modify the outputs of the organization to more fully meet the needs of its clientele or stakeholders. To accomplish this objective, it is possible to alter the inputs to the system, reorder the processes within the system, rearrange the structural components, or introduce new states into the structure of the system.

The characteristic behavior of a system is conditioned primarily by its structure—the basis upon which a system is organized. The structure, in turn, is the consequence of the interaction of a set of functional prerequisites. That is to say, a given organizational structure emerges and is sustained in response to certain organizational needs. Therefore, the most critical component of any organization is its structure, and strategic management must be directed primarily toward the introduction of new states within the structure of the organization. This conclusion assumes that the structure of an organization as an open system is exceedingly complex, full of interaction, and organized in a hierarchical fashion. It also is rich in negative feedback to permit self-correcting action.

In Alvin Toffler's book *Future Shock,* we are told that rapid change is endangering the very foundations of our society, that the human species is on the brink of its own self-made destruction. But change in modern society is inevitable. The question is not how change can be held back, but rather how it can be channeled effectively to produce positive results, while minimizing the dysfunctional consequences. Change for the sake of change is not the appropriate objective. Progress is *not* our most important product if we cannot define what we are progressing toward. *Planned change* must be undertaken in full recognition of the by-products and side effects of our actions. It must begin with an understanding of the system, the society, within which we operate and the functional exigencies of that society.

Adaptive, Self-Regulating Systems

Most modern organizations are characterized by rather complex internal relationships in terms of structure and processes. What goes on within organizations often is unintelligible to outsiders. Admission to organizational activities cannot be gained without appropriate credentials. As a consequence, complex organizations may be labeled "esoteric" functional systems, that is, systems designed to carry out certain basic functions necessary for the continued operation (and survival) of the total society but understood by, or meant for only, specially instructed or initiated individuals.[12] This is not to suggest that complex organizations are closed systems, only that they tend to be self-organizing and self-regulating.

Adaptiveness and Teleological Behavior

The properties of adaptiveness and self-regulation are very important to the operations of complex organizations. An adaptive system continues to achieve its objectives regardless of a changing environment or deterioration in the performance of some of its internal elements. A *self-regulating system* is one in which internally determined behavior is continually modified by environmental inputs. Any effort to restructure complex organizations should attempt to capitalize on these propensities. To do so, a conceptual framework must be created so that the organizing power of the systems themselves, and the professionalism, knowledge, and energy of their participants, can be released and channeled to produce more effective responses to environmental change.

To understand the dynamics of complex organizations, it is necessary to begin with a corresponding understanding of adaptiveness or teleological behavior within such a conceptual framework. Von Bertalanffy defines *teleology* as "directed behavior" and as "directiveness of processes."[13] Coulter presents the following minimum capabilities for a control mechanism based on goal-directedness or teleos:

1. *Teleological (goal-seeking) behavior.* The mechanism should be capable of controlling the output of the system so that it conforms to "goal signals," that is, predetermined ends or objectives.
2. *Teleogenesis (goal formulation).* The control mechanism should be capable of proposing goals within the range of the system's overall capacity to respond to such goals.
3. *Forecasting.* On the basis of sensed data about the controlled quantity, the control mechanism should be capable of predicting outcomes if a proposed goal is adopted by the system.
4. *Evaluation.* The control mechanism should be capable of assigning worth-values to the range of outcomes predicted for each goal and of computing an overall worth-function for the decision process.
5. *Decision making.* In accordance with some decision procedures, the system should be capable of selecting one of the proposed goals and of making commitments to that goal.[14]

The dynamic self-regulation of a system is achieved through feedback and adaptation, that is, "the ability to react to the environment in a way that is favorable . . . to the continued operation of the system."[15] Adaptation is concerned with the *essential variables* that determine the desired state(s) of an open system. These essential variables possess a degree of flexibility in that they can move and adjust within certain limits without appreciably changing the system. Such flexibility permits the system to maintain the condition of stability. The set of stable states may have variability, but such variability can be tolerated.

Control and Regulation

Control systems applicable to complex organizations may be modeled by utilizing the general concepts of feedback. Simply stated, feedback is output that subsequently is reintroduced into the system as input. A product of this modeling should involve the control of entropy among interconnected functional elements or subsystems that comprise the total organization.

To begin with a very simple feedback model, figure 2–3 illustrates an assumed relationship between "the public" and any given organization. Demands are identified by the organization, and attempts are made to meet these demands (at least those demands considered to be above some threshold of concern). When the supply of services does not match up with the level of

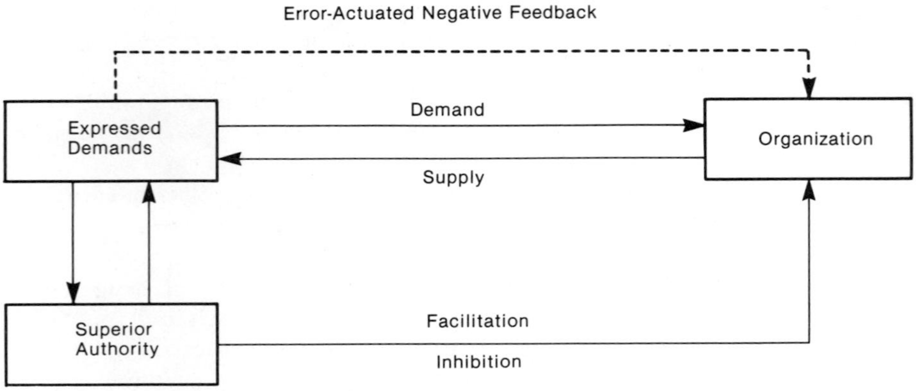

Error-Actuated Negative Feedback

Figure 2–3. Interaction between Demands and an Organization

demands, however, a process occurs that systems theorists call "error-actu-ated negative feedback." As a consequence, with subsequent attempts to sup-ply services, the system may more closely approximate the actual level of de-mand. Demands also may be monitored by some superior authority (such as government), which, in turn, may take steps to facilitate or inhibit the opera-tions of the functional systems. This fundamental feedback model, based on demand for and the supply of organizational services, will be further elaborated upon in a subsequent section.

Self-regulation in an organization can be accomplished through such feedback mechanisms. Organizational responses may be modified on the basis of information inputs that deal with actual performance, measured against some established criteria (goals and objectives). Or such responses may be triggered by something as subtle as a slight increase in some complex production function. The control mechanism may operate entirely within the organization and be termed *closed,* or may derive its information from out-side the system, and be termed *open.* Haberstroh illustrates this control func-tion when he says:

The study of self-regulating systems, now generally known as cybernetics, explores the ways in which some output of a dynamic system can be main-tained in a more-or-less invariant equilibrium, or steady state, in the face of disrupting external forces. The most general answer to this question is that

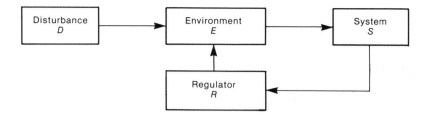

Figure 2–4. Error-Controlled Servo-Mechanism

the system must somehow be supplied with information about the disrupting forces that is used to offset their effect.[16]

Consider the basic feedback model depicted in figure 2–4. A disturbance, *D*, acts through the environment, *E*, on the system *S*. Feedback as to the state of *S* is provided to a regulator, *R*, which can then act on *S* through its environment to maintain the system in some set of desirable states. The function of the regulator is to block the transfer of the disturbance to the system. However, the system must experience the disturbance (and a changed state) before *R* can act. Hence, regulation, at best, will be imperfect. This is because *R* can receive only imperfect information about the original disturbance.

R's capacity as a regulator cannot exceed its capacity as a communication channel. A fundamental theorem of information theory states that the amount of noise (disturbance) in a communication channel that can be countered by a correction channel (regulator) is limited to the information capacity of the correction channel.[17] Stated in other terms, a regulator must have sufficient degrees of freedom to counter a disturbance.

Adequate capacity is a necessary but not a sufficient condition for achieving adequate regulation, however. The quality of information transmitted through the channel identified as a regulator is as important as the quantity. If the information available to the regulator (*R*) about the state of the system is not relevant to the disturbing influence, then no effective regulation can take place.

In general, the essential role of a good regulator is to maintain stability, that is, to keep the system within the desired stable set of states. The environment *E* usually is a given; it cannot be abolished, but usually, it can be manipulated in some fashion. The problem of regulation is as follows: given *E*, *S*, and *D*, form the mechanism *R* so that *R* and *S*, when coupled, act to keep *S* within the desired range of stability. This coupling may take place in one of five ways:

1. *R* may be introduced between the disturbance and the environment so as to be directly sensitive to *D* and, in turn, serve as an input in determining the state of *E* (and therefore of *S*).

2. The disturbance may act simultaneously on *R* and *E*, with a second link between *R* and *E*.

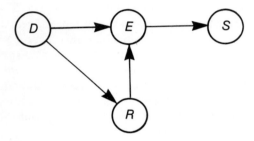

3. The disturbance may be sensed by *R* only indirectly through *E*, from which *R* provides an input back to *E*.

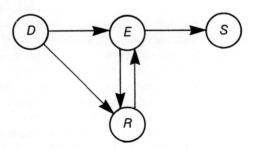

4. The regulator may be interposed between *E* and *S*, such that the system, the environment, and the regulator are coupled so as to act as a whole.

5. The sensitivity of R to some disturbance may be dependent upon the actual effect of D on S acting through E.

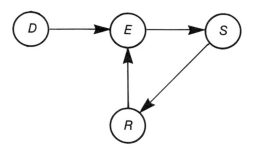

The first type of coupling, of course, is the ideal type. Here, the regulator acts in such a way as to serve as an input in determining the state of the environment, which, in turn, governs the desired conditions of the system. However, such cases of perfect regulations are relatively limited when dealing with real phenomena. As noted, the most common form of coupling is illustrated by the fifth example, known as an "error-controlled servomechanism" or a "closed loop regulator."

Goal Setting and Forecasting

The effectiveness of an organization can be measured by how well resources are allocated to achieve agreed-upon goals. Goals must be based on a careful analysis of the expressed and unexpressed demands of the various clientele served. In many organizations, however, resource allocations are directed toward a relatively narrow clientele, with inadequate attention given to the implications for other groups in the society. This short-sighted allocation of resources often reflects an inadequacy of the structural arrangements within these organization entrusted with the setting of priorities (strategic management).

Three specific areas of information provide the basis of the formulation of organizational goals: (1) *auto-intelligence* provides information about the particular organization under study and the component elements of that organization, (2) *environmental intelligence* provides information about the broader environment—the "out there"—of which the particular organization is a part, and (3) *historical data* brings together and analyzes the lessons of the past (see figure 2–5). From intelligence studies in these three areas, it is possible to develop probabilistic forecasts. Such forecasts represent a weighed and balanced analysis, rather than an intuitive impression of current trends and their possible effect on the future.

These forecasts provides the first and fundamental part of a strategic planning process. The forecast for any particular time period must be based

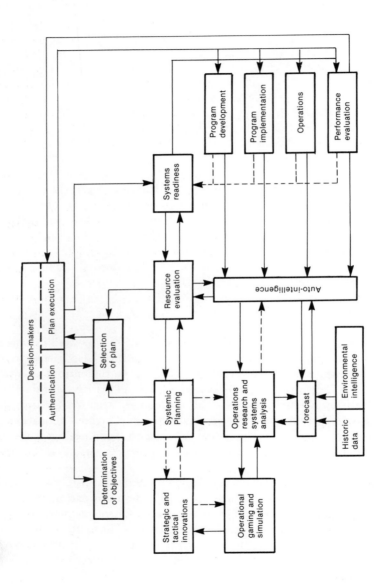

Figure 2–5. A Strategic Decision System

Source: Alan Walter Steiss and Anthony J. Catanese, *Systemic Planning: Theory and Application* (Lexington, Mass.: Lexington Books, 1970), p. 50. Reprinted with permission.

on existing trends in relation to the values and objectives chosen. A prognosis can be made of future situations that may arise if these trends continue. It may be argued that with experience, such forecasts can be made with sufficient certainty to provide a far better basis for rational action than available through the present informal and almost random decision making that characterizes many organizations.

In view of these forecasts, strategic planning can focus on determining new strategic, technical, and tactical courses of action to enhance the overall performance of the organization. The ultimate functional outcome of such a process would be to add new states to the system—new options in response to a network of goal perceptions. A basic problem of most modern organizations, whether in the public or private sector, is achieving a balance of programs and resource commitments so as to ensure *systems readiness* in the short-, mid-, and long-range futures. This requires a posture of sufficient flexibility to meet a wide range of possible competitive situations.

All too often, organizational decisions are based on intuitive methods that may have been sufficient in the past when problems were comprehensible to a single human mind or a small board of advisors. In many organizations, decision makers have not come to recognize that in truly complex situations this approach is outmoded. In today's decision environment, the available tools of analysis and synthesis must be utilized in combination with intuition developed through experience. The strategic planning task force must include more than merely planning technicians—strategic planning is a principal responsibility of high-level administrators and policymakers. Their participation is vital to the success of the strategic planning process. By the same token, a rapport and level of confidence must be developed whereby the decision makers can accept the result of the analyses with the assurance that they are valid without having to question them in detail.

The organizational executive should have the benefit of all the sophisticated management and planning techniques when individual plans and sets of objectives are presented, covering proposed strategies, tactics, and action programs. The executive, then, has the responsibility for the final decision that determines whether a particular proposal is to be implemented. This implementation may require further program development and specification before action programs can be put into operation. Finally, some mechanism of performance evaluation must be built into action programs to provide further inputs into the autointelligence system for subsequent problem situations.

Organizational Stability

Among the inputs to any complex organization are various clientele groups, that is, persons for whom the organization has been designed to serve. For the most part, these clientele groups have relatively little effect on the structure or processes of an organization as they pass through it (or are served by it). Whatever else happens, a complex organization is very powerfully arranged to maintain its internal stability.

Stability-Seeking Character of Open Systems

At any point in time, the stability of a complex organization is determined by the relationship among a set of systemic variables. Any change in one of these variables may cause a shift in the position of dynamic equilibrium (stability) of that variable. The variable affected by the change is modified slightly so that the effects of the disturbance are offset, and the organization continues its original pattern of behavior. This is a consequence of the stability-seeking character of any open system.

No system, of course, can survive environmental disturbances so great as to be extirpating. Up to this final threshold of disturbance, however, complex organizations are machines for survival, and indeed they do survive. The operations within an organization that produce this survival behavior are social mechanisms, including the socialization to a particular belief structure and a complicated set of organizational rules and regulations, conventions, norms, values, and so forth that supports this belief structure.

It is important to any society, of course, that its organizations do have such solidarity, that they are "ultrastable." Although this characteristic may impede change, it also is what gives the prevailing society its strength. Society would be constantly on a threshold of chaos if organizations could be toppled under the pressures from anarchists or maniacs, or even through the incompetence of individuals concerned with the operations of these systems.

Those who seek changes in the prevailing social system—social critics, reformers, and innovators—often fail to recognize the ultrastable character of modern organizations. As a consequence, they cannot understand why their criticisms, demands, or advice fail to produce more effective results. Direct frontal attacks on the internal mechanisms (structure and process) of complex organizations yield little but frustration. Would-be reformers may become even more frustrated when an organization does not mount a direct counterattack in response to their efforts. This is a measure of the extent to which organizations have developed self-sustaining devices to maintain stability.

When faced with an outside disturbance, certain processes within an equilibrium-seeking system may act in reverse. Thus, a functional system may maintain its stability and from the outside, may look very much the same. The extent of the changes which may have occurred within the system (and the implications of these changes) may not be realized, however. Despite these internal changes, the system has maintained its overall integrity. In fact, a reversal of the line of behavior may have an even more detrimental impact on the broader society than the operations of the system prior to the efforts of reform.

An example of such detrimental effects might be drawn from our legal institutions. Suppose that the desired reforms related to the manner in which the judicial system dispenses justice in matters of criminal litigation. The principle that a man is innocent until proven guilty might be represented by the system before the disturbance. After the disturbance (for example, an external threat to the society such as was perceived during the McCarthy era), the judicial system might operate under the principle that a man is guilty until proven innocent. The structure of the justice system might remain unchanged (the available states might remain constant). However, the procedures of litigation would obviously be quite different.

General systems theory would predict three characteristic outcomes (ultrastable responses) when a complex organization is faced with serious disturbances:

1. The organization survives as an integral system; it is still recognizable as the original esoteric functional system.
2. The organization maintains equilibrium relationships with other functional systems, although the form of these relationships may change.
3. Extensive realignments within the organization may be required to achieve its integral survival; in particular, these adjustments may involve actual reversals of internal roles or in the specific conditions whereby the role of the organization is defined in terms of variables most responsive to changes in the broader environment.

Social Metasystems

Most activities in modern society are carried out through a collection of organizations and institutions. These functional systems, in turn, are connected together under some set of rules to constitute a social metasystem. The term *metasystem* is used in general systems theory to refer to a combination of systems which, when linked together, transcends the limitations of their own parameters (that is, where the whole is greater than the sum of the parts).

In linking together a series of functional systems to form a social metasystem, it must be recognized that the result should be more than the collective attributes of the individual social institutions and organizations. "Something more" essentially refers to what, following Hegal, could be called a higher-order synthesis. The resulting social metasystem should be capable of survival even when its component institutions and organizations (despite their stability) may finally begin to fail.

The linking of complex organizations and social institutions to form a social metasystem, in one sense, can be likened to stringing a set of beads. A string of beads can be stable, but it is not ultrastable. If the cord is cut, nothing is left but the individual beads, and they may be widely scattered.

In contemporary society, established practices appear to be adrift in several dimensions simultaneously. Modern technology has not been properly related to the various functional systems, and as a consequence, the full potential of this technology has not been realized. At the same time, the ultrastable metasystem once provided by religion has largely disappeared, and with it, its ethical language. The metasystem of temporal power (government) that has emerged in modern society turns out to be spurious—and no real metasystem at all. The society is faced with a set of outmoded, possibly archaic, functional systems, the modus operandi of which is governed by anachronistic technology. Functional systems are strung together, not in a true metasystem, but in accordance with rules which themselves are the product of a functional system: the social institution of the status quo.

Thus, what is required to create an *ultrastable metasystem* is a set of relationships among social institutions and organizations which are more (a) elaborately structured, (b) cleverly connected, and (c) carefully planned and controlled than might emerge merely by assuming an association among the functional systems. Since the integration of key social institutions and organizations is important to the overall well-being of society, it may be necessary to establish a metasystemic mechanism which can influence the course of events by intervening in definitive ways.

The Search for a Hybrid Approach

It is far easier to advocate a systems approach to the analysis of complex organizations than it is to apply such an approach. A great deal of groundwork must be laid before a wholesale transfer of general systems techniques can be made to the field of organizational analysis. In fact, it may well be that such outright transfers are neither possible nor desirable. Rather, it may be necessary to formulate a hybrid approach in order to retain the scientific applications of the systems-oriented disciplines and the social and human value orientation of more traditional approaches to organizational analysis.

Problems most adaptable to systemic methodologies tend to be univariate in nature. An optimal solution may involve only a single problem dimension, and may result in the suboptimation of many other related systems or subsystems. Problems confronting complex organizations, on the other hand, often are multivariate. In dealing with such problems, it is necessary to anticipate possible by-products or side effects that might occur throughout a broader environment. Thus, strategies applicable to the solution of such organizational problems must seek to achieve one set of goals with minimum loss to the realization of other desired goals.

Systemic methodologies may not be directly applicable as tools of analysis in long-range problem situations. To handle such long-range problems, it is necessary to deal with *possible* situations, which can only be forecast. In a very real sense, it may be said that the functional systems (organizations) to be analyzed do not exist but must be invented. The operational situations envisaged do not as yet exist, and furthermore, they have only a probability of actually existing at some time in the future. By the same token, the operational laws governing the behavior of these functional systems must be brought into being through proper manipulation of the operational environment. Both the invented system and the operational laws must be conceptualized and analyzed.

It must be recognized that there are no immutable laws governing the operations of complex systems (or, for that matter, no immutable systems). It is possible, however, to identify a set of constraints and associated laws governing the behavior of selected systems or subsystems. If these characteristics can be accepted empirically and intellectually for a sufficient time period, it is possible to describe and, subsequently, to manipulate variables so as to optimize some set of desired goals and objectives in the actual operations of complex organizations. These are the necessary and sufficient conditions to permit the application of systemic techniques in dealing with complex organizations.

Past efforts to analyze the dynamics of complex organizations, for the most part, have been characterized by intuitive approaches.[18] As Forrester has observed, intuitive solutions to the problems of complex systems will be wrong most of the time.[19] Intuition gained through experience must be combined with available systemic tools of analysis and synthesis. Such an approach should be developed in such a way as to have the advantages of both "hard" systems (scientific applications) and intuitive or value-oriented applications.[20] The concepts of strategic management, as developed herein, are presented with these objectives in mind.

Notes

1. H.D.F. Kitto, *The Greeks* (Baltimore, Md.: Penguin Press, 1951), p. 175.

2. Ludwig von Bertalanffy, *General Systems Theory* (New York: George Braziller, 1968), p. 37.

3. Ludwig von Bertalanffy, "General Systems Theory," *Main Currents in Modern Thought,* vol. 71 (1955). In this assertion von Bertalanffy echoed the observation made twenty years earlier by Robert S. Lynd in *Knowledge for What* (Princeton: Princeton University Press, 1967).

4. Ibid.

5. Von Bertalanffy, *General Systems Theory,* p. 33.

6. D. Stanley-Jones, "The Role of Positive Feedback," *Progress in Cybernetics,* vol. 1 (London: Gordon and Breach Science Publishers, 1970), p. 251.

7. Gregory Bateson, *Naven* (Cambridge: Cambridge University Press, 1936), p. 175.

8. Ludwig von Bertalanffy, *Biophysik des Fliessgleichgewichts,* translated by W. Westphal (Braunschweig, 1953).

9. Von Bertalanffy, "General Systems Theory," p. 42.

10. Ibid., p. 41. For a further discussion of the application of these concepts in management and planning, see Alan Walter Steiss, *Models for the Analysis and Planning of Urban Systems* (Lexington, Mass.: Lexington Books, 1974), chap. 7.

11. Alvin Toffler, *Future Shock* (New York: Random House, 1970).

12. See Steiss, *Models for the Analysis and Planning of Urban Systems,* chap. 9, for further elaboration on this point.

13. Von Bertalanffy, *General Systems Theory,* p. 78.

14. N.A. Coulter, Jr., "Toward a Theory of Teleogentic Control Systems," *General Systems* (Ann Arbor: Society for General Systems Research, 1968), p. 86.

15. A.D. Hall and R.E. Fagan, "Definition of System," in *Modern Systems Research for the Behavioral Scientist,* edited by Walter Buckley (Chicago: Aldine, 1968), p. 87.

16. Chadwick J. Haberstroh, "Control as an Organizational Process," in *Organizations: Systems, Control, and Adaptation,* edited by Joseph A. Litterner (New York: John Wiley & Sons, 1969), p. 308.

17. Claude E. Shannon and Warren Weaver, *The Mathematical Theory of Communication* (Urbana: University of Illinois Press, 1949), p. 37.

18. Jerald Hage, *Theories of Organizations: Form, Process and Transformation* (New York: Wiley-Interscience Publication, John Wiley & Sons, 1980).

19. Author's notes from "Should We Improve Our Cities? Can We?", paper presented by Jay W. Forrester at the NATO International Conference on Cities (Indianapolis, May 25–28, 1971).

20. For a further discussion of this point, see Anthony J. Catanese and Alan Walter Steiss, *Systemic Planning: Theory and Application* (Lexington, Mass.: Lexington Books, 1970), chap. 1.

3
Decision Making as a Multistage Process

S
tudies of complex organizations often fail to give adequate attention to the more dynamic aspects of the decision process. By concentrating on a particular aspect or phase of decision making, these studies present a somewhat static picture, even though the dynamic characteristics of the decision process often are acknowledged.

In the context of strategic management, decision making is viewed as a multistage process involving the gathering, evaluating, recombining, and disseminating of information. It is a dynamic process, within which communication both binds the process together and moves it from stage to stage in response to demands for both tactical and strategic decisions.

A Dynamic, Open, Goal-Directed, Stochastic System

Viewed in terms of a general systems model, organizational decision making can be considered an open system which seeks relative stability through a stochastic search process. Even though the decision-making process appears to operate on a trial-and-error basis, its behavior is teleological or goal directed. In the search process, the decision system of an organization may pass through a number of critical stages until eventually it settles down in a stable region, wherein conflicts with some larger environment can be held to a minimum.

Adaptation to Change

An effective decision system does not merely seek equilibrium. The classic equilibrium model assumes that, in the face of change, a system is compelled by an overriding force to reestablish some preexisting state of equilibrium. This traditional concept of equilibrium is incapable of describing important ranges of dynamic phenomena. An open system does not merely seek static continuity at some fixed point or level of equilibrium. Rather, in responding to forces of change, an open system frequently strives to create conditions that, under favorable circumstances, will permit the system to achieve some new level of stability. At times, positive action may even be taken to destroy a previous equilibrium or even to achieve some new point of continuing disequilibrium. These dynamic qualities of open systems also require that a more thorough examination be given to the temporal sequences by which the structure of a system shapes its functions, and which, in turn, is altered by functional change.

Adaptation to change represents more than simple adjustments to events which impose themselves on the structure of the system. A primary characteristic of all open systems is that they are able to manifest a wide range of actions of a positive, constructive, and innovative sort for warding off or absorbing forces of displacement.

The range of possible adjustments is governed by the relative number of responses available to the decision system when confronted by decision-demanding situations. In general systems terms, this is analogous to the Law of Requisite Variety—a set of regulators (R) only can be successful in warding off a set of disturbances (D) if the number of alternatives available to R (R's variety) is equal to, or greater than, those available to D (D's variety).[1] It is possible to increase the range of variety available to regulatory devices through coupling. In this sense, coupling can be equated to increased access to information and channels of communication within the decision-making process.

Recognition must be given to the fact that an organization, operating as a dynamic, open system, interacts continually with its broader environment. Expressed and unexpressed demands, emanating from the broader environment and from within the organization, continue to act as disturbances to the stability of the organization. These disturbances force the organization to develop and employ regulatory devices to counter these "dysfunctional" aspects.

Tactical, Adaptive, and Strategic Decisions

The elementary components of organizational decision making often are characterized by a good deal of randomness. Efforts to describe the sequence of steps taken in the process may be somewhat arbitrary. Running through the decision process, however, are two elements that give it structure and permit the process to yield a relatively well-organized product. These elements are (1) the broad procedural stages recognizable in most problem-solving situations; and (2) the substantive parameters; that is, the structure elements of the decision process which, in turn, reflect the structure of the problem.

In their landmark work on organization, Simon and March suggest a three-stage process of problem solving. This process begins with a *disaggre-*

gation of the problem to permit the solution of the parts; is followed by a *search stage,* which may be physical, perceptual, or cognitive; and culminates in a *screening stage,* in which the items identified in the search stage are examined to see if they qualify as possible solutions or components of solutions to the problem at hand.[2] Simon and March also make the following distinction between programmed and nonprogrammed problem solving: "Programmed activity generally involves a great deal of problem-solving of a rather routine and reproductive sort. . . . Contrariwise, the unprogrammed activity in innovation generally requires a great deal of "productive" problem-solving."[3]

Programmed problem solving generally involves *tactical decisions.* If both the underlying conditions of the problem and the requirements that must be satisfied by the solution are known, then a routine problem-solving approach may well be applicable. In such cases, the task is merely one of choosing from among a few obvious alternatives. The decision criterion usually is one of economy (least cost). While many tactical decisions reached through the use of well-established problem-solving techniques may be relatively important and complicated, invariably they are unidimensional in nature.

Decisions with far-reaching implications generally are decisions of *strategy.* To arrive at effective decisions in such instances, it is necessary (1) to find out what the general problem situation is, (2) to determine what alternative courses are open to change the situation, (3) to identify the most effective solution in light of available resources, and (4) to determine what additional resources might be necessary (and feasible) to achieve a more effective solution. A rational choice as to the course of action to be pursued can only be reached after these steps have been taken.

A third category should be inserted in the tactical-strategic continuum to account for *adaptive decisions.* Adaptive decisions begin with programmed responses but require considerable reconstruction of programmed details before they are applicable to a given problem situation. Such decisions seek to alleviate built-up pressures by removing the more immediate sources of demand or by providing a satisfactory alternative solution to that which is sought. Adaptive decisions provide a means of modifying established patterns of responses. Such decisions reestablish a flow of productive activity on a more or less stable basis. Since adaptations may not eliminate the root causes of the problem, they often are only temporary solutions. As pressures of displacement continue to mount, adaptive decisions may no longer suffice, and, in some instance, may even contribute to the total stress on the organization.

Since accommodation is relatively less painful and less disruptive to the status quo, most dysfunctional patterns of activity are dealt with through adaptive rather than strategic decisions. Adaptive decisions lead to certain minor revisions in expectations, whereas strategic decisions may lead to new expectations or to major adjustments in existing expectations. The term *expectations* is used in this connection to denote the indigenous criteria against which persons gauge the efficacy of a particular decision. The principal test of new patterns produced by a decision is their compliance with the minimal expectations sanctioned by the organization.

When the organization's expectations are met through adaptive decisions, fine adjustments are initiated that lead to routinization of the response. The revised pattern gradually is "programmed" as a legitimized response, that is, as a regulatory mechanism. Even though adaptive decisions may dissipate those stresses which evoked the initial need for adjustment, such decisions may include some ill-conceived steps or unanticipated side effects which, in turn, produce new and unfamiliar stresses. In such cases, further adaptive decisions may be required to produce more satisfactory patterns.

There are limits to the malleability of the structure of a decision system, however. Adaptive adjustments must be devised within these limits. When the suggested accommodations call for changes which exceed these boundaries, a major problem emerges. Such situations require innovative, strategic decisions to bring about major modifications in ends as well as means.

A strategic decision differs from an adaptive decision principally in the rate at which changes comes about. A series of adaptive decisions may eventually lead to the introduction of substantial changes in the structure of the system. The two modes differ in intent, however. The strategic decision is a deliberate attempt to deal with an intolerable situation through a direct frontal attack rather than through oblique incremental operations.

This is not to deny the value of incremental decisions. It may be said that the highest art of decision making lies in knowing when to induce change in genuine increments and when to use the bold stroke of innovation. Situations requiring innovative decisions usually involve issues that run to the roots of the organization—issues so central and compelling that they cannot be disposed of either obliquely or incrementally.

Once the need for a strategic decision is apparent and accepted, an overt appraisal should be made of the goals and objectives of the organization. The purpose of this assessment is to place the strategic innovation in its proper perspective. This appraisal often brings to the surface conflicting motives distributed among several otherwise discontinuous roles within the structure of the organization.

Decision making involves an aggregate of people collaborating through some imposed system (a system which they have inherited and continually remake). As a consequence, individual goals frequently diverge and become inconsistent with the overall goals of the organization. So long as conflicting goals remain unstated (that is, are not explicitly held up to the light for examination), these inconsistencies may go unnoticed, even though they may be dysfunctional to the organization. When innovation is introduced, however, and these goals must be made explicit, conflict becomes evident and must be dealt with if the organization is to retain its stability.

Stages of Decision Making

While attempts have been made to analyze decision making as a universal process, considerable differences exist in the ways in which these decision responses—tactical, adaptive, and strategic—are handled by an organization's decision system. It is important to recognize these differences and to examine systematically the unique attributes of the general classes of regulatory devices and their impact on the decision process.

Demands as the Inputs of a Decision System

As a rule, the decision process becomes more orderly and identifiable at the stage in which alternative solutions are formulated and evaluated. The earlier stages of decision making, however, often are characterized by a good deal of randomness, with considerable arbitrariness in the sequence of steps taken. If meaningful insights are to be derived, however, a systematic approach is required in the analysis of these early stages. As Northrup has so aptly pointed out, "One may have the most rigorous of methods during the later stages of investigation but if a false or superficial beginning has been made, rigor later on will never retrieve the situation."[4]

A particular organization under study often is set apart from its broader environment. It must be recognized, however, that many aspects of this environment have important impacts on the organization insofar as decision demands are concerned. Decision demands enter the system in the form of inputs. As noted previously, Easton has defined a *demand* as "an expressed opinion that an authoritative allocation with regard to a particular subject matter should or should not be made by those responsible for doing so."[5] A demand does not necessarily reflect the value preferences of the demand maker. In fact, demands may be used to conceal true preferences, as when a program is promoted for the purposes of generating support for some other, unexpressed course of action.

Demands may also arise from dysfunctional conditions in a given situation without taking the form of expressed opinions. Such conditions may be interpreted from within the system as constituting demand inputs, even though in the larger environment they have not been identified or verbalized as such.

A demand may be narrow, specific, and relatively simple; or it may be general, vague, and complex. Demands may be expressed as specific grievances associated with a particular situation; or they may be generalized. Such generalized demands seldom include proposals for specific courses of action, although they may embody ill-defined, all-encompassing programs. Expressed demands may be directed toward specific individuals or groups within an organization, or may be ubiquitously oriented. However, every expressed demand carries with it a set of expectations concerning the responses that should come from the organization.

Unexpressed demands also arise from a variety of sources and assume multifaceted characteristics. As with expressed demands, they are evidence that someone within the organization recognizes the existence of unacceptable conditions. In other words, before demands can gain entry as inputs into the decision system, they must be sensed as demands. Someone within the organization must recognize that the conditions giving rise to the demands are "out of phase" with some acceptable norm or condition within the desired state of the organization.

It is this perception of a demand that sets the decision process in motion. Very often, this perception is merely a sense of uncertainty or doubt that exists because the constituent elements of a segment of the broader environment are unsettled or are not unified. As Dewey has observed, "It is the very nature of the indeterminate situation which evokes inquiry to be questionable . . . to be uncertain, unsettled, disturbed."[6]

This concept of uncertainty is a positive one, meaning more than a mere subjective sense of absence or deprivation. The uncertainty that exists stems from a particular uncertain objective situation. Objective observations of the situation do not coincide with the definition of what *should be,* a concept that may be subjectively or objectively defined.

An individual's conceptual frame of reference, in large measure, governs the way in which he or she approaches an uncertain situation. Furthermore, this frame of reference will contribute to the identification of a situation as being "out of phase" with the presently accepted system. Background and training may provide individuals with well-constructed sets of concepts which make them more sensitive to certain problems that others might pass over unobserved.

Thus the role of the strategic manager, as an initiator in the decision process, can be identified more clearly. The strategic manager must continually appraise various aspects of the accepted system and identify any elements in the broader environment that may seem to be potential disturbances to the organization. This role might be likened to a regulator which acts as a warning device against disturbances which threaten to drive a system out of some desirable set of states.

Decision demands may originate from within the organization itself, as well as coming from sources external to the organization.[7] The manner by which these inputs or demands are handled within the organization, however, varies only slightly whether the sources of uncertainty are external or internal.

Screening Demands to Determine Intakes

Once a situation has been identified as uncertain or potential, four responses are possible (see figure 3–1). Each of these responses involves a different degree of commitment to the decision process.

The first possibility is to disregard the uncertain situation, that is, to decide to do nothing about it. Such a response is likely when the demand is below some threshold of tolerance. If for some reason, such as time, cost, or effort, this response is invoked, the decision process will be cut short. For the purposes of this discussion, we have no further interest in such negative behavior.

The second possible response is to identify further the uncertain situation as one which can be handled through programmed decision mechanisms. This response would suggest that some sort of memory bank exists within the decision system in which these programmed decision mechanisms are stored and against which uncertain situations can be tested to determine if an appropriate programmed decision is available. Again, the decision process is cut short by the application of a programmed response.

If either of the two remaining possible responses is invoked, the decision process moves to the next stage—that of *classification* and *definition*. Inputs are screened to determine the actual intakes into the decision system. This screening filters out those demands for which no further action will be taken at present and those which can be handled through programmed mechanisms. The individuals responsible for this screening are analogous to the "gatekeepers" in Easton's conceptual schema.

Although uncertainty is essential to an initiation of the decision process, it is not sufficient to create a problematic situation, that is, one for which decision makers are likely to seek alternative solutions. As Dewey has stated, the uncertain situation "becomes problematic in the very process of being subjected to inquiry."[8] Analysis does not begin with the uncertain or unsettled situation, that is, anticipatory to analysis. Under analysis, the problematic situation is made more explicit. As Rapoport has noted, the first step in solving a problem is to state it.

> The statement usually involves a description of an existing state and desirable state of affairs where the factors involved in the discrepancy are explicitly pointed out. The success with which any problem is solved depends to a great extent on the clarity with which it is stated. In fact, the solution of the problem is, in a sense, a clarification (or concretization) of the objectives.[9]

Vague statements of the situation lead to vague methods, where success is erratic and questionable. The more a given problem situation can be extended, the better the classification, and the greater the promise of a successful solution.

The first question to be asked about an uncertain situation is: Is this a

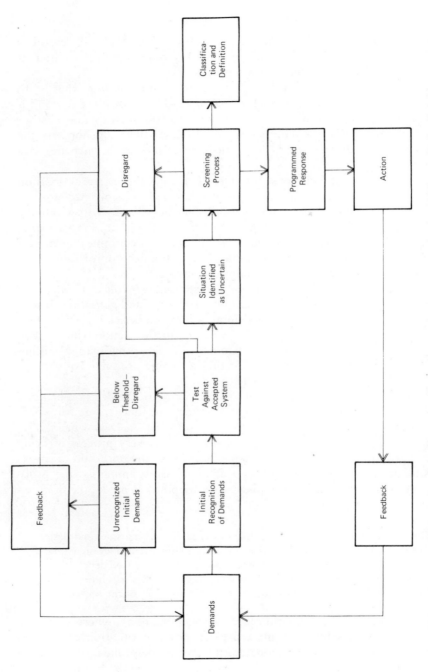

Source: Alan Walter Steiss, Public Budgeting and Management (Lexington, Mass.: Lexington Books, 1972), p. 127. Reprinted by permission.

Figure 3–1. Screening Demands to Determine Intakes

symptom of a fundamental or generic problem or merely a stray event? A generic problem often can be handled through the application of pro-grammed or adaptive responses. The truly exceptional event, however, must be handled as it is encountered.[10]

Strictly speaking, a distinction should be made among four, rather than two, different types of problem sets. First, there is the truly *generic event,* of which the individual occurrence is only a symptom. Most of the problems confronting complex organizations fall into this category. As a rule, such generic situations require adaptive decisions. Frequently, programmed deci-sion mechanisms are applied to the symptoms of a generic problem. Until the generic problem is identified, however, significant amounts of time and energy may be spent in the piecemeal application of programmed decisions to the symptoms without ever gaining control of the generic situation.

The second type of occurrence is one that, although unique in a given organization, is actually a generic event. For example, when a company must choose a location for a new processing plant, this may be a unique situation as far as the current decision makers in the company are concerned. It is, of course, a generic situation that has confronted many other companies in the past, however. Some general rules exist for deciding on the best location for such facilities, and the decision makers can turn to the experience of others for these guidelines.

The third possible classification is the truly *unique situation.* Here, the event itself may be unique or the circumstances in which the event has occurred may be unique. For example, the huge power failure of November 1965, which plunged northeastern North America into darkness, was a truly exceptional or unique event, at least according to first explanations. On the other hand, the collision of two airplanes miles from any air terminal is a unique situation, not because airplanes do not run the risk of collision, but because of the unique circumstances under which the event occurred.

The fourth type of event confronting the decision process is the *early manifestation* of a new generic problem. Both the power failure and the colli-sion of the two airplanes, for example, turned out to be only the first occur-rences of what are likely to become fairly frequent events unless generic solu-tions are found to certain basic problems of modern technology.

General rules, policies, or principles usually can be developed or adapted to deal with generic situations. Once the right decision has been found, all manifestations of the same generic situation can be handled fairly pragmati-cally by adapting the rules or principles to the concrete circumstances of the situation. In short, such problems can be handled through adaptive decision making.

The unique problem and the first manifestation of a generic problem, however, often require greater innovation in the search for successful solu-tions. As illustrated in figure 3–2, the relationships among these four catego-

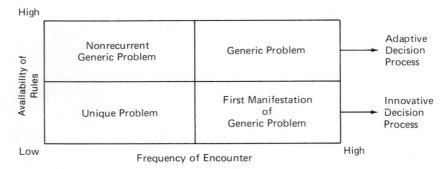

Source: Alan Walter Steiss and Gregory A. Daneke, *Performance Administration* (Lexington, Mass.: Lexington Books, 1980), p. 106. Reprinted by permission.

Figure 3–2. Classification and Definitions of Basic Problems

ries can be described in terms of the two fundamental dimensions of *availability of rules and principles* for dealing with such problems and the *frequency of encounter* of these situations.

By far the most common mistake in decision making is to treat a generic problem as if it were a series of unique events. The other extreme, that of treating every problem incrementally (that is, treating a unique event as if it were just another example of the same old problem to which the same old rule should be applied), can have equally negative repercussions.

The role of the experienced strategic manager is to avoid incomplete solutions to problems that are only partially understood. The technical expertise of those closest to the situation should be used to classify the problem. Once a problem has been classified, it is usually relatively easy to define. A further danger in this step, however, is that of finding not the wrong definition of the problem, but a plausible albeit incomplete one. Safeguards against an incomplete definition include checking it against all observable facts and discarding the definition if and when it fails to encompass any of these facts.

The outcome of the analysis of a problem should be a clear definition of that problem. If the problem cannot be stated specifically, preferably in one interrogative sentence, including one or more objectives, then the analysis has been inadequate or of insufficient depth. Emotional bias, habitual or traditional behavior, and the human tendency to seek the path of least resistance may contribute to a superficial analysis, followed by a statement of the apparent rather than the real problem. An excellent solution to an apparent problem will not work in practice, because it is the solution to a problem that does not exist in fact. Short-circuiting this phase of the decision process may actually result in more time spent later to get at the real problem when it becomes painfully evident that further analysis is required.

Identification of Constraints and Boundary Conditions

The next major step in the decision process involves the clear specification of what the decision must accomplish. Five basic questions must be answered:

1. What objectives must be met and what are the minimum goals to be obtained?
2. What are the existing or potential constraints to an effective solution?
3. What measure(s) of efficiency can be used relative to each of the objectives?
4. What standard(s) can be applied for the evaluation of possible courses of action?
5. What definition of "most effective" is to be applied in judging the possible solutions to any given problem set?

These questions aid in the establishment of *boundary conditions*—the set of factors that define the field within which a feasible solution can and should be found. When techniques of operations research, such as linear or dynamic programming, can be applied, boundary conditions can be clearly identified and even given numerical values. In most organizational decision situations, however, the identification of boundary conditions may be a most difficult undertaking.

Nevertheless, this stage of the decision process is crucial. A decision that does not meet the boundary conditions is worse than one that incorrectly identifies the problem. It is all but impossible to salvage a decision that starts with the right premise but stops short of the right conclusions. Furthermore, clear thinking about boundary conditons is essential to recognize when a course of action, brought about by a given decision, should be abandoned. Decision makers must be able to recognize a subsequent shift in objectives—in specifications—that may make a prior "right" decision suddenly inappropriate. As Drucker has observed, "Unless the decision maker has kept the boundary conditions clear, so as to make possible the immediate replacement of the outflanked decision with a new and appropriate policy, he may not even notice that things have changed.[11]

Often the decision specifications to be satisfied essentially are incompatible. In other words, to achieve goal *A* through the course of action prescribed by the decision may preclude the achievement of goal *B,* or at best, makes this achievement highly unlikely. This dilemma represents a classic case in which boundary conditions were not fully and clearly identified. Similarly, decisions often are made which involve a gamble or so-called calculated risk. This type of decision, which may work if nothing whatsoever goes wrong, often emerges from something less rational than a gamble, a futile hope that two or more clearly imcompatible specifications can be fulfilled simultaneously.

Determining boundary conditions require a clear view of organizational goals and objectives. All too often, however, organizational goals are too vague to establish boundary conditions applicable to any particular decision situation. What is required is some mechanism whereby overall goals can be translated into more specific program objectives and through which identifiable boundary conditions can be tested against the more general (and remote) organizational goals. In deterministic decision situations, such mechanisms are generally available. In stochastic situations, such mechanisms are more difficult to develop and apply.

Formulation of Alternatives

Several alternatives should be developed for every problem situation. Otherwise, there is a danger of falling into the trap of a false "either-or" proposition. There is a common confusion in human thinking between a true contradiction, embracing all possibilities, and a contrast listing only two out of a number of possibilities. This danger is heightened by a tendency to focus on the extremes in any problem situation.

In adaptive decision making, for example, a standard set of alternatives may be selected for analysis, the outcome being limited by some initial set of "givens." This procedure tends to limit the evolutionary nature of alternative formulation. And as a consequence, this approach should be avoided, if possible, even in adaptive decision making.

Alternative solutions are the primary means of bringing to light the basic assumptions concerning a given problem situation, thereby forcing an examination of their validity. Alternative solutions are no guarantee, however, of wisdom or the right decision. Nevertheless, an examination of alternatives can guard against making a decision that would have been seen to be wrong if the problem had been thought through more carefully.

Alternative approaches to a given decision-demanding situation differ according to the level of reflection reached. At first, they may be relatively vague; but as the alternatives posed direct further observation, they become more suitable for resolving the problem. As alternatives become more appropriate, empirical observations likewise become more acute. Perception and conception work together, the former locates and describes the problem, while the latter represents possible methods of solution.[12]

The next step is to develop an understanding of the possible consequences, by-products, and side effects associated with each of the suggested alternatives (see figure 3–3). This examination consists of an identification of the implications of particular courses of action in relation to other aspects of the organization. This formulation leads to a proposition: If such and such

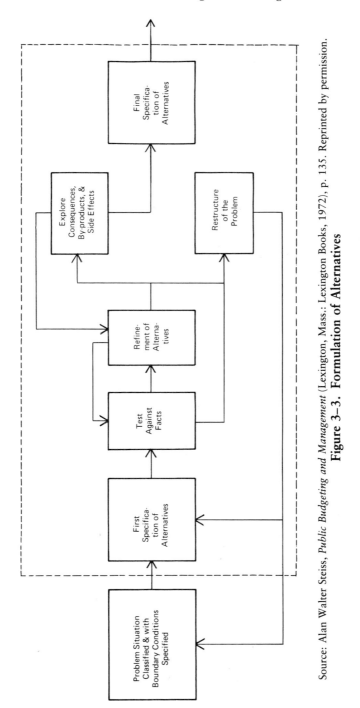

Source: Alan Walter Steiss, *Public Budgeting and Management* (Lexington, Mass.: Lexington Books, 1972), p. 135. Reprinted by permission.

Figure 3–3. Formulation of Alternatives

relation is accepted, then we are committed to such and such other courses of action because of their membership in the same set. A series of such intermediate examinations leads to an understanding of the problem that often is more relevant to the decision-demanding situation than was the original conception.

The examination of suggested alternatives for their operational fitness involves an investigation of their capacity to direct further observation aimed at securing additional factual material. This examination may result in the rejection, acceptance, or modification of ideas in an attempt to arrive at more relevant alternatives. The possible range of alternatives will vary with the problem. It must be recognized, however, that alternatives, in part, are a function of the data and concepts at the disposal of the organization. When these are sufficient, useful alternatives are likely to emerge.

One possible alternative is always that of taking no action at all. This alternative seldom is recognized as a decision, although it is no less a commitment than any specific positive action. An unpleasant or difficult decision cannot be avoided by doing nothing, however. The potential consequences of a decision not to act must be clearly spelled out. By carefully considering the alternative of doing nothing, the traditional ways of doing things, which often reflect past needs rather than those of the present, can be examined more carefully.

Frequently an impasse is reached in the search for alternatives. In such cases, restructuring the problem may lead to new insights into possible alternatives. Problem restructuring involves the manipulation of the elements of the problem. It may involve, for example, a change of viewpoint, or a permissible modification of objectives, or a rearrangement of other problem elements. Framing and analyzing alternatives and their consequences in light of the problem and the relevant facts of the situation is a major part of all rational decision making. In spite of its primacy to the decision process, there are no simple hard-and-fast rules for hitting upon the right set of alternatives.

The Search for a Best Solution

Only after a number of alternatives have been formulated and evaluated is it possible to determine the best solution. If an adequate job has been done to this point, it likely will be found that there are several alternatives from which to choose. There may be half a dozen or so, all of which fall short of perfection, but differ among themselves as to the area of shortcoming. It is a rare situation in which there is one and only one right solution. In fact, whenever analyses lead to this comforting conclusion, one may reasonably suspect the conclusion as being little more than a plausible argument for a preconceived idea.

There are two basic modes of operation for finding the best solution from among several alternatives (see figure 3–4). The mode selected depends on the general class of decision sought, adaptive or strategic. Since adaptive decisions merely require that the alternative meet certain minimal expectations sanctioned by the organization, the best alternative can be selected on the basis of relatively simple criteria. The selected alternative should be one that provides a satisfactory solution to the problem (thereby alleviating the pressures created by the demand). At the same time, the selected course of action should create a minimum disturbance to established expectations. No single alternative may satisfy these conditions, and therefore, it may be necessary to combine elements from several alternatives to achieve these objectives.

The strategic decision requires a more rigorous analysis and testing, since it ultimately will result in the modification or substitution of expectations. Several criteria may be useful in seeking the best strategic decision. These criteria deal with such issues as (1) uncertainty, (2) risks and expected gains, (3) economy of effort, (4) timing of alternatives, and (5) limitations of resources.

Most strategic decisions involve major conditions of uncertainty. In such cases, therefore, analyses of alternatives must provide for explicit treatment of uncertainty. Several techniques, applicable under varying circumstances, have been developed for this purpose. Since problems of uncertainty are so crucial to effective strategic decisions, a major section of chapter 5 will be devoted to these techniques.

The risks associated with each proposed course of action must be weighed against expected gains. The terms *risks* and *gains* are used here rather than the more conventional concepts of costs and benefits for several reasons. Efforts to convert the positive and negative aspects of any alternative into dollars and cents frequently result in too narrow a frame of reference. The concept of costs associated with strategic decision alternatives means something more than that which shows up on a profit and loss statement. In developing a cost-benefit analysis, items often are omitted because they are intangibles. Many of these intangibles are important risks that may seriously affect the outcomes of a strategic decision. Assessments of benefits, on the other hand, frequently involves a form of double accounting. Direct benefits, for which dollar figures can be derived, often are counted again in terms of more indirect benefits. In arriving at a net-gains figure, therefore, such indirect benefits must be discounted in order to avoid an unrealistic assessment.

There is no riskless action nor even riskless nonaction. What is important, however, is neither the expected gain nor the anticipated risk, but the relationship between them. Every alternative should be evaluated on this basis. The value of such an analysis lies not in the end result but in the process pursued in arriving at this result.

The third criterion involves an assessment of the economy of effort. The various alternatives must be examined to determine which course of action

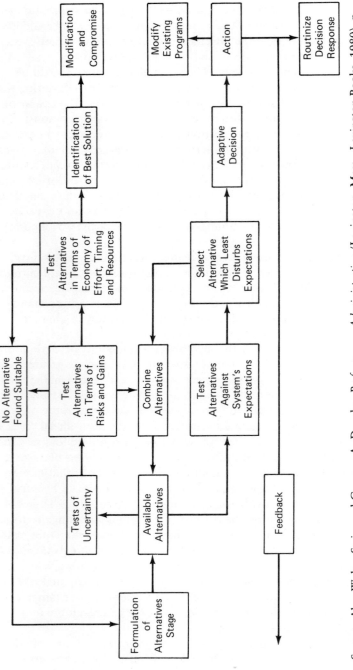

Figure 3–4. Finding the Best Solution

Source: Alan Walter Steiss and Gregory A. Daneke, *Performance Administration* (Lexington, Mass.: Lexington Books, 1980), p. 112. Reprinted by permission.

will give the greatest results with the least effort. As Drucker has observed, decision makers often use an elephant gun to chase sparrows or a slingshot against forty-ton tanks.[13] Grandiose schemes have many hidden risks which, if carefully considered, would reduce the overall economy of effort. By the same token, solutions that fail to set their sights high enough to produce optimal results may yield a series of incremental actions that, in the long run, will involve a much higher expenditure of effort.

The fourth criterion is concerned with the timing of the possible alternatives. If the situation is urgent, the preferable course of action may be one that dramatizes the decision and serves notice that something important is happening. If, on the other hand, long, consistent effort is needed, a slow start that gains momentum may be preferable. In some situations, the decision must be final and must immediately inspire those involved to seek new goals and objectives. In other situations, the first step is the most important— the final goal may be shrouded in obscurity for the time being.

Timing decisions is often extremely difficult to systematize; they may elude analysis and depend on perception. There is one guide, however: whenever a decision requires a change in vision to accomplish something new, it is best to be ambitious, to present the complete program and the ultimate aim. When a decision necessitates a change in people's long-standing habits, however, it may be best to take one step at a time, to start slowly and modestly, to do no more at first than is absolutely necessary.

The final criterion deals with the limitation of resources and is closely related to the notion of systems readiness. A basic problem of organizational decision making in both the public and private sectors is to achieve a balance in programs and the allocation of resources that will ensure a systems readiness in the short-, medium-, and long-term futures. Achieving this objective requires flexibility in confronting a wide range of competing actions.

Decisions often are made, procedures developed, and policies formulated without first asking: Are the means available for carrying out these actions? Perhaps the most important resource are the personnel who will be called upon to execute the decision. A less-than-optimal decision should not be adopted simply because the competence to do what is required is lacking. The best decision should always lie among genuine alternatives, that is, among courses of action which will adequately solve the problem. If such solutions demand greater competence, skill, and understanding than is available, then provision must be made to raise the capacity of those who must implement the programs associated with the best solution. All too often, substantial investments are made in organizational programs without adequate consideration given to the training of personnel necessary to effectively carry the requisite activities.

Modification to Gain an Acceptable Decision

The effective decision maker must start out with what is right or best rather than what is merely acceptable or possible because in the end compromises invariably will be necessary.[14] This factor relates back to the specification of boundary conditions, for if it is not clearly known what will satisfy the boundary conditions, the decision maker cannot distinguish between an appropriate and an inappropriate compromise. The decision maker gains relatively little if the decision process starts out with the question: What is acceptable? In the process of answering this question, important things usually are overlooked, and any chance of coming up with an effective solution—let alone the right answer—may be lost. The things one worries about seldom happen, while difficulties no one thought about initially may suddenly turn out to be almost insurmountable obstacles.

After a best solution has been identified, the first step in seeking an acceptable decision is to make a reconnaissance of the expectations of those segments of the organization most likely impacted by this decision (see figure 3–5). Unlike adaptive decisions, strategic decisions almost always require that expectations be altered and modified. Therefore, a careful appraisal must be made of expectations both internal and external to the organization. These expectations are relevant factors which must be accommodated by the decision.

Upon matching the proposed solution against the expectations of people within the organization, it may be anticipated that one of three conditions will prevail: (1) the expectations are in accord with the proposed solution, in which case an acceptable decision has been found; (2) the people are ambivalent with respect to the proposed solution; or (3) there is hostility with regard to the proposed solution. In the latter two cases, some means must be devised to divert the hostile attitudes and engender support for the proposed solution. If no acceptable means are found, internal demands will be heightened, and a further reconnaissance of the organization's expectations will be required.

This process of modification and compromise is somewhat akin to what other decision models have identified as "accommodating to the power structure." The more neutral notion of system expectations has been used here to give recognition to the role of the internal structure of the decision process, as well as to provide a model which is adaptable to both the power-structure and pluralistic approaches to decision making. The term *expectations* can include all factors, both internal and external to the decision system.

Converting the Decision into Action

Although thinking through the boundary condition may be the most difficult phase in the decision process, converting the decision into effective action is

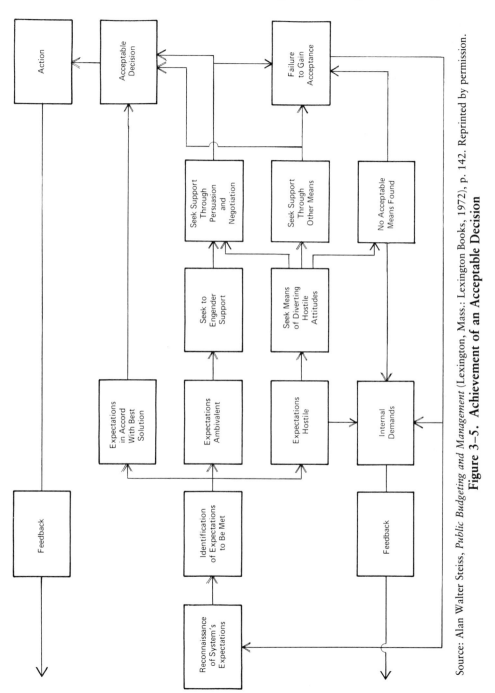

Source: Alan Walter Steiss, *Public Budgeting and Management* (Lexington, Mass.: Lexington Books, 1972), p. 142. Reprinted by permission.

Figure 3–5. Achievement of an Acceptable Decision

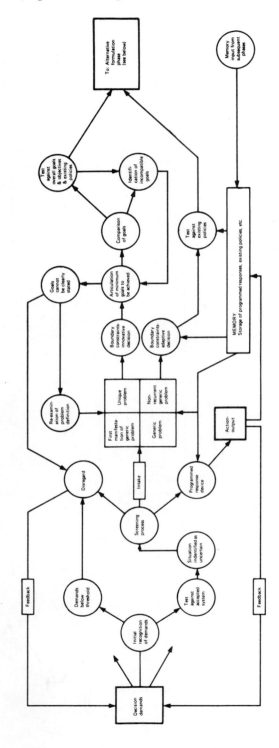

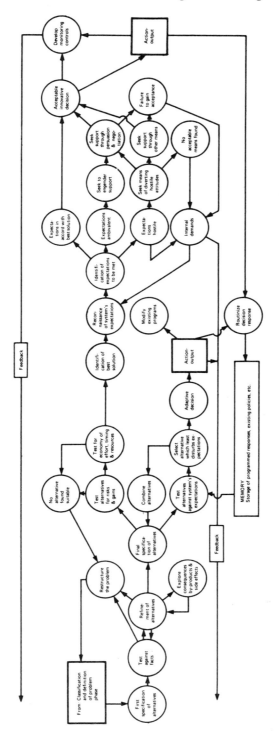

Source: Alan Walter Steiss, *Public Budgeting and Management* (Lexington, Mass.: Lexington Books, 1972), p. 145. Reprinted by permission.

Figure 3–6. A General Systems Model of Decision Making

usually the most time-consuming. Yet a decision will not become effective unless action commitments have been built in from the start. In fact, no decision has been made unless carrying it out in specific steps has become someone's work assignment. Until this is accomplished, the decision is only a good intention.

The flaw in many policy statements is that they contain no action commitments; they fail to designate specific areas of responsibility for their effective implementation. Converting a decision into action requires that several distinct questions be answered: (1) Who has to know about the decision?, (2) What action has to be taken?, (3) Who is to take this action?, and (4) What does the action have to be, so that people who have to do it can do it? All too often, the first and last of these questions are overlooked, with dire consequences.

Action commitments become doubly important when people must change their behavior, habits, or attitudes in order for a decision to become effective. Care must be taken to see that responsibility of the action is clearly assigned and that the people are capable of carrying it out. Measurement, standards for accomplishment, and incentives associated with the proposed action must be changed simultaneously with the introduction of the decision.

Feedback Phase

Provision must be made throughout the decision process for feedback. Feedback occurs, intentionally or unintentionally, at many stages in the decision process. Much of this feedback is internal to the process, resulting in a recycling of a particular phase in order to achieve further refinements and modifications. The feedback which has an impact on the entire decision process generally occurs at two points: (1) after the decision has been made and action programs have been initiated, and (2) whenever internal demands are created within the organization. In both cases, new demands (inputs) may be generated, causing the decision process to recycle.

Information monitoring and reporting are particularly important after a decision has been reached. This feedback is necessary to provide continuous testing of expectations against actual results. Even the best decision has a high probability of being wrong; even the most effective decision eventually becomes obsolete. Failure to provide for adequate feedback is one of the primary reasons for persisting in a course of action long after it has ceased to be appropriate or rational. The advent of the computer has made it possible to compile and analyze great quantities of feedback data in a relatively short time period. It must be recognized, however, that computers can handle only abstractions. Abstractions can be relied upon only if they are constantly checked against concrete results. Unless decision makers build their feedback around direct exposure to reality, their decisions may result in sterile dogmatism.[15]

A basic aspect of the decision process is the development of a predictive capacity within the organization to identify changing conditions which might necessitate modifications in the selected course of action. Controls should be developed for a given solution by:

1. defining what constitutes a significant change for each variable and relationship which appears as a component in the decision,
2. establishing procedures for detecting the occurrence of such changes, and
3. specifying the tolerable range within which the solution can be modified if such changes occur and beyond which new solutions must be sought.

Although this prescriptive model (figure 3–6) is presented in eight distinct stages, it would be misleading to assume that real-life problems are obliging enough to permit an easy, logical sequence of attention. As Joseph Cooper has observed, problems

> conceal their true nature so that halfway down the path of a decision you may find that you must retrace your steps for a new beginning. Or you may have alternatives for decisions presented to you which, in your belief, are not the only and best possible courses. This, too, will send you back to the beginning.[16]

Alternatives seldom are created by moving in an orderly sequence from the first stage to the last. It is not uncommon for new alternatives to occur from time to time while data are still being collected. Moreover, in a complex situation different phases of the process may develop at different rates. For example, the stage of alternative formulation may be reached for one aspect of a complex problem, while other parts of the same problem are still at the stage of definition and analysis. Thus, in a complex, difficult problems situation, various stages may appear simultaneously in different aspects of the same problem. Nevertheless, it is necessary to approach the patterns of decision making stage by stage in order to adequately analyze the process. Only in this way is it possible to uncover meaningful and useful insights into how the process can be improved.

Notes

1. W. Ross Ashby, *An Introduction to Cybernetics* (New York: John Wiley & Sons, 1963), p. 206.
2. Herbert A. Simon and James G. March, *Organizations* (New York: John Wiley & Sons, 1958), pp. 178–179.
3. Ibid.

4. Filmer S.C. Northrup, *The Logic of the Sciences and the Humanities* (New York: Macmillan, 1947), p. 1.

5. David A. Easton, *A Systems Analysis of Political Life* (New York: John Wiley & Sons, 1965), p. 38.

6. John Dewey, *Logic, The Theory of Inquiry* (New York: Holt, Rinehart and Winston, 1938), p. 105.

7. Easton, *Systems Analysis of Political Life,* p. 21. Easton makes a distinction between inputs and withinputs, the latter referring to demands which are generated from within the organization.

8. Dewey, *Logic,* p. 105.

9. Anatol Rapoport, "What Is Information?" *ETC: A Review of General Semantics* 10 (Summer 1953), 252.

10. Peter F. Drucker, "The Effective Decision," *Harvard Business Review* 45 (January-February 1967), pp. 92–104.

11. Ibid., p. 95.

12. Robert W. Morell, *Managerial Decision-Making* (Milwaukee, Wisc.: Bruce Publishing, 1960), p. 22.

13. Peter F. Drucker, *The Practice of Management* (New York: Harper and Brothers, 1954), p. 363.

14. Drucker, "Effective Decision," p. 95.

15. Ibid., p. 95.

16. Joseph D. Cooper, *The Art of Decision-Making* (Garden City, N.Y.: Doubleday, 1961), pp. 15–16.

4
Strategic Planning

S trategic planning has been a vital ingredient of corporate decision making for some time. As King and Cleland explain, strategic planning in the private sector

> involves the development of objectives and the linking of these objectives with the resources which will be employed to attain them. Since these objectives and resource deployments will have impact in the future, strategic planning is inherently future oriented. Strategic planning, therefore, deals primarily with the contrivance of organizational efforts directed to *the development of organizational purpose, direction, and future generation of products and services,* and the design of implementation policies by which the goals and objectives of the organization can be accomplished.[1]

The term *strategic* is applied to these planning activities to denote linkage with the goal-setting process, the formulation of more immediate objectives to move the organization toward its goals, and the selection of specific actions (or strategies) required in the development of organizational resources to assist in achieving these objectives. The term also was adopted to distinguish the scope of this process from the forecasting and other piecemeal efforts undertaken by industry, business, and government in the name of "planning."

The Origins of Strategic Planning

Many organizations that undertake long-range planning place considerable emphasis on the extrapolation of expected developments of their activities into the future, so that top management can get a better picture of where the organization is going. Managers may compare this forecast of future performance with what might be desirable according to a set of goals and objectives for the organization. The discrepancy between desirable goals and expected performance according to the forecast is commonly called the *planning gap.*

Forecasting is only one of the ingredients in the planning process, however. Forecasts involve educated guesses about the future. A major purpose of planning is to support strategic decision making with the formulation of alternative courses of actions that will have long-term, desirable consequences.

Strategic Planning in the Private Sector

The concept of strategic planning first found application in the private sector in the late 1950s and early 1960s. As B.W. Scott observed in a 1965 publication of the American Management Association:

> Strategic planning is a systematic approach by a given organization to make decisions about issues which are of a fundamental and crucial importance to its continuous long-term health and vitality. These issues provide an underlying and unifying basis for all the other plans to be developed within the organization over a determinant period of time. Thus a long-range strategy is designed to provide information about an organization's basic direction and purpose, information which will guide all its operational activities.[2]

When Robert S. McNamara left the presidency of Ford Motor Company in 1961 to become secretary of defense in the Kennedy administration, he took with him a method of multiyear planning which had helped him gain a perspective on the key strategic decisions in that company. McNamara's abilities as a manager, and the role of long-range planning as an essential ingredient to his effectiveness, were widely discussed in the media. As a consequence, managers of large organizations all over the country began to wonder if they too should attempt such a planning effort.

While some companies attempted to formalize a planning process during the 1960s simply because it was the thing to do, there were substantial reasons as well for this movement toward a more comprehensive and long-range approach to organizational decisions.[3] The 1960s was a period of steady economic growth and general prosperity, especially in the United States. Many corporate executives realized that, while they had many attractive opportunities for growth, they also had to choose carefully from among these opportunities. During this period, many businesses chose to diversify, sometimes through acquisition, and to enter into international markets. Such strategic moves increased in geometric fashion the managerial complexity of large corporations. The problem was particularly intense at the top of such corporations. And new methods and technologies clearly were needed to help top management cope with an increasing array of strategic decisions. Formal, long-range planning seemed almost like a godsend to these top managers.

Based on their studies of planning in numerous corporations, Lorange

and Vancil suggest five fundamental characteristics of effective st.
ning systems:

1. Strategic planning is a line-management function. The corollar
   strategic planning system must be designed by the organizatio.
   agers who will use it.
2. An effective strategic planning system must help line managers make
   important decisions: "Line managers are not interested in plans; they
   make decisions. If the planning system helps their decision-making process, they will devote vast amounts of time to it."[4]
3. An effective strategic planning involves a process by which line managers
   work together in resolving strategic issues.
4. Strategic planning systems are unique to the corporate environments in
   which they reside: "The overriding design rule is that there is no general
   design."[5]
5. An effective strategic planning system changes continually: "The corporate situation is always changing as a result of changes in the external
   environment as well as shifts in organizational structure and power."[6]

Strategic Planning in the Public Sector

Efforts to apply strategic planning in the public sector began to surface in the
late 1960s and early 1970s, in part as a response to criticisms of *comprehensive planning*—advocated (but seldom achieved) in government for over three
decades. Catanese and Steiss describe an alternative to the traditional planning approach in their book entitled *Systemic Planning: Theory and Application.* This hybrid model, they suggest, focuses on probabilistic futures and
combines the best features of more sophisticated analytical techniques with
humanistic traditions of public planning.[7] Systemic planning presents a challenge to a new generation of planners to avoid technocratic determinism,
while attaining a more systematic approach to public decision making.[8]

The initial *P* in PPBS (Planning-Programming-Budgeting Systems) was a
reflection of the same general concern for a longer-range perspective to the
formulation of goals and objectives. It was assumed that such planning could
provide a broader framework within which the more detailed functions of
programming and budgeting could be undertaken. Unfortunately, the PPBS
approach was a top-down model in which goals and objectives were formulated in the upper echelons of the organization (much as envisioned in the
corporate approach to strategic planning). These goals were then filtered
down through a series of what Herbert Simon has called "means-ends
chains." At the end of a lengthy process, specific programs were to be developed and implemented to achieve these goals and objectives. Central direction from the top, however, often was poorly coordinated, contradictory,

often counterproductive, or nonexistent. As a consequence, many public agencies operating under a PPBS mandate went through the motions of fulfilling the procedural requirements, using the appropriate buzzwords, but with little change in their traditional incremental approaches the programming and budgeting of activities.

Short-Range Planning and Disjointed Incrementalism

The common approach to public planning for many years has involved the formulation of a plan for some specific target date ten to twenty years in the future. Under this approach, various demographic and economic factors are projected for a defined period of time, suggesting that by 1990 or the year 2000, the population of a particular jurisdiction will be of such-and-such a magnitude (often expressed as a range). Based on these projections, it is then suggested that public services and facilities will have to be expanded accordingly, employment opportunities will have to be provided in a given quantity, land consumption will be of a given quantity (and perhaps quality), and so forth. As a rule, considerable attention is also devoted to an identification of more immediate problems of growth (or the lack of it) and to suggested solutions to those problems. Many organizations outside the government have adopted a similar short-range approach to planning.

Under such an approach, problem solving often takes precedence over the establishment of long-range goals and objectives. Program proposals frequently are based on anticipated demographic and economic conditions—a simple extrapolation of the status quo. When the overriding focus is on solutions to more immediate problems, the cumulative process becomes short-range planning, albeit applied to a relatively long time period. The results, benefits, and profits to be gained from such short-range plans cannot be assured in the long run and, in fact, may be lost in the crisis of disjointed problem solving. A plan is of relatively little value if it does not look far enough into the future to provide a basis on which change can be logically anticipated and rationally accommodated.

Charles Lindblom has described decision making in the public sector as a process with little concern for goals and objectives. Public objectives are difficult to define and consensus rarely can be achieved, according to Lindblom. Therefore, the best course of action is *incrementalism*.[9] Incrementalism results from competition among interest groups and produces short-range programs rather than long-range policies. Democracies are composed on widely differing factions that compete for the public's interests (and resources). Even if these interests were not contradictory, our ability to foresee the full consequences of our actions (to plan) is so limited that, according to Lindblom, objectives must be approached in small, manageable steps, that is, incrementally.

Thus, Lindblom dismisses categorically any attempt to develop more synoptic or comprehensive approaches to decision making on the grounds that such approaches do not conform to reality. Some writers have argued that *disjointed incrementalism* is a necessary—and desirable—consequence of the democratic process.[10] An extension of this assertion, some would argue, is that planning is contrary to, or at least inappropriate and difficult to achieve within, a democracy.

The most significant flaw in the concept of disjointed incrementalism is that it fails to consider all the incremental alternatives between existing approaches to decision making and the strawman extreme of synoptic planning. Lindblom and his followers have oversimplified the alternatives and, thus, have stacked the argument in their favor. A planning approach that recognizes the need for inputs from the bottom up, which conforms to or adapts to the ideals of the democratic process, and that, at the same time, secures a more rational basis for decision making, also is an option on this continuum. The "pragmatic incrementalists" seem to ignore this alternative.

From One-Shot Optimizations to a Planning Process

Many traditional planning efforts, in both the public and private sectors, have tended to be one-shot optimizations, drawn together periodically, often under conditions of stress. Once the best plans were laid, there was little attempt to test their continued efficacy against the realities of current conditions.

It has been said that few plans survive contact with the enemy. And indeed, rarely are organizational policies and programs executed exactly as initially conceived. Random events, environmental disturbances, competitive tactics, and unforeseen circumstances may all conspire to thwart the smooth implementation of plans, policies, and programs. In short, the traditional processes of planning do not provide an adequate framework for more rational decision making. Fixed targets, static plans, and repetitive programs are of relatively little value in a dynamic society.

What is required is a planning framework within which strategic decisions can be subjected to continuous testing, correction, and refinement. Through such an approach, alternative courses of action can be identified and analyzed, and a desirable range can be established within which choices can and should be made. The concept of strategic planning, as it has evolved over the past twenty-five years, offers an important response to this need for a more dynamic planning process.

Another important component in the development of strategic planning was the recognition of a planning hierarchy in which the respective responsibilities at various levels within an organization are more clearly articulated. In private sector applications, Robert Anthony describes this hierarchy as consisting of (1) strategic planning, (2) management planning, and (3) operational control.[11] Management planning is a pivotal ingredient in this approach, involving "(1) the programming of approved goals into specific projects, programs, and activities; (2) the design of organizational units to carry out approved programs; and (3) the staffing of those units and the procurement of necessary revenues."[12]

In the absence of a strategic planning framework, however, management planning can become disjointed and counterproductive. At the same time, without the consistent follow-through of management planning (programming and budgeting) and operations scheduling and control, strategic planning may be little more than a set of good intentions with little hope of realization. Thus, as emphasized in strategic management, the linkages among these three basic components are as important as the component themselves.

A Strategic Planning Model

From a total systems perspective, strategic planning should be part of a continuous process that includes the allocation and management resources, as well as performance evaluation and feedback. It should involve an examination of alternative courses of actions and estimates of the impacts and consequences that are likely to result from their implementation. Explicit provision should be made for dealing with the uncertainties of probabilistic futures. The art of management is to reduce uncertainty and to bring risk within the bounds of tolerance. In this context, strategic planning can play an important role by assisting managers in organizing goals and objectives and in developing feasible action plans to achieve them. In so doing, major priorities can be ordered, the impacts of resource decisions can be assessed, and the activities and functions of the organization can be integrated into a more cohesive whole.

Basic Components of the Model

The strategic planning model advocated herein consists of five basic components:

1. Basic research and analysis
   a. basic data collection, inventories, and broad needs assessments
   b. external and internal environmental analyses to determine system readiness
   c. identification of planning horizon and levels of client groups to be served.

2. Diagnosis of trends and needs

    a. macrolevel trends and related considerations
    b. microlevel technical and applied studies, including facilities analyses and specific needs assessments

3. Statements of goals and objectives

    a. formulation of hypotheses concerning conceptual aspects of the organization's mission
    b. delineation of significant structural changes required to realize the mission statement
    c. definition of the desired state of the system
    d. identification of program objectives to achieve the desired state.

4. Formulation and analysis of alternatives

    a. development of an objectives matrix
    b. redefinition of the desired state of the system in light of more detailed objectives.

5. Policy alternatives and resource recommendations

    a. translation of goals and objectives into general policies
    b. formulation of explicit policy sets
    c. delineation of effectiveness and efficiency measures
    d. establishment of decision guidelines for the allocation of financial resources.

Linkages among these basic components are shown in figure 4–1.

It is assumed in this model of strategic planning that a concentration of systemic data can provide the basis for theoretical constructs—preliminary goals and objectives—as to the desired future state of the organization. The emphasis in strategic planning is on an orderly evolution—from a broad mission statement, to statements of more specific goals and objectives consistent with the organization's mission, to more explicit policies and implementing decisions. This emphasis seeks to establish or to reinforce linkages that are missing in the disjointed incremental approach. The absence of consistency from the general to the specific also is one of the major shortcomings of more traditional planning efforts.

The goal formulation process also serves as a vehicle for avoiding the tendency to posit future plans merely on the basis of existing conditions. Through a goal-oriented mode, policies, *factual premises* representing what can be done, can be tested against goals, *value premises* representing what should be done. Thus statements of goals and objectives play a vital role in the day-to-day process of decision making. The danger of sacrificing the basic merits of the strategic plan to technical or politically expedient considera-

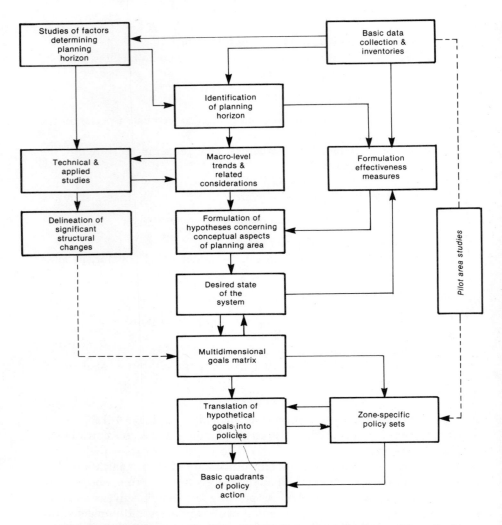

Source: Alan Walter Steiss, *Public Budgeting and Management* (Lexington, Mass.: Lexington Books, 1972), p. 205. Reprinted by permission.

Figure 4–1. Schematic Diagram of the Strategic Planning Process

tions, in large measure, can be circumvented through the application of this approach. When compromises must be made, as they always will, the decisions can be more clearly based on the optimal or normative conditions outlined in the statements of goals and objectives.

Several of the steps outlined in the strategic planning model are common to most planning approaches. Other are unique to this model, however, and therefore merit further discussion, including (1) the planning horizon, (2) the emphasis on program objectives, (3) the objectives matrix, (4) formulation of policy sets, and (5) the use of effectiveness measures.

The Horizon Concept

Basic to this strategic planning model is the use of a *planning horizon,* the farthest point than can be anticipated based on an interpretation of what is known about existing conditions and emerging trends. Applying this concept, a series of plans can be developed for given levels of service at the planning horizon. Each plan represents an alternative mix of clientele groups and organizational programs. Just as with the natural horizon, as the specific service level is approached, the organization's planning horizon continues to recede, making adjustments in long-range goals and objectives both necessary and possible. Therefore, the horizon concept provides a more dynamic approach to strategic planning. The planning horizon can (and should) be changed, revised, or even dismissed as the body of information on which it is based is enlarged and clarified.

The planning horizon of any organization can be determined through the application of both objective (measurable) and subjective criteria. The service capacity of the organization, for example, may represent one such criterion; optimal staff-client ratios might provide another criterion. In both these examples, the criteria are closely tied to the availability of resources; and as resource availability changes, the criteria must also be adjusted. Some horizon criteria are products of the level of technology at any given time. Other criteria are established on a somewhat more subjective basis, which may be altered (and should be reevaluated) from time to time as, for example, the organization's client profiles change.

A strategic plan formulated on the horizon concept yields a series of policy alternatives to guide future organizational activities toward some desired state. The horizon concept offers the basis for thesis rather than merely a synthesis, that is, the more traditional cumulative approach to planning. This thesis emerges from a series of hypotheses or "what-if" studies, whereby various mixes of clientele groups and programs are explored with the overall parameters of the planning horizon.

Each plan alternative has different implications for the distribution and management of resource requirements. A number of combinations and permutations are possible based on a relatively well-defined set of pure alternatives. From these hypotheses, the mix that best fits the mission statement of the organization can be identified and set forth as the *thesis* of what should be (that is, the desired future state of the organization). Policies and programs can then be developed to implement this chosen alternative.

Programs: The Pivotal Ingredients

Programs provide the fundamental building blocks for strategic planning. A program can be defined as *a group of interdependent, closely related activities or services* which contribute to a common objective or set of objectives. Each program should bring together all costs associated with its execution. A program is concerned with a time-span of expenditures that extends beyond the current fiscal period.

A set of activities, cutting across several public agencies or departments, focusing on problems of juvenile delinquency can constitute a program. The establishment of a trauma unit in a hospital emergency room is an example of a program. The internal auditing process within the controller's office may be defined as a program. A university research center concentrating on the environmental sciences may be treated as a program or may have a number of programs associated with its research mission.

Under traditional management processes, decision making frequently becomes input-oriented. That is to say, the analysis of objectives and alternative methods of achieving these objectives is based on expenditure-related issues rather than being policy-based. Seldom is an assessment made of the effectiveness of these inputs in terms of meeting identified client needs or the performance of services. As a consequence, there is no guarantee that decisions will be coherently responsive to comprehensive objectives.

The formulation of precise, qualitative statements that are output-oriented, however, is not an easy task. A common tendency is to describe what the organization does, instead of addressing the question of why these activities are appropriate within its mandate. The purpose of a public employment assistance agency, for example, is not: *To interview, test, counsel, and place unemployed persons in jobs.* This statement focuses on a process, on what the agency does, rather than on the mission of the agency. A more appropriate statement of purpose would be: *To assist the unemployed and underemployed in securing satisfactory jobs appropriate to their abilities so as to contribute to an increased standard of living for individuals and families within the community.* More specific objectives might be concerned with accomplishing the principal purpose for specific target groups, such as the disadvantaged, handicapped, youths, residents of urban ghettos, and the rural unemployed.

The setting of program objectives is perhaps the most critical part of the strategic planning process, as these objectives become the building blocks of the organization's work programs and management controls. In identifying program objectives, an effort should be made to specify the key results to be accomplished within a specific time period. Program objectives should be quantifiable. While they should be realistic and attainable, they also should present a challenge to improve conditions consistent with existing organizational policies, practices, and procedures. A program objective must also be consistent with the resources available (or anticipated) and should assign singular responsibility and accountability, even in joint efforts.

Program objectives should specify the *what* and the *when* of anticipated organizational activities. There is a tendency, however, to focus on the *how*. Thus, an appropriate program objective of a municipal fire department would be: *To reduce current response time to all fire and emergency vehicles by 25 percent over a period of two years.* The statement *to build, equip, and man a third fire station during the next two years* tells how the program objective might be accomplished and should be reserved for the delineation of specific strategies.

Strategy statements describe how and where specific resources (personnel, equipment, materials, capital expenditures, and so on) will be used. Such statements specify the means for achieving a single key result based on the resources (fiscal and personnel) available or anticipated. These statements, in turn, should be related to performance measures and measures of effectiveness that identify the products, service units, and/or clients associated with the activities of the organization in carrying out the operations of a program. Appropriate measures of efficiency and effectiveness provide a base line against which to test the notion of adequacy. In the absence of such measures, the traditional "least cost" compromise is likely to prevail.

While these procedural steps may be initiated sequentially, more often they are performed through a series of iterations (see figure 4-2). In identifying objectives, for example, further clarification may be achieved as to the appropriate programs and subprograms of an organization. This amplification, in turn, may assist in determining which activities should be placed within each subprogram. Sometimes it will not be possible, however, to formulate precise statements of objectives until the schedule of activities has been examined in some detail. The establishment of such schedules, in turn, may require careful examination of alternative strategies and associated measures of efficiency, economy, and effectiveness.

The Objectives Matrix

In strategic planning, a deductive approach replaces the more typical inductive techniques of planning. Tentative goals sets are formulated and then tested in the context of specific horizon alternatives, allowing new factors to emerge and be considered. Thus, goal formulation can serve as an educational device as well as a planning tool. It should increase the awareness of the participants with respect to the changes that may be taking place within the organization. However, it also allows these participants to react to these changes in accordance with their own values, norms, and expectations.

Explicit recognition is given in the strategic planning model to the fact

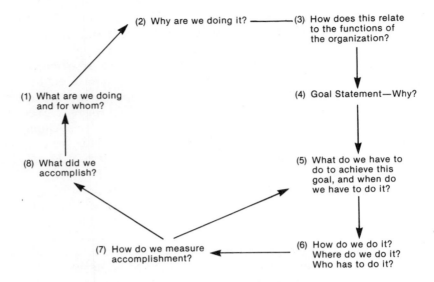

Figure 4–2. Iterative Process for Setting Goals

that value inputs (personal biases) are likely to occur at critical points, namely, in connection with the formulation of more explicit objectives. This tendency can never be completely eliminated. Therefore, statements of objectives must be formulated within a concise framework that provides an opportunity to clearly identify conflict positions, that is, statements of existing or potential value conflicts. As shown in figure 4–3, the objectives matrix provides a basis for the identification of conflict situations.

Conflicts can emerge on several different levels. The first conflict dimension is between the overall objectives of the organization and those of individuals or groups within the organization or serviced by the organization. A second level of possible conflict arises from territorial considerations, that is, the prerogatives of various units within the organization. A third level of conflict emerges with regards to explicit issues and the various viewpoints that can be brought to bear on their resolution.

The purpose of this analysis is to more clearly identify both the potential conflicts and the areas of agreement and congruence. The objectives matrix merely provides a convenient scorecard for recording these points, so as to avoid the tendency to assume that objectives are mutually exclusive.

The matrix is built through a series of iterations, involving a broad cross-section of participants. First, an objective statement is posited for each identified issue area. These objectives are then categorized according to the three conflict levels. At the end of the first iteration, a number of cells in the matrix

	Organization			Individuals		
	Territorial Prerogatives			Territorial Prerogatives		
	Unit *A*	Unit *B*	Unit *n*	Unit *n*	Unit *B*	Unit *A*
Viewpoint 1						
Viewpoint 2						
Viewpoint *n*						

Figure 4–3. Illustrative Format for Objectives Matrix

should be filled and others likely will remain empty. The next iteration should focus on filling the empty cells by identifying objectives that parallel (that is, complement or are in conflict with) those previously identified in the particular dimensions. This iteration may reveal additional issue areas, which produces yet another cycle. The end product of this phase of the analysis should be a fully articulated matrix, with each cell containing one or more objectives. Finally, those objectives should be identified that (1) are clearly in conflict with one another, (2) evidence potential conflict or consensus, and (3) are mutually reinforcing.

This approach has been successfully applied in small groups through the use of a modified Delphi technique and on a broader basis using a series of questionnaires and public meetings.[13] The matrix can reveal different levels of understanding regarding the broader goals of the organization. Respondent conflict must be expected and analyzed. The general premise underlying this matrix approach is that information regarding conflicts among participants will be valuable in identifying levels of comprehension with respect to complex organizational issues. That is, it is better to know about these existing and potential conflicts at the outset than to get part way into a course of action and have it rapidly deteriorate when they surface.

Explicit Policy Sets

In the context of the strategic plan, policy statements are intended to cover the entire range of actions required from the identification of a goal to the point at which that goal is attained. The formulation of policy, therefore, embraces various points on a continuum of means, ranging from long-range, general, and educational objectives to more immediate, specific, and action-oriented programs. The number of points along this continuum, of course, will vary from situation to situation. Five categories of policy were suggested in an earlier chapter, spanning a range from norms and values, on the one hand, to relatively specific procedural guidelines on the other (see figure 4–4). General policies anchor one end of the continuum and control policies on the other. Between these extremes are arrayed strategic policies, program policies, and implementation policies.

The other dimension of this policy matrix is defined by (1) what is to be accomplished (objectives), (2) when it is to be accomplished (priorities), (3) where it is to be accomplished (locus), (4) how it is to be accomplished (means), and (5) standards for the evaluation of accomplishments. These five factors relate to and help to define the content of policy statements.

As shown in figure 4–4, four quadrants in the policy matrix require the attention of various participants in the policy-making process. *Basic policy* is primarily of a strategic nature and focuses on objectives and priorities. *Exec-*

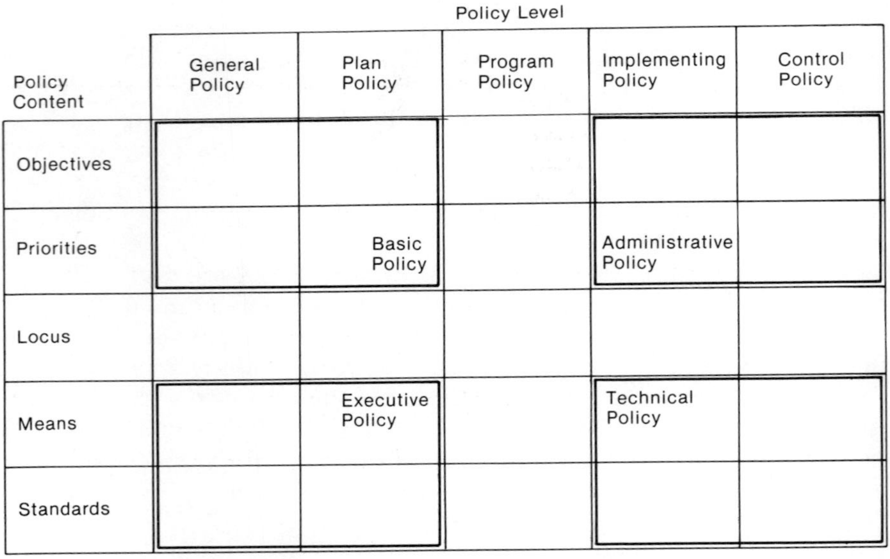

Policy Level

Policy Content	General Policy	Plan Policy	Program Policy	Implementing Policy	Control Policy
Objectives					
Priorities		Basic Policy		Administrative Policy	
Locus					
Means		Executive Policy		Technical Policy	
Standards					

Source: Adapted from Alan Walter Steiss, *Management Control in Government* (Lexington, Mass.: Lexington Books, 1982), p. 273. Reprinted by permission.

Figure 4–4. Multiple-Policy Matrix

utive policy is required to establish operational means and standards within the framework of strategic planning. The objectives and priorities of implementation and control are part of the realm of *administrative policy,* whereas the means and standards of implementation and control are, in most instances, technical in nature. Each of these quadrants suggest a particular realm of policy formulation responsibility and, furthermore, delimits the focus and emphasis appropriate to each of these realms. The notion of specific policy sets, therefore, underlines the importance of maintaining these parameters to ensure that one policy quadrant does not encroach unduly on the responsibilities of another quadrant.

The area formed by the demarcation between these four quadrants also is important to define. The vertical plane represents the trade-offs that must be made between executive and administrative policy, while the horizontal plane represents the overlap between strategical, managerial, and operational considerations. It is in these areas that conflicts between policies are inevitable.

Effectiveness Measures

Effectiveness measures must be formulated and applied to measure goal achievement. Effectiveness measures involve a scoring technique for determining the status of an organization at a certain point. They are indicators that measure both direct and indirect impacts of specific resource allocations in the pursuit of certain goals and objectives.

Effectiveness measures can be defined by (1) establishing current levels and types of performance in the organization in discrete categories, (2) estimating the current impacts of resources on this performance, and (3) then defining the desired levels and types of performance. The development of positive statements of performance provides a base from which change may be defined and evaluated.

Performance must be defined in output-oriented terms based on a vocabulary of understandable policy and program variables. Policy and program variables, in turn, must identify administrative and executive policy and those patterns of performance to be affected. An important assumption in the development of effectiveness measures is that they can be derived or inferred from current conditions (but are not limited to those conditions). This means that current operations and their effects must be continually monitored (that is, the basic data collection component of the strategic planning model). This continuous evaluation is probably the most effective means available for initiating a goal-oriented planning and decision-making system within an existing organizational structure.

The Information Requirements of Strategic Planning

The strategic planning process can be characterized by (a) an emphasis on a more comprehensive program structure, (b) a concern with the processes by which goals and objectives are formulated and policy decisions are made, (c) application of quantitative techniques of analysis, (d) an extended time horizon on which to base decisions, and (e) formal mechanisms for ongoing evaluation in terms of the attainment of agreed-upon program objectives.[14] Each of these elements has special information needs, as outlined in the following section. The inability to provide for these needs, in large measure, accounts for the limited success of strategic planning in the public sector.

The emphasis on *program structure* involves a shift in focus from traditional groupings of activities, based on organizational lines of responsibilities, to programs and subprograms. These programs, in turn, are directed toward the achievement of explicitly identified public objectives. It also results in a shift in the approach to resource allocation (budgeting). The traditional line-item budget focuses on inputs, such as expenditures for personnel, materials and supplies, and equipment. The programmatic approach tends to emphasize the outputs of particular efforts which may involve more than one department or agency.

A more comprehensive program structure can provide a better basis for the comparison of program outputs to resource inputs in terms of cost-benefit or cost-effectiveness measures. The presumption is that alternative program approaches can be ranked with respect to their capacity to meet objectives, and that more rational expenditures decisions can be made on this basis. To date, however, the analysis of program alternatives has met with only limited success in application. The information required to carry out full-blown analyses of this sort has yet to be fully developed in readily accessible formats.

The concern with the *decision-making process* builds on the assumption that more rational decisions will be made if management is provided with well-organized, factual information at key points in its deliberations. Any decision, of course, is based on both value and fact. The principal contribution of the strategic planning approach is the strengthening of the factual basis for decision through the development of management information and program evaluation systems (MIPES).

Such information systems, however, are highly dependent upon the storage and retrieval capacity of modern data-processing equipment. These systems, in turn, are vulnerable to the GIGO problems ("garbage in—garbage out") that confront any use of computers in decision making. Various standardized reporting formats and "turnaround documents" may be required in an effort to increase the consistency, reliability, and validity of information. Turnaround documents are periodic reports that provide data inputs to the information system and information back to the originating agency. Unfortunately, as more attention is devoted to the form of the report and less to the content, the medium often does becomes the message.

Quantitative analysis, the third element of strategic planning, involves the application of more systematic techniques to public decision making. The techniques are derived, in large measure, from systems analysis, operations research, and the management sciences. Since these techniques are dependent on the successful development of the management information system, they share some of the same problems in application.

Many of the activities of government cannot be sufficiently quantified for successful application of the techniques of cost-benefit analysis. As a consequence, rough surrogates often are developed to approximate the monetary measures of costs and benefits. It is important to recognize, however, that many decisions regarding the delivery of public services cannot be predicated solely on a positive benefit-cost ratio (in which the measurable benefits exceed the costs). It may be necessary to commit public resources to the resolution of critical problems where the benefits are long-term, intangible, and/or unmeasurable in specific monetary terms.

The *extended time horizon* of strategic planning makes explicit provision for this characteristic of public resource commitments by shifting the focus of decision from the traditional one-year cycle to a longer time frame. Most public programs extend beyond the period of the annual budget. Therefore, decisions regarding the allocation of resources can have significant implications well beyond the fiscal year under consideration. Multiyear program plans should be developed as inputs to each year's budget deliberations. In application, however, such multiyear statements often are little more than linear extrapolations of the current commitments and do not reflect the complex shifts in demands from increasing or decreasing client groups.

Evaluation has been a watchword in both the public and private sectors for over two decades. Despite considerable fanfare, however, systematic evaluation of public programs remains more a promise than a practice. Public goals and objectives are often nebulous and ill-defined. Consequently, the measurement of programs results is often even more elusive. As Wholey has pointed out, "From the point of view of decision-makers, evaluation is a dangerous weapon. They don't want evaluation if it will yield the 'wrong' answers about programs in which they are interested."[15] Thus, in spite of the emphasis placed upon evaluation in strategic planning, its application has largely been limited to postmortems of abandoned or drastically altered programs or has focused on isolated components of larger program issues.[16]

A Continuous Process, Not a Panacea

This overview of the rudiments of the strategic planning process runs the risk of generating an impression that the process is simple and relatively easy to implement. This is not the case, however. Organizations that have adopted this approach are well aware it is not a panacea. Strategic planning will not immediately resolve all problems confronting an organization, nor is its implementation easy to administer. A firm commitment by those who will be involved to see the process through is essential to its success.

Strategic planning must be a continuous process performed in annual cycles and coupled with continuing involvement of management personnel and other participants in different phases of the process. The cyclical nature of this process, however, does offer an opportunity to introduce the various components in a series of refinements rather than on a whole-cloth basis. Formalization of the process, however, is at the very root of successful strategic planning, as distinguished from forecasting and the rather piecemeal analytical efforts of the past.

Notes

1. William R. King and David I. Cleland, *Strategic Planning and Policy* (New York: Van Nostrand Reinhold, 1978), p. 6.

2. B.W. Scott, *Long-Range Planning in American Industry* (New York: American Management Association, 1965), p. 63.

3. Peter Lorange and Richard F. Vancil, *Strategic Planning Systems* (Englewood Cliffs, N.J.: Prentice-Hall, 1977), p. x.

4. Ibid., p. xii.

5. Ibid., p. xiii.

6. Ibid., pp. xiii–xiv.

7. Anthony J. Catanese and Alan Walter Steiss, *Systemic Planning: Theory and Application* (Lexington, Mass.: Lexington Books, 1970), chap. 16.

8. Ibid.

9. Charles E. Lindblom, "The Science of 'Muddling Through,'" *Public Administration Review* 19 (1959), pp. 79–88; Charles E. Lindblom and David Braybrooke, *A Strategy of Decision* (New York: Free Press, 1964); Charles E. Lindblom, *The Intelligence of Democracy: Decision Making through Mutual Adjustment* (New York: Free Press, 1965).

10. Lindblom, *The Intelligence of Democracy;* Aaron Wildavsky, *The Politics of the Budgetary Process* (Boston: Little, Brown, 1964).

11. Robert N. Anthony and Glenn W. Welsch, *Fundamentals of Management Accounting* (Homewood, Ill.: Richard D. Irwin, 1974), p. 303.

12. Alan Walter Steiss, *Public Budgeting and Management* (Lexington, Mass.: Lexington Books, 1972), p. 148.

13. N.B. Mutunayagam, "Cooperative Management: An Alternative Approach to Multijurisdictional Management of Resources" (Ph.D. dissertation, Virginia Polytechnic Institute and State University, 1981).

14. James C. Snyder, *Financial Planning and Management in Local Government* (Lexington, Mass.: Lexington Books, 1977), p. 107.

15. Joseph S. Wholey, "What Can We Actually Get from Program Evaluation?" *Policy Sciences,* vol. 3, no. 3 (1972): 362.

16. For a further discussion of these points, see Steiss and Gregory A. Daneke, *Performance Administration* (Lexington, Mass.: Lexington Books, 1980), chap. 11.

5
Resource Management: Financial Planning and Cost Analysis

R esource management involves a determination of how the resources of the organization can be employed most effectively to achieve strategic objectives. Most often the focus is on financial resources, since the common denominator among the various resources of any organization is the cost involved in their utilization. The primary emphasis of this chapter will be financial planning and analysis. The concepts and techniques of cost-benefit analysis will be discussed in a subsequent chapter. Procedures for the allocation of resources through the budget process provides the basis for a third chapter dealing with this pivotal component of strategic management.

Analysis of Financial Data

Extensive data on the use of financial resources can be derived from the accounting system of any organization. An effective accounting system should provide quantitative information for three broad purposes: (1) *external reporting* to various constituencies or client groups (for example, stockholders), regulatory bodies, and the general public; (2) *internal reporting* for use in the planning and analysis of ongoing operations; and (3) *strategic planning* to assist in the formulation of long-range policies and plans. Traditional accounting procedures have served the first of these broad purposes reasonably well. With some interpretation, accounting records of financial transactions have been used successfully in the operational planning and control activities. Traditional financial accounting systems, however, have provided relatively little direct assistance in the activities of strategic planning.

The Accounting Equation and Financial Reporting

While accountants must collect data in considerable detail, financial analysts must group data (accounts) to facilitate their analyses. The two major sources of data for financial analysis are (1) the balance sheet and (2) the income statement. Before proceeding with a discussion of the some of the basic techniques of financial analysis, it is important to define some fundamental accounting terminology.

Simply stated, a *balance sheet* is a statement of the financial position of an organization as of a specific date. All accounting transactions must balance: the sum of the assets shown on the balance sheet should agree with the equities, that is, liabilities plus owner equity.

Assets are things of value or resources owned by the organization. Assets may be in the form of cash, amounts owed to the organization by others, equipment, inventory, and so forth. Assets are recorded based on total cost incurred at the time of acquisition. This leads to the traditional caveat that a balance sheet presents historical rather than current market value of assets. The *liabilities* of an organization represent obligations or debts and include amounts owed to creditors for goods and services purchased, salaries owed employees, taxes due, notes payable, and other forms of debt.

To be profitable, a business must increase the amount of assets and/or reduce its liabilities. The balancing residual is included as an increase in owner equity. *Equity* is always equal to the assets of an organization minus its liabilities. Equity comes from two sources: (1) contributed amounts resulting from investments and (2) earnings retained in the organization.

The equilibrium between assets and liabilities plus owner equities is known as the basic accounting equation. The concept of double-entry accounting is derived from this equilibrium. Regardless of the number or type of transactions for a given organization, the accounting equation must always remain in balance.

An *income statement* is based on the following fundamental relationship:

$$\text{net income} = \text{revenue} - \text{expenses}$$

The goal of profit-seeking entities is to generate revenue in excess of the expenses required to produce the income. Sales of merchandise from a retail store represent revenue; services rendered by a lawyer are revenues to the law firm; interest received by a bank represents revenue; taxes billed and fines collected by a city are revenues to the municipal government. Although many transactions may be classified as balance sheet entires, few relate completely to income statement transactions, that is, involve revenue or expenses. Thus the basic accounting equation must be expanded as follows:

$$\text{assets} = \text{liabilities} + \text{owner equity} + \text{revenue} - \text{expenses}$$

Profit-seeking entities strive to generate net income. Not-for-profit organizations, however, strive to break even, that is, to balance revenues and expenses. In the not-for-profit area, revenues are matched against *expenditures*. Although expenditures do not generate revenues, this match must be made because of accountability requirements. Thus if a balance sheet is prepared for a governmental entity (agency, program, or fund), it would likely reflect only those items properly classified as current assets and current liabilities. At the same time, some type of balancing item (free balance or uncommitted appropriation) would be used in lieu of owner's equity.

The basic accounting equation must be altered to reflect the accounting equilibrium of governmental funds, as follows:

$$\text{assets } + \text{ estimated revenue } + \text{ expenditures } =$$
$$\text{liabilities } + \text{ fund balance } + \text{ revenues } + \text{ appropriations}$$

If a system of *encumbrances* has been adopted, then two additional components must be added to the equation: (1) to the asset side, an amount expected to be paid for goods and services (*encumbrance*), and (2) to the liabilities side, a part of the appropriation (called *reserve for encumbrance* or *reserved appropriations*) to pay for the obligation when the goods are received. In this way, the governing body is assured that the amount appropriated during the accounting period will not be overexpended.

Financial Ratio Analysis

Accounting data can be a valuable source of information in assessing the internal strengths and weaknesses of an organization. Numbers connote precision. It is important to bear in mind, however, that the numbers provided in balance sheets and income statements are condensed from many detailed accounting reports. Therefore, any further analyses based on these data must be undertaken with full awareness of the condensations and abstractions that have already been made. Accounting data merely reflect the financial dimension of an organization. Other important aspects, such as behavioral factors that may impinge on the overall performance of the organization, also must be considered.

Financial ratio analysis is a widely used technique for comparing an organization with other similar entities. Financial ratios have been used for many years in the private sector as indicators of the well-being of a business with respect to liquidity, leverage, profitability, and the utilization of assets. These ratios tend to be retrospective and static in nature. Therefore, they may be of only limited use in strategic management.

Three different methods can be applied to evaluate the performance of an organization with respect to financial ratios:

1. *Organizational comparisons:* Data should encompass organizations of similar size, serving the same or similar clientele with similar products or services.
2. *Time series analysis:* Ratios may be plotted for several periods to determine whether significant changes have occurred and, in turn, to project the future financial performance of the organization.
3. *Absolute standards:* Minimum requirements can be established appropriate to the expectations of a given organization.

Liquidity measures are based on the simple notion that an organization cannot operate if it is unable to pay its bills. A sufficient amount of cash and other short-term assets must be available when needed. On the other hand, most short-term assets do not produce any significant return. A strong liquidity position can be damaging to profits. Therefore, management must try to keep the liquidity of the organization low, while ensuring that short-term obligations can be met. Liquidity is essential for survival, and therefore, it should take priority in financial analysis.

A so-called current ratio is determined by dividing current assets by current liabilities. This ratio indicates the extent to which the claims of short-term creditors can be covered by short-term assets. The higher the ratio, the greater the presumed ability of the organization to meet its current obligations. Organizations with stable and predictable conditions generally require smaller current ratios than will more volatile organizations.

Other liquidity measures include the following:

a. *Quick ratio:* indicates an ability to pay off short-term obligations without having to sell current inventory. Inventories are subtracted because they are the least liquid of current assets; in a forced sale, inventories may be worth very little. Substantial deviations below 1:1 may indicate a cash crisis; a ratio of 3:1 or higher suggests a cash rich organization.
b. *Ratio of inventory to net working capital:* indicates the extent to which the working capital of an organization is tied up in inventory. This ratio is calculated by subtracting current liabilities from current assets and dividing the result into the value of inventory.

Leverage ratios (sometimes labelled *debt management ratios*) show how the operations of an organization are financed. Debt (and leasing) entails fixed obligations. Positive leveraging occurs when the organization has the opportunity to borrow at a low rate and to invest this borrowed money at higher rates of return.

The use of debt financing implies both opportunity and risk. Too much equity often means that management is not taking advantage of the leverage effect associated with long-term debt. On the other hand, outside financing will become more expensive as the debt-to-equity ratio increases. Thus, the leverage of an organization must be viewed with respect to its profitability and the volatility of activities in which it is engaged. The use of debt implies both opportunity and risk. The three principal measures of leverage are:

1. *Debt-to-assets ratio:* the extent to which borrowed funds are used to finance the organization's operation. The higher the ratio, the greater the leveraging.
2. *Debt-to-equity ratio:* ratio of funds from creditors to funds from stock-holders.
3. *Long-term debt to equity ratio:* the balance between long-term borrowing and equity.

Profits are limited by the cost of production on the one hand and by the marketability of the product or service on the other. Therefore, profit maximization entails the most efficient allocation of resources by management. There are two categories of profit ratios. The first consists of *margin ratios,* which proportion profit to sales and are derived from the income statement. Margin ratios measure the performance of cost controls. The second category is *return ratios,* which measure profit against resources committed to the organization.

Among the profit ratios most often used are:

1. *Gross profit margin:* the total margin available to cover operating expenses and yield a profit. This ratio is calculated by subtracting the cost of goods sold from total sales and dividing the result (gross profit) by total sales.
2. *Net profit margin:* the return on sales, determined by dividing profits after taxes by total sales.
3. *Return on assets:* represents the return on the total investment from both stockholders and creditors. This ratio is calculated by dividing earnings before interest and taxes by total assets.
4. *Return on equity:* the rate of return on stockholder's investment in the firm, calculated by dividing profits after taxes by total equity. This ratio will be most affected by positive or negative leveraging.

These measures also can be applied, with some obvious modifications, to not-for-profit and nonprofit organizations. The basic objective with such organizations is to break even.

Asset utilization ratios measure the productivity and efficiency of an organization. A fixed asset turnover ratio, for example, when compared to industry averages, will show how well a company is using its productive capacity. Similarly, an inventory turnover ratio can indicate whether the company is producing too much inventory in generating its sales and whether the company may be carrying too much obsolete inventory. Assess utilization ratios can be tailored to the needs of nonprofit and not-for-profit organizations as well. Such measures usually entail some measure of volume of activity or work load (for example, cases per caseworker) divided by some measure of cost or time.

Strategic Funds Programming

Introducing a new strategy often is like attempting to rebuild a ship while at sea. The current organization must be kept afloat and operating properly, while at the same time, the strategic manager must introduce programs to move the organization into new areas. Managers may become so enamored with the potential opportunities of a new strategy that they fail to provide sufficient support to current operations.[1] To avoid this pitfall, it is important to identify a source of funds to initiate the new strategy. A budgeting and control system must be designed to provide the decision information required to implement the strategy, while balancing the financial needs for maintaining the current organization.

A second type of financial analysis, therefore, considers the flow, sources, and uses of funds. Such analysis can be helpful in determining areas in which discretionary funds, available in the past, might be applied in the implementation of new programs and strategies. Unlike most other accounting methods, this technique provides a future-oriented perspective of the financial requirements of the organization and the potential sources to meet these needs.

The first step is to identify how the organization allocates its financial resources from period to period. This *cash flow analysis* can help to identify sources of discretionary funds and show where potential adjustments may be made. Funds can be obtained either by selling off assets or by increasing liabilities or owner's equity. In turn, these funds will be used to increase other assets or to reduce liabilities or equity.

Generally speaking, an organization can generate new funds from three sources:

1. from regular operations and other internal sources (for example, profits after taxes, depreciation, or disposition of excess inventory or unused facilities),
2. from expansion of short-term debt consistent with the financial structure of the organization (for example, having banks provide extended lines of credit, leasing rather than buying equipment, or factoring accounts receivable),
3. by changing the financial structure of the organization to permit the addition of new long-term debt or equity funds.

Funds accumulated from these sources generally comprise the total funds available to the organization for managing its operations. These funds are used in the following ways:

Baseline funds support the current, ongoing operations of the organization.

Strategic funds are invested in the new programs required to meet the goals and objectives of the organization.

Baseline funds are used to pay current operating expenses, maintain adequate working capital, or maintain current plant and equipment. Baselines funds are used to maintain the same level of production or services, to maintain the organization's market share, or to maintain a specified, ongoing growth rate.

Strategic funds are allocated to (a) purchase new assets, such as equipment, facilities, and inventory; (b) increase working capital; and (c) support direct expenses for research and development, marketing, advertising, and promotions. Strategic funds also are used for mergers and acquisitions. A market penetration strategy, for example, may call for a more intensive investment of funds in the current business. A market expansion strategy usually requires an aggressive use of strategic funds for advertising and promotion. A company must use strategic funds to produce more diverse products or services and to develop new markets for these products/services.

The programming of strategic funds begins with an identification of basic organizational units (budget or program units) and the formulation of goals and objectives for these units. The total amount of strategic funds available to the organization can be determined by subtracting baseline funds from total assets (revenue or appropriations). Strategies must be formulated to carry out the goals and objectives within each unit. Once estimates are made as to the amount of funds required for each strategy, the strategies can be ranked according to their potential contribution to the achievement of the identified goal and objectives. In undertaking this ranking, the kinds of strategic funds available and the level of risk involved must be taken into account. Procedures for dealing with risk will be described in greater detail in a subsequent section.

The available strategic funds should be allocated to each program in priority order. Key decision points concerning risk and return are encountered when (a) funds available from internal sources have been fully consumed and (b) readily available credit sources have been exhausted. At this point, proposed strategies must be evaluated in terms of the changes required in the financial structure of the organization. The final step is to establish a management control system to monitor the generation and application of funds to achieve the desired results. Management control procedures will be discussed in some detail in later chapters.

The programming of strategic funds only identifies *feasible options* under different financial assumptions. The strategic manager must make an assessment of risk and return before the final option is chosen.

Computer-Assisted Financial Planning

In recent years, computer-based methods of analysis have become a significant tool for the financial planning. Interactive financial planning software allows the nonprogrammer to use the computer as an on-line, real-time decision support system (DSS) to (1) test assumptions on which a plan is based, (2) consider the risk associated with different available alternatives, and (3) explore a range of possible decision scenarios. Traditional methods of financial analysis often can only explain from hindsight why things went right or wrong in a particular plan of action. Computer-assisted methods of financial planning, on the other hand, allow the strategic manager to constantly fine-tune the plan so as to anticipate things to come (and to adjust to the unanticipated things that may arise as the plan is implemented).

In early approaches to interactive financial planning, a fixed structure was used to provide the manager with the capacity to pose "what if" questions about certain input variables. These programs usually displayed the results as pro forma balance sheets or income statements. Simultaneous equations frequently were used in these models to project the financial performance of an organization. Sales revenues often are the driving force in these models: by using different sales forecasts, alternative income and balance sheet projections could be made. The balance sheets show expected changes in assets and liabilities based on the various scenarios with regards to sales.

Obviously the results of such analyses are only as valid as the sales forecasts made by the planners. However, by being able to run through different financial scenarios, the strategic manager could increase his or her awareness of potential problems and be prepared to deal with them when they occur.

Individuals lacking experience in computer programming often were unable to use these early models because of (1) the need to learn a new, unfamiliar, computer language that often was difficult to communicate, and (2) the inflexibility associated with procedural languages, which force the user to make input statements in a sequence difference from the structure of the actual problem. Software packages designed to eliminate these problems are now available. Such software is, in the jargon, user friendly—menus and submenus are written in English and allow users with very little programming experience to select the analytical steps appropriate to their needs. These packaged programs use a nonprocedural approach in which there is no "correct" or predetermined sequence of statements required to describe the problem. Therefore, a great deal of flexibility is provided in terms of both model design and subsequent modifications that may be necessary.

Modern interactive packages for financial planning provide a number of important options in addition to generating automatic reports for various "what if" questions. It is possible to develop a model applicable to the particular conditions confronting an organization and to use this model to (a) project financial statements, (b) analyze cash flow requirements, (c) optimize financial leverage, (d) compare lease versus purchase options for difference depreciation schedules, and (e) evaluate the impacts of proposed mergers or acquisitions. Models frequently can be consolidated or combined so that managers in different functional areas can use the same financial planning package (and assumptions) and design models to their particular needs. By combining these models, it may be possible to attain an overall model for the whole organization.

Goal-seeking procedures can be applied in such models. The computer works back from certain targets (goals) set by management to determine the conditions that will have to prevail to permit these goals to be achieved. Goals can be viewed as constraints to the problem, and in some instances, it may be necessary to relax some of the constraints (lower the targets) in order to arrive at a feasible solution.

Available software packages also make it possible to perform *sensitivity analyses* to determine how an optimal solution might change if some of the variables in the model should change. A model often responds to key assumptions, while the majority of variables may have little consequence on the results. Thus, the strategic manager has a means of selecting those variables that require a more detailed analysis. This selection is the first step in performing a *risk analysis*.

In the application of *deterministic models,* it is assumed that a single estimate can be specified for each of the input variables. As Hertz has pointed out, however, behind any precise calculation are data that are not precise, and taken together, these combined uncertainties could result in a total uncertainty of major proportions.[2] Most computer-based systems for financial planning have the capacity of introducing and analyzing risk and uncertainty in the manner outlined in the following section.

Risk and Uncertainty

Strategic management is concerned with the future, often the distant future. And because of this focus, the environment in which the organization must operate often is characterized by uncertainty. This is an important facet of the strategic decision problem that must be recognized and treated explicitly from the outset. Strategic managers must continually assess opportunities, risks, and innovations. A risk is taken no matter what the decision; even the decision to do nothing involves the risk of lost opportunity. An effective manager, whether in the public or private sector, must be aware of how opportunity, innovation, and risk are interrelated and must be willing to take risks appropriate to his or her level of responsibility. Strategic decisions must involve an assessment of risk and uncertainty based on the weighing of available information and an estimate of alternative payoffs or gains.

Economic versus Satisficing Man

Nearly all economic decision theory is based on the notion of riskless choice, or decision making under certainty. This realm of theory is based on the assumption that a person faced with a decision situation will act as an *Economic Man,* defined as someone who is (1) completely informed, (2) infinitely sensitive to changes in the decision environment, and most importantly, (3) rational.

Economic Man is assumed to know not only what courses of action are available, but also what the outcomes of any action will be. The assumption that Economic Man is rational has two corollaries: (1) he can weakly order all the states or choices open to him (that is, he can rank A over B, B over C, and so forth), and (2) he can make his choices so as to maximize or minimize something. These conditions assume a complete utility-ordering or preference hierarchy that can rank all sets of consequences from the most preferred to the least preferred. Therefore, the decision maker has only to select the most preferred consequences in terms of what he seeks to maximize or minimize.

Almost no discussion is offered in the field of economic decision theory as to the possibility that the essential components of rationality might be in conflict with one another. It is conceivable, for example, that it might be very costly in time and effort to continuously maintain a weakly ordered preference field in order to have sufficient knowledge about all available choices to put them in rank order. Such conditions, therefore, would result in a negative utility. And under such conditions, would it be rational for the decision maker to have such a preference field?

Herbert Simon was not the first to be struck by the unreality of the concept of Economic Man, with its attributes of complete information and rationality. He took the lead, however, in offering an alternative model of decision making—the concept of *Satisficing Man.* [3] Economic Man is assumed to make decisions as would an owner in an environment of predominantly small firms in a perfectly competitive market. Decision makers in contemporary organizations, however, tend to be professional managers in an environment fraught with imperfectly competitive market conditions. The theory of Economic Man is normative (it reflects what *should* be done). The theory of Satisficing Man tends to be descriptive (it deals with what *is* done).

Satisficing Man has various motivations in the search for the best alternative. When an alternative is found that is good enough—one that suffices or that resolves the dilemma for the moment—he refrains from further search; that is, he is satisfied. Thereby, time, energy, and resources can be conserved by suspending any further analysis. Satisficing Man is not necessarily concerned with the best or optimal solution, only with moving toward a better position or more satisfactory state. The path through which Satisficing Man moves, therefore, is characterized by a trial-and-error process, based on the incremental feedback of information. Since many organizational decisions rarely exhibit the use of feedback and periodic adjustments, in some quarters, Simon's model unfortunately has become a defense of the status quo.

Using the satisficing model, however, requires considerable knowledge of such variables as the values of individual actors, the cost of the search, and the obstacles to the implementation of particular proposals. Unless such knowledge is available, the satisficing model reveals relatively little about why any particular actor considers any particular alternative to be "good enough."

Converting Uncertainty to Risk

One manager's uncertainty may be another's acceptable risk. What one manager may interpret as an uncertain situation to be avoided, another may see as an opportunity, albeit involving some risk. While the two terms often are mistakenly used interchangeably, the distinction between uncertainty and risk is an important concept in strategic management.

Certainty may be defined as a state of knowledge in which the specific and invariable outcomes of each alternative course of action are known in advance. The key to certainty is the presence of only one state of nature (although under some circumstances, there may be numerous strategies to achieve that state). This condition enables the manager to predict the outcome of a decision with 100 percent probability.

Uncertainty may be defined as a state of knowledge in which one or more courses of action may result in a set of possible specific outcomes. The probabilities of these outcomes, however, are neither known or meaningful. As Archer has observed, uncertainty involves a range of conditions in which probability distributions vary from a condition of relative confidence, based on objective probabilities, to at the other extreme, a condition of uncertainty with little or no information as to the probable relative frequency of particular events.[4]

If the strategic manager is willing to assign objective or subjective probabilities to the outcome of uncertain events, then such events may be said to involve risk. *Risk* is a state of knowledge in which each alternative leads to one of a set of specific outcomes, each outcome occurring with a probability that is known to the decision maker. More succinctly, risk is reassurable uncertainty. Risk is measurable when decision expectations or outcomes can be based on statistical probabilities. The event of drawing a red card from a well-shuffled deck is an example of a risky outcome with a probability of 50 percent. The event of the election of a Democratic president in 1988 is an uncertain outcome.

The relationship between Economic Man, Satisficing Man, and the problems of risk and uncertainty are summarized in figure 5–1. The range of risk between Economic Man, who operates under complete certainty, and Satisficing Man frequently can be defined in terms of *objective probabilities*. The conventional methods of probability theory can be applied to reduce uncertainty under such conditions. The range of risk between Satisficing Man and an ignoramus (the individual who operates in the realm of complete uncertainty, often out of an unwillingness to accept any risk) can be defined in terms of *subjective probabilities*. Methods of statistical inference and the Bayesian approach to probability provide a basis for dealing with such uncertainty in some cases. The effective manager willingly accepts both the notion of risk and the application of objective and subjective probabilities.

Uncertainty, Risk, and Probability Functions

The uncertainty and risk that strategic managers face come from two primary sources: (1) statistical uncertainty, and (2) uncertainty about the state of the real world in the future. The first type of uncertainty usually is the least troublesome to handle. This type of uncertainty arises from chance elements in the real world and would exist even if the second type of uncertainty were zero. When encountered, so-called Monte Carlo and related probability techniques can be applied to deal with statistical uncertainty.[5]

Establishing a probability function can bring problems within more manageable bounds by reducing uncertainty to some level of risk that may be tolerated by the strategic manager, depending on his or her *risk threshold*. Probabilities can be established either *a posteriori* (by induction or empirical measurement) or *a priori* (by deduction or statistical inference). The basic conditions necessary to establish an empirically based probability are that (1) the number of cases or observations must be sufficiently large to exhibit statistical stability, (2) the observations must be repeated in the appropriate population or universe, and (3) the observations must be made on a random basis. The inductive approach offers the maximum opportunity for applied decision theory, because the number of situations in which such objective probabilities can be used is increasing significantly.

Under the deductive approach, probability statements are not intended to predict a particular outcome for a given event. Rather, this approach asserts that in a large number of situations, with certain common characteristics, a particular outcome is likely to occur. In short, a statistical inference

Figure 5-1. The Certainty-Uncertainty Spectrum

is made regarding the probable outcomes arising from a somewhat uncertain event or series of events.

Thomas Bayes (1702–1761), an English mathematician, first expressed in precise, quantitative form the mode of statistical inference. The Bayesian approach to decision making tends to treat problems of uncertainty as if they were problems of risk by relying on personal, subjective probabilities, rather than the relatively frequency, or objective probabilities. In effect, the Bayesian approach bases probabilities on the strategic manager's confidence in the validity of specific propositions. Such confidence, in turn, depends on how well prepared the manager is to deal with uncertainty (which may reflect the quality and quantity of available management information).

Uncertainty and Cost Sensitivity

It is the second type of uncertainty—uncertainty about the future state of the real world—that is dominant in most strategic management problems. In such cases, the use of sophisticated techniques to deal with statistical may be little more than expensive window dressing.[6] When the environment is uncertain, an *expected value* approach often can be applied. Expected value is determined by multiplying the value products across all possible outcomes. In mathematical terms, expected value (EV) can be expressed as:

$$EV = P1\$1 + P2\$2 + \ldots Pn\$n$$

where P stands for probability, $ stands for the value of an outcome, and

$$P1 + P2 + \ldots Pn = 1.$$

Several techniques, utilizing the concept of expected value, have been developed to analyze uncertainty about the future state of events. These techniques include (1) sensitivity analysis, (2) contingency analysis, and (3) a fortiori analysis. Each of these techniques is applicable under varying circumstances. In describing these techniques, the purpose is not to present a "how-to-do-it" approach, but rather to identify the underlying conceptual framework.

Sensitivity analysis is designed to measure (often quite crudely) the possible effects that variations in uncertain elements (for example, costs) may have on the alternatives under analysis. In most strategic decisions, there is considerable uncertainty among a few key parameters. The analyst must determine a set of expected values for these parameters (as well as other parameters). Recognizing that these expected values, at best, may be "guesstimations," the analyst may use several values (optimistic, pessimistic, and most likely) in an attempt to ascertain how sensitive the results might be in light of these variations in the uncertain parameters.

Table 5–1 illustrates how sensitivity analysis can be used to determine the variations in rankings among several alternatives based on anticipated costs. First, the analyst sets the expected values for all costs which are certain (for which there is some reliable basis for establishing an estimated cost). Three values for the uncertain costs, optimistic, most likely, and pessimistic, are then determined. The optimistic cost represents an assessment of cost based on the assumption that everything goes right with the project, that all of the uncertainty is resolved favorably. The pessimistic cost represents the opposite assumption. Given these two extremes, the most likely cost figure is somewhere in between.

Two related points concerning uncertainty are illustrated in table 5–1. First, it points up that the range of uncertainty may vary from alternative to alternative. (For alternative *A*, the range is 100–1,100; for alternative *B*, 300–1,150; and for alternative *C*, 200–900). Second, this illustration under-

Table 5–1
Illustration of Sensitivity Analysis

Cost Levels	Alternative A	Alternative B	Alternative C
Expected values of certain costs	900	800	1,000
Most likely expected values of uncertain costs	600	400	700
Expected values of all costs	1,500	1,200	1,700
Rankings	2	1	3
Pessimistic expected values	1,100	1,150	900
Expected values of all costs	2,000	1,950	1,900
Rankings	3	2	1
Optimistic expected values	100	300	200
Expected values of all costs	1,000	1,100	1,200
Rankings	1	2	3

lines the fact that uncertain costs may not always be the critical factor in determining the best alternative. For example, although uncertain costs are lowest in the case of alternative *C,* it still ranks third except under conditions of high or "pessimistic" uncertain costs.

Contingency analysis is designed to examine the effects on alternative choices when a relevant change is postulated in the criteria for evaluating the alternatives. This approach also can be used to ascertain the effects of a major change in the general decision environment or ground rules under which the problem situation is operative. In short, contingency analysis is a "with and without" approach. In the field of public health, for example, various alternatives to the responsibilities of state government for environmental health might be evaluated with and without a major new program in code enforcement. In a more local context, an organization might evaluate various sites for the location of its headquarters under existing conditions of client distribution and access routes. Additional evaluations might then be made, assuming different client distributions and under various route configurations.

A fortiori analysis (from the Latin for "with stronger reason") is a method of deliberately "stacking the deck" in favor of one alternative to determine how it might stand up in comparison to other alternatives.[7] Suppose that in a particular decision situation, the general accepted judgment of the governing board prior to analysis strongly favors alternative *C.* In performing the analysis on *C* in comparison to the other feasible alternatives, the analyst would deliberately choose to resolve any major uncertainties in favor of *C.* The analyst would then determine how each of the other alternatives compared under these adverse conditions. If some alternative other than *C* looks good (that is, if *C* does not show up to be the best alternative), there may be a very strong case for dismissing the initial intuitive judgment concerning *C.* Such analysis can be carried out in a series of trials, with each alternative, in turn, being favored in terms of the major uncertainties.

While these three techniques for dealing with uncertainty may be useful in a direct analytical sense, they also can contribute indirectly to the resolution of problem situations.[8] Through sensitivity and contingency analyses, for example, it may be possible to gain a better understanding of the really critical uncertainties of a given strategic problem. With this knowledge, a newly designed alternative might be formulated that would provide a reasonably good hedge against a range of more significant uncertainties. While this often is difficult to do, when it can be accomplished, it may offer one of the best ways to offset the uncertainties of a problem situation.

Payoff Matrices and Decision Trees

The review of expected values arising from choices in the decision environment often is facilitated by the construction of a probability payoff matrix or decision tree. These analytical tools represent combinations of the feasible strategies, the states of nature (with their probabilities of occurrence), and the strategies used.

A decision tree is used to enumerate all the possible outcomes of a sequence of events where each event can occur in a finite number of ways. The construction of a simple decision tree is illustrated in figure 5–2. Three machines—A, B, and C—produce respectively 50 percent, 30 percent, and 20 percent of the total number of items manufactured by a particular factory. For each machine, there is a definable level of defective output (D)—3 percent, 4 percent, and 5 percent, respectively. If an item is selected at random from the factory's daily output, what is the probability that it will be defective?

The decision tree illustrates the various "paths" that influence the problem outcome. A fundamental theorem in probability theory states that sequential or conditional probabilities (that is, where the probability of one event occurring is conditioned by the occurrence of the previous event) can be calculated by multiplying the probabilities associated with each event. In other words, the probability of a defective item coming from machine A is .50 times .03 or .015.

A second basic theorem is that all probability paths leading to the same outcome are additive. Therefore, the probability of a defective item being selected from all items produced by these machines is:

$$(.50)(.03) + (.30)(.04) + (.20)(.05) \text{ or } .037.$$

With these data it also is possible to determine the probability that the defective item was produced by a particular machine, for example, machine A. This is done by dividing the probability of a defective item from that machine (.015) by the total probability of a defective item being produced (.037).

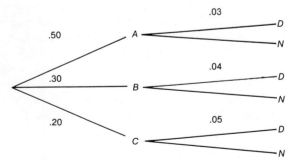

Figure 5–2. A Simple Decision Tree

Thus, the probability of a defective item, if found, coming from machine *A* is .4054 (40.54 percent).

Uncertainty, Risk, and Expected Utility

The assumption that people actually behave rationally in the manner suggested by the mathematical notion of expected value often is contradicted by observable behavior in risky situations. People are willing to buy insurance even though they are well aware that the insurance company makes a profit. People are willing to buy lottery tickets even though the lottery makes a profit. Consideration of the problem of insurance and the so-called St. Petersburg paradox led Daniel Bernoulli, an eighteenth-century mathematician, to propose that these apparent contradictions could be resolved by assuming that people act so as to maximize their expected utility rather than expected value.[9] Thus, people buy insurance because the consequences against which they are insured are significant in view of the costs, including the profit made by the insurance company. People are willing to invest a small amount of money in a lottery ticket, even though the probability outcome is highly uncertain insofar as any individual is concerned, because the payoff is quite high relative to their expected utility.

Extensive research has been performed in the area of risk and uncertainty because the behavior of decision makers often appears to violate commonly accepted axioms of rational behavior. While no exact probabilities may exist for the success or failure of a particular event, Kassouf has observed that an individual with "clear-cut, consistent preference over a specified set of strategies . . . will act as if he has assigned probabilities to various outcomes."[10] The values for the probabilities will be unique for each individual and not unlike the values of utility that might be assigned to an individual through a study of his or her social preferences. The obverse of social preferences, of course, is social risk aversion, a subject on which there are various opinions.[11]

As most economists will now admit, utility theory alone will not resolve the disputes over social preference and/or aversion to risk. There are numerous situations in which strategic managers will have to obtain a more careful reading of the various utility functions or preferences of their clientele and the organization as a whole. As Stokey and Zechhauser explain, strategic choice under uncertainty is a threefold process.[12]

1. Alternatives must be assess to determine what lotteries (probabilities and payoffs) are implied for individual members of the organization and clientele.
2. Attitudes toward risk for these individuals must be evaluated to determine the certainty equivalents of these lotteries.

3. Having estimated the equivalent benefits that each alternative offers to different members of the organization/clientele, the decision maker must select the preferred outcome.

While this process may sound simple, it is very complex in application. Some basic tools been developed to aid the strategic manager in unraveling these complexities. These include (1) dynamic equilibrium analysis, designed to identify relative aversion to risk; (2) Markov chains, a highly instrumental modeling technique which traces probabilities for various states of the system over time; and (3) distribution analysis, which provides for the calculation of the level of divergence from an equal distribution of policy payoffs.[13]

These relatively mechanical techniques can be brought into play only after the manager has a fairly good understanding of organizational and/or clientele preferences. Once the groundwork for approximating utility has been laid, the strategic manager is prepared to address uncertainties in a more systematic fashion.

A basic objective of strategic management is to reduce uncertainty by bringing to light information that will clarify relationships among elements or variables in the decision process. This reduction of uncertainty may cause the risk associated with a particular choice: (1) to remain unchanged, (2) to decrease (as in the case where a reduction in uncertainty permits the assessment of more definitive probabilities), or even (3) to increase (as happens when the additional information reveals risk factors previously unknown). Thus, although risk and uncertainty are interrelated, they must be treated independently in many situations.

Cost Analysis

Factors that influence future costs must be examined as part of the financial planning process so as to be reflected in strategic management decisions. There is a tendency to think of costs strictly in terms of inputs—the financial resources required to support organizational personnel, equipment, materials, and so forth. Costs that cannot be conveniently measured in dollar terms all too often are dismissed as noncost consideration. Future costs, however, may have important economic implications beyond their measurable monetary value. When estimating future costs, it is important to ask: Who will benefit from this expenditure, when, and by how much? It also is important to extend the question of how much a program will cost by asking: To whom?

Factors Influencing Future Costs

No program decision is free of cost, whether or not the decision leads to the actual expenditures of organizational resources. And certainly, the choices among alternative strategies for the accomplishment of an organization's goals and objectives are likely to involve many costs. Such choices include not only the expenditure of money but also the consumption of physical resources, the employment of human resources, and the use of time—all critical commodities in any organization.

The strategic manager must be cognizant of the following factors that influence future costs:

1. scope and quality of the services or products to be delivered;
2. volume of activity required to deliver these services or products;
3. methods, facilities, and organization required to perform these activities;
4. qualities and types of labor, materials, equipment and other cost elements required by these programs;
5. price levels of the various cost elements.

These factors which influence cost must be analyzed as they relate to the various programs, activities, and operations to be performed. This analysis should be a continuous process. Cost factors should be considered (1) in developing plans and programs, (2) in preparing budget requests, and (3) after commitments have been authorized and a program or project enters the implementation phase.

Many organizational activities can be measured in terms of units of production (workload measures). Current records of personnel activities may provide sufficiently accurate and reliable data to determine workloads. In some cases, however, it may be necessary to undertake more extensive, descriptive analyses of the nature and scope of the organizational activities to be initiated. Further refinements are possible where cost accounting systems have been adopted.

Having established the volume of work required to perform certain activities under existing organization and methods, it may be appropriate to examine alternative approaches to determine if greater efficiency and effectiveness can be attained. The analysis of alternatives should both precede the formulation of a financial plan (that is, the identification of program strategies) and follow the actual allocation of resources (to ensure that the approach which is adopted fits the resources available). Work methods should be analyzed to establish the appropriate mix of personnel, equipment, supplies, and other operating requirements to do the job with the least effort and at the least cost. Particular attention should be given to possible increases in productivity through simplified procedures and the use of labor-saving equipment.

Personnel (labor) is the most critical cost element for most organizational operations. Therefore, performance measures that interpret the volume of work in terms of man-hours required to carry out an activity or program are most useful to program managers. It may be possible to establish unit cost standards for activities that are of a type and importance to justify cost accounting procedures. For nonroutine (nonrepetitive) activities, however, workload and unit cost measures may not provide the basis for determining the quantities of various cost elements required. In such cases, management may have to rely on more subjective measures to provide an adequate basis for strategic decisions.

Personnel costs are subject to management control in two important areas: salary rates and job classifications. Periodic reviews should be made to see that each employee has the proper work assignment in view of his or her pay rate. All too often, skilled employees with higher pay classifications are assigned tasks that lower-rated persons should perform. Eliminating positions at the lower end of the pay scale may result in false economies if higher-paid personnel eventually have to do the work.

Changes in salary plans should be made only after a thorough study of such factors as (1) trends in the cost of living; (2) rates paid by comparable organizations; and (3) evaluation of fringe benefits, including sick leave, vacations, extra holidays, and security of tenure. Often improved fringe benefits can provide a bigger payoff to employees than increases in the salary and wage scale, which are likely to be subject to a larger "tax bite." Sound personnel and pay policies will prove to be a long-run economy.

Prices for materials and equipment can be controlled only to the extent that scheduling these requirements may enable purchases to be made at the lowest price, consistent with necessary quality. Continuous analysis should be made of price trends of frequently used commodities. Appropriate inventories should be maintained of items subject to price fluctuations. The cost of maintaining inventory (space requirements, shelf life, anticipated price changes, and so forth) also must be considered.

Monetary Costs and Economic Costs

Monetary costs are those commonly reflected in financial accounts and include research and development costs, investment costs, as well as the cost of operations, maintenance, and replacement. At times, it is necessary in financial planning to look beyond these monetary costs to what economists call opportunity costs, associated costs, and social costs.

Research and development (R&D) involve front-end costs that may or may not figure into the actual expenses of a given project or program. R&D costs incurred explicitly for a given project should be included as a project expense. However, general R&D costs that eventually benefit more than one project or program must be considered as *sunk costs.* Such costs should not be included in the direct cost estimate for a specific project or program.

Investment costs are expenses incurred to obtain benefits in future periods. Such investments may also result in sunk costs or in actual project outlays, depending on their timing. Consider the decision to build a public health clinic on land that was purchased some years earlier for some other public purpose. Only those additional investment costs required to prepare the site for the clinic should be considered as project outlays. The previous investment for the land purchase is a sunk cost.

Sunk costs can become an *inheritable asset* if previous investments can be used to the particular advantage of one alternative over another. The decision as to the site of the health clinic should not be based on the past investment, however, if that location for the clinic would be an inferior alternative in view of identified client needs. This decision would simply result in throwing good money after bad.

Investment costs vary primarily with the size of a particular program or project but not with its duration. *Recurring costs,* on the other hand, include those operating and maintenance costs that vary with both the size and duration of the program. Such recurring costs include salaries and wages, employee benefits, maintenance and repair of equipment, miscellaneous materials and supplies, transfer payments, insurance, and direct overhead costs. These recurring or operating costs do not add to the stock of capital. Rather, they are incurred to maintain, insofar as possible, the value of the existing stock. In preparing cost estimates, it is important that these recurring costs be considered over the life cycle of the project or program and not just the costs that might be incurred in the initial fiscal period.

As these distinctions suggest, some program costs are fixed, that is, are the same regardless of the size or duration of the program. Other costs are variable; that is, may change significantly as the scope of the project or program is increase. Often some uncertainty may exist regarding these costs, particularly if the project has a relatively long duration. It is important, therefore, to consider the *marginal* or *incremental costs* of increasing the size or scope of a program or project.

Suppose, for example, that the decision was whether to build one or two public health clinics. It might be possible, for example, to get quantity discounts on materials and equipment that would reduce the cost of a second clinic. If it is possible to build one clinic for, say, $300,000 and two clinics for $500,000, then the marginal cost of the second clinic is $200,000 (and not the average cost of $250,000).

Costs should be considered regardless of where they are carried on the accounts, what organizational units they are connected with, or where the money will come from. Once these costs have been identified, however, it may be important in the final strategic decision to determine where these costs must be borne.

This leads to the concept of *opportunity costs*. If resources are committed to one program, the opportunity has been preempted to use these resources elsewhere. The concept of opportunity costs can be illustrated by returning to the health clinic example. Having determined the monetary costs required for the proposed facility, it may be appropriate to describe some of the alternative uses of these resources. For example, what other purpose could the land be put? What other use could be made of the required staff salaries? If bonds are to be issued, what other uses might be made of the funds required for interest and principal payments?

If these alternative uses are sufficiently important, attempts should be made to estimate the value of such alternatives. This evaluation would consider the benefits that must be given up if the decision is made to go ahead with the proposed clinic. Keep in mind that a basic purpose of cost analysis is to estimate the value of alternatives forgone. Opportunity costs may be extremely important in making decisions among alternative program strategies.

Associated costs are "any costs involved in utilizing project services in the process of converting them into a form suitable for use or sale at the stage benefits are evaluated."[14] Associated costs are often incurred by the beneficiaries of public programs and services. The incremental costs of travel, food, lodging, and so forth represent the associated costs that must be borne by users of public recreational facilities, for example. If access to the facility is improved, so that the users' travel costs are reduced, then these savings in associated costs might be attributed as benefits arising from improved access. *Social costs* may be defined as the subsidies that would have to be paid to compensate persons adversely affected by a project or program for their disbenefits. Rarely is such compensation actually made (except perhaps when affected individuals enter into litigation and are awarded damages). Therefore, social costs represent an analytical concept.

In making a cost analysis, social costs can be handled in one of two ways.[15] They may be treated as external costs and subtracted from the market value of the output of the project to obtain a net social value. Or they may be treated as opportunity costs, whereby the potential benefits to those who are likely to be adversely affected are examined on the assumption that the project resources were to be spent on some other program. For example, the location of a sewage treatment facility may result in reduced property values in adjacent residential areas. These losses may be treated as disbenefits and subtracted from the overall benefits of the project to the larger community. Alternatively, the benefits accruing to these property owners from an alternative use of project funds (for example, for the development of a park site) might be calculated. The project with the larger yield would represent the better use of these resources.

Unfortunately, social costs, if included at all in a cost analysis, seldom are treated fairly. Such cost consideration are either underplayed by proponents of the project or overplayed by the opponents of the project. Social costs often carry significant emotional overtones and, therefore, may be difficult to evaluate. Nevertheless, such an evaluation may be a very important part of the overall strategic decision.

Summary

Accounting data form the basis for much of the financial and cost analysis conducted in complex organizations. Such data provide a retrospective view of the consequences of past decisions. The conceptual framework of strategic management, however, demands analytical techniques that can accommodate some dimensions of risk and uncertainty that are inevitable in future decision environments.

The various techniques of *financial ratio analysis,* such as liquidity measures, leverage ratios, measures of profitability, and assess utilization ratios, have been widely used for many years as indicators of the relative well-being of business organizations. These ratios, however, also tend to be retrospective and static in nature and of only limited application in strategic management.

Strategic funds programming, on the other hand, is more future-oriented and can be helpful in determining where discretionary funds may be available within the financial structure of an organization to implement new programs and strategies. The techniques available for programming strategic funds assist in identifying feasible options under various financial assumptions. The strategic manager still must make an assessment of risks and payoffs before the best option is selected.

In recent years, interactive computer software has become a significant analytical tool for financial planning, making possible on-line, real-time decision support systems. While traditional methods of financial analysis use hindsight to determine why things went wrong, computer-assisted methods of financial planning provide a basis on which to anticipate (and accommodate) change before its full impact occurs. Most computer-based systems for financial planning provide a capacity to analyze risk and uncertainty.

In this connection, important distinctions must be recognized between the concept of Economic Man, based on the notion of riskless choice, and the concept of Satisficing Man, as defined by Herbert Simon. Decision processes pursued by Satisficing Man more closely mirror the imperfectly competitive market conditions that confront professional managers in contemporary organizations. Satisficing Man is not concerned with the best or optimal solution. Rather, he seeks a solution that suffices, that moves the organization toward a better or more satisfactory state.

A basic objective of strategic management is to reduce uncertainty and bring risk within tolerable limits. This is accomplished through the generation of management information that clarifies critical relationships among elements or variables in the decision process. Various methods for converting uncertainty to risk, including the use of objective and subjective probabilities and the techniques of sensitivity analysis, contingency analysis, and a fortiori analysis, were outlined in this chapter. The use of payoff matrices and decision trees, and the concept of expected utility were also touched upon in an effort to provide the reader with a broader understanding of the critical dimensions of strategic decisions.

Factors influencing future costs must be examined as part of the financial planning process. Monetary costs—research and development costs, investment costs, and the cost of operations, maintenance, and replacement—are commonly reflected in financial accounts. In financial planning, however, it often is necessary to look beyond these monetary costs to what economists refer to as opportunity costs, associated costs, and social costs. A thorough cost analysis must also distinguish between (1) fixed and variable costs, (2) recurring costs, and (3) marginal or incremental costs. These costs should be examined over the life cycle of the project or program under analysis. The need to adopt an extended time dimension in such cost assessments led to techniques of cost-benefit analysis—the topic to be addressed in the next chapter.

Notes

1. Alan J. Rowe, Richard O. Mason, and Karl E. Dickel, *Strategic Management and Business Policy: A Methodological Approach* (Reading, Mass.: Addison-Wesley, 1982), p. 102.

2. David B. Hertz, "Risk Analysis in Capital Investment," *Harvard Business Review,* vol. 42. no. 1 (January–February 1964).

3. Herbert A. Simon, *Administrative Behavior,* 2d ed. (New York: Macmillan, 1957).

4. Stephen H. Archer, "The Structure of Management Decision Theory," *Academy of Management Journal* 8 (December 1964), p. 283.

5. For a basic discussion of Monte Carlo techniques, see E.S. Quade, *Analysis for Public Decisions* (New York: American Elsevier, 1975), and Herman Kahn and Irwin Mann, *Monte Carlo,* P–1165 (Santa Monica, Calif.: Rand, July 30, 1957).

6. C.J. Hitch, *Appreciation of Systems Analysis,* P–699 (Santa Monica, Calif.: Rand, August 18, 1955).

7. Ibid.

8. Gene H. Fisher, "The Analytical Bases of Systems Analysis" (paper presented at a symposium on "Systems Analysis in Decision-Making," sponsored by the Electronics Industries Association, Washington, D.C., June 23, 1966).

9. L. Sommer, trans., "Specimen Theoriae Nove de Mensura Sortis," *Econometrica* 22 (1954), p. 46.

10. Sheen Kassouf, *Normative Decision-Making* (Englewood Cliffs, N.J.: Prentice-Hall, 1970), p. 46.

11. For a broader discussion of this point, see Jack Hirshleifer and David L. Shapiro, "The Treatment of Risk and Uncertainty," *Public Expenditures and Policy Analysis,* 2d ed., edited by Robert H. Haveman and Julius Margolis (Chicago, Ill.: Rand McNally, 1977), pp. 180–203.

12. Edith Stokey and Richard Zeckhauser, *A Primer for Policy Analysis* (New York: W.W. Norton, 1978), p. 252.

13. For a more detailed discussion of decisions under uncertainty, see Howard Raiffa, *Decision Analysis* (Reading, Mass.: Addison-Wesley, 1968). For more about dynamic equilibrium, see Stuart Nagel and Marian Neef, *Operations Research Methods* (Beverly Hills, Calif.: Sage Publications, 1976). For an introductory discussion of Markov chains, see Stokey and Zeckhauser, *A Primer for Policy Analysis,* chap. 7.

14. U.S. Congress, House Subcommittee on Evaluation Standards, Report to the Interagency Committee on Water Resources, *Proposed Practices for Economic Analysis of River Basin Projects* (Washington, D.C., May 1958), p. 9.

15. Ronald H. Coase, "The Problem of Social Cost, *Journal of Law and Economics* (October 1960), pp. 1–44.

6
Resource Management: Cost-Benefit Analysis

T he resource management problem is as old as mankind. Ever since the Garden of Eden, people have been concerned with the allocation of scarce resources to achieve specific objectives. In theory, the problem is quite simple—it is difficult only in practice. One merely has to decide what is wanted (specification of goals and objectives), measure these wants (quantification of benefits sought), and then apply the available means to achieve the greatest possible value of the identified wants (maximize benefits). In contemporary society, the means become the resources of complex organizations. And therefore, the problem is one of maximizing benefits (once specified and quantified) for any given set of financial inputs (that is, specified and quantified costs).[1]

Elements of Cost-Benefit Analysis

Cost-benefit analysis can be defined as a systematic approach which seeks to (1) determine whether or not a particular program or proposal is justified, (2) rank various alternatives appropriate to a given set of objectives, and (3) ascertain the optimal course of action to attain these objectives. Cost-benefit analysis operates within an extended time horizon in contrast to more traditional forms of evaluation that tend to be short-range and narrow in scope. And, insofar as possible, cost-benefit analysis considers both the direct and indirect factors involved in the allocation of resources.

Basic Components

As Prest and Turvey have observed, "One can view cost-benefit analysis as anything from an infallible means of reaching the new Utopia to a waste of resources in attempting to measure the unmeasurable."[2] Although some of the criticisms of cost-benefit analysis are based on misconception, others are perfectly valid. Many of the valid criticisms, however, are applicable *a for-*

tiori to other analytical techniques as well. All too often, the argument for replacing relatively poor analysis with better approaches degenerates to assertions that, since analysis is difficult, costly, and troublesome, it should be abandoned in favor of more intuitive approaches.

Cost-benefit studies may be undertaken as a preliminary to the allocation of resources or as a continuing effort to ascertain optimal expenditure patterns in light of budget recommendations. In general, there are two principal approaches to cost-benefit analysis: (1) the fixed costs or fixed budget approach, where the objective is to maximize benefits for an established level of costs or a predetermined budget allocation; and (2) the fixed benefits approach, where the objective is to ascertain the minimum level of expenditures necessary to achieve some specified level of benefits. As discussed in further detail in a subsequent section, this second approach is sometimes called cost-effectiveness analysis.

The fixed level of costs or benefits may be a given, that is, it may be specified by someone other than the analyst. Very often, however, a major part of the analysis will center upon a determination of this constraint. Either (or both) of these approaches may be used, depending on the context of the resource management problem. In any event, the objective is to facilitate comparisons among alternatives, and for this purpose, it generally is necessary to hold something constant.

The crux of cost-benefit analysis lies in a statement of the problem, for if the problem is explicitly known, one already has a basis for its solution. As Anatol Rapoport has observed, the first step in solving a problem is to state it. "The statement usually involves a description of an existing state and a desirable state of affairs where the factors involved in the discrepancy are explicitly pointed out."[3]

A common source of error in allocation decisions arises from a traditional emphasis on finding the right answer rather than on asking the right question. As Peter Drucker has observed, "There are few things as useless—if not as dangerous—as the right answer to the wrong question."[4]

The traditional formulation of the cost-benefit approach was first outlined by Otto Eckstein.[5] The allocation problem is clarified through the identification of (1) an objective functions, (2) constraints, (3) externalities, (4) time dimensions, and (5) risk and uncertainty. Selecting an *objective function* involves the identification and quantification (in dollar terms, to the extent possible) of the costs and benefits associated with each alternative under consideration. In this way, various alternatives can be compared with each other and against the cost of attaining the desired benefits. *Constraints* specify the "rules of the game", that is, the limitations within which a solution must be sought. Frequently, solutions that are otherwise optimal must be discarded because they do not conform to these imposed rules. Constraints are incorporated into mathematical models as parameters or boundary conditions.

Externalities are those factors—inputs (costs), outputs (benefits), and constraints—that initially are excluded from the problem statement in order to make it more manageable. Ultimately, the long-range effects of these phenomena must be considered, however, usually after the objective function and model have been tested and the range of feasible alternatives has been narrowed.

In examining the *time dimensions* of various alternatives, it is necessary to delineate life-cycle costs and benefits. Life-cycle costs can be grouped as follows:

1. *Research and development costs:* one-time costs associated primarily with the development of new programs or capabilities to the point where they are ready for operational use; such costs are generally insensitive to the length of time a project or program will operational or the number of operational units;
2. *Investment costs:* costs incurred beyond the "start-up" development phase, frequently in the form of capital equipment or construction costs; investment costs may be a function of the number of units planned—the greater the number of units the planned, the higher the investment costs;
3. *Operations:* recurring costs of operating, supporting, and maintaining a program or capability; operating costs vary with both the number of units in a project or program and the length of time that such units must function.

Direct and indirect benefits also must be delineated carefully over the expected life of the proposed undertaking. There may be a time lag between the initiation of a project and the realization of the first increment of benefits. Benefits may build up gradually or may accumulate rapidly; they may reach a peak and decline rapidly or may taper off slowly. In short, the timing of costs and benefits cannot be ignored. It is not sufficient merely to add the total benefits and subtract the total costs estimated for a given alternative. Rather, it is necessary to consider a measure that reflects the impacts of deferred benefits and future costs. And in so doing, the analyst encounters the problems of risk and uncertainty.

Selecting an Objective Function

Decision making frequently involves a process of choosing a more immediate objective that is one of many means to a further end. As Herbert Simon has observed:

> In the process of decision those alternatives are chosen which are considered to be appropriate means for reaching desired ends. Ends themselves, how-

ever, are often merely instrumental to more final objectives. We are thus led to the conception of a series, or hierarchy, of ends. Rationality has to do with the construction of means-ends chains of this kind.[6]

The issue often is how far back along a means-ends chain should the analyst go in selecting an objective function appropriate to a particular area of concern. Not going back far enough may result in "suboptimization," involving attempts to achieve means that may or may not be correct or most efficient (or most effective) in achieving the specified ends. Failure to give adequate consideration to appropriate alternative ends may result in an incomplete or incorrect statement of the objectives to be attained. As Simon has observed, "Rational decision-making always requires the comparison of alternative means in terms of the respective ends to which they will lead."[7]

The choice of ends in a means-ends chain also involves the element of time. This, in turn, imposes two problems: the achievement of a particular end at a given time (1) may result in the need to relinquish other alternative ends for that same time period and (2) may result in limitations being placed on the ends that may be achieved at other times.

Paradoxically, the second classic mistake in identifying objective functions is the failure to consider a means as an end when indeed it is.[8] At times, a process may be highly valued, in and of itself, over any set of finite objectives that might be identified. In a democracy, for example, effective justice is not a legal system that fills the jails or maximizes convictions per dollar expenditure for law enforcement. Rather, it is a system that guarantees due process, wherein the rights of the individual are preserved. Thus, while decision makers may be accused of not seeing the forest for the trees (that is, for assuming means to be ends), they also may be guilty of sacrificing the trees to preserve what they believe to be the forest.

Quantification is at the very core of science. The improper use of quantification, however, may lead to distorted results in the art and science of organizational decision making. If critical means or ends are unable to be quantified, then superficial precision with numbers within the analysis may be irrelevant, and even harmful, to the solution. Indeed, many ends may be obscured by a myopic, fetishlike preoccupation with numbers.

An objective of cost-benefit analysis is to select that alternative which involves the lowest total cost at the highest ratio of user benefits to total costs. An inability to quantify more fundamental measures of systems effectiveness, however, has led to the identification of cost minimization as the most important goal in many such analyses. Evaluating alternatives by focusing on measurable costs and benefits may be applicable to some strategic decisions situations.

In many areas of strategic management, however, alternatives must be evaluated by somewhat more subjective considerations, by careful "guesstimations," and even by "gut feelings." As Simon Ramo has observed, the critical task of analysis "is the handling of the 'unknown' factors . . . weighing the importance of human reactions, for example, or guessing political influences, or generally dealing with technological issues that lend themselves little to measurement and quantification."[9]

There are situations, times, and places in strategic management where it may be inappropriate to try to achieve agreement on objectives or even to spell out precisely the objectives sought. To gain total clarity of objectives might result in a breakdown of some tenuous unity in an organization. The premature establishment of objectives in such situations may result in a decision inertia of dysfunctional proportions. It may be more appropriate to formulate objectives on the basis of feedback as the situation unfolds. Thus, obscure and obfuscated objectives are not always a sign of ineptness in application of the concepts of strategic management.

Criteria for Analysis

Once an objective function has been identified, the next step in cost-benefit analysis is to select an indicator of success, that is, an index that will yield a higher value for more desirable alternatives and lower values for less desirable ones.[10] Conceptually, such an indicator involves the maximization of something. Businessmen, for example, are reputed to maximize profits. Public officials are presumed to seek the maximum benefits for their constituencies. At times, however, the maximization problem can be dealt with more effectively by minimizing something, for example, costs.

The goal of cost-benefit analysis frequently is cited as the maximization of benefits and the minimization of costs. In reality, however, both cannot be accomplished simultaneously.[11] Costs can be minimized by spending nothing and doing nothing, but in that case, no benefits result. Benefits can be maximized within a particular project or program by committing organizational resources until marginal benefits are zero. But such action may require much more resources than are available. Therefore, some composite criterion is needed. Three obvious choices are:

1. maximize benefits for given costs
2. minimize costs while achieving a fixed level of benefits
3. maximize net benefits (benefits minus costs)

The first cost-benefit criterion to be used in the quantitative evaluation of alternatives was the *benefit/cost ratio,* introduced as part of the Flood Control Act of 1936. This act established the requirement that water resource development projects could not be initiated unless the evaluation showed that a project's expected benefits are in excess of the estimated costs. A second criterion is the *internal rate of return*. This approach to costs and benefits is widely used in business and reflects a legacy of prominent economists such as John Maynard Keynes and Kenneth Boulding. A third, more recently developed indicator is *net benefits,* that is, benefits minus costs. This criterion is intuitively appealing as it is purported to summarize all relevant factors. Before discussing each of these criteria in more detail, however, it is necessary to examine the concept of present value and the techniques of discounting as applied in cost-benefit analysis.

Discounting Future Costs and Benefits

Time is a valuable resource in any organization. And yet, the value of time often is overlooked, particularly when dollars spent this year are compared with those of last year or next year. It is important in developing a cost analysis, however, to recognize that dollar values are not equal over time. Benefits that accrue in the present are worth more to their recipients than benefits that occur at some time in the more distant future. Similarly, funds that must be invested today "cost more" than funds that must be invested in the future, since presumably one alternative use of such funds would be to invest them at some rate of return that would increase their value.

Therefore, the strategic manager must determine the equivalent *present value* of both costs and benefits by multiplying each stream by an appropriate *discount factor*. This factor gets smaller as the costs or benefits occur farther in the future. If the alternative is to invest available funds at some interest rate (i), then an appropriate discount factor can be expressed as:

$$\frac{1}{(1 + i)^n}$$

where i is the relevant interest rate per period and n is the number of periods into the future that the benefits and costs will accrue. If, as is the usual case, i is positive, the farther an event is in the future, the smaller is its present value. A high discount rate means that the present is valued considerably over the future; that is, there is a significant time preference, a higher regard for present benefits than for equal future benefits, and/or a willingness to trade some amount of future benefits for current benefits.

The choice of the discount rate may make the difference between the acceptance and rejection of a project. Unfortunately, there are no simple guidelines for determining an appropriate discount rate for organizational investments.

In theory, the proper criterion on which to judge the desirability of a project is the value of the opportunities bypassed in some other sector when the resources are withdrawn from that sector. It follows that an appropriate discount rate is the rate of return that the resources would otherwise provide if the same dollars were invested.

For several reasons, however, this theoretical approach to determine a discount rate often fails to yield a fair figure in the public sector. Private sector investments seldom have the life span of public sector commitments. The rate of return on a five-year investment seldom provides an equitable basis on which to judge a twenty-year public debt commitment. Public funds frequently must be invested in facilities and services for which no private sector incentives for investment exist.

In lieu of these theoretical constructs, various standard discount rates have been established for the evaluation of investments in the public sectors. Many economists argue, however, that these rates are too low to provide a fair evaluation.

An alternative approach reflects both local conditions and the marketplace for investments. Under this approach, either (1) the cost of borrowing the capital necessary to finance the project or program is determined or (2) a rate of return is calculated on the basis of what could be earned by the organization is an equivalent amount were to be invested for the same period of time. Thus, if the project could be financed through borrowing at an 11 percent interest rate, or if an investment of equivalent organizational funds would yield 10 percent, these percentages might be appropriately applied for the purposes of discounting future costs and benefits.

Although the choice of the particular discount rate may be difficult to justify, the procedures for discounting are quite simple. Once an appropriate rate is chosen, a table of discount factors can be consulted to determine the appropriate figure to apply to each year in the stream of costs and benefits. However, as the data in table 6-1 illustrate, the selection of the discount rate can significantly affect the final decision.

Benefit-Cost Ratio

The benefit-cost ratio is the present value of the benefits divided by the present value of the costs (or average annual benefits over average annual costs). This ratio can be expressed mathematically as follows:

$$R = \frac{\sum_{n=0}^{N} B_n(1 + i)^{-n}}{\sum_{n=0}^{N} C_n(1 + i)^{-n}} = \frac{B}{C}$$

Thus, if the discounted stream of benefits over the expected duration of the program or project equals $400,000 and the discounted stream of costs equals $320,000, the benefit/cost ratio is 1.25.

Table 6–1
Discounting $10,000 Annually over Ten Years

Year	Discount Factor at 8 Percent	Value	Discount Factor at 10 Percent	Value
1	0.925926	$ 9,259.26	0.909090	$ 9,9090.90
2	0.857339	8,573.39	0.826446	8,264.46
3	0.793832	7,938.32	0.751315	7,513.15
4	0.735030	7,350.30	0.683013	6,830.13
5	0.680583	6,805.83	0.620920	6,209.20
6	0.630170	6,301.70	0.564472	5,644.72
7	0.583490	5,834.90	0.513156	5,131.56
8	0.540269	5,402.69	0.466505	4,665.05
9	0.500249	5,002.49	0.424095	4,240.95
10	0.463193	4,631.93	0.385541	3,855.41
Total		67,100.81		61,445.53

A variation on the basic benefit/cost ratio tends to emphasize the return on invested capital by segregating operational costs and subtracting them from both sides of the ratio. In the previous example, assume that the present value of operational costs represents $160,000 of the total stream of costs. Subtracting operational costs from both benefits and total costs results in the following net benefit/cost ratio:

$$\frac{\$400,000 - \$160,000}{\$320,000 - \$160,000} = 1.50$$

As operational costs account for an increasingly larger portion of total costs, the net benefit/cost ratio becomes larger. Net benefit/cost ratios may be preferable for private enterprises in which capital is more constraining than operational expenses, especially when taxes are considered. However, a number of economists argue for the use of gross ratios in public sector application. They base this opinion on the notion that legislative bodies should consider operational costs as well as capital costs and should give agencies credit for savings on operational costs by permitting them to spend more on capital costs.

Internal Rate of Return

Since the costs associated with any investment decision usually accrue first, the undiscounted sum of benefits must be considerably larger in order to yield a favorable project. This characteristic of long-term investments is implicit in the analytical technique of internal rate of return (r), which is defined by the following equation:

$$r = \sum_{}^{N} \frac{B_n}{(1 + r)^n} :: \sum_{}^{N} \frac{C_n}{(1 + r)^n}$$

Note that the internal rate of return is not set equal to anything, the right-hand side of the equation is the present value of costs and the left-hand side is the present value of benefits. The internal rate of return is that interest rate r that brings the two sides of the equation into equilibrium, that is, when the return on investment (discounted benefits) equals the cost of capital.

To illustrate the application of this criterion, assume that a firm is confronted with the decision whether or not to initiate a new product line that will require a first-year investment in start-up costs of $100,000, with estimated annual operating costs of $40,000. In the fifth year of operations, it is anticipated that major modifications in the product line will be required and the current line will be shut down at a cost of $70,000. It is estimated that the firm will have three years of operations in this product line during which time gross profits will average $100,000 annually. In short, for an investment of $290,000 over five years the firm will obtain a return of $300,000. The costs and benefits of this project are illustrated in table 6–2.

As illustrated by the calculations on the right-hand side of table 6–2, an internal rate of return of approximately 11.6 percent provides one solution to the equation. If capital costs less than 11.6 percent (in terms of the interest rate in the current market), the proposed project would be desirable. In practice, of course, the firm would likely examine several alternative investments and select that alternative that exhibits the greatest margin of return. One problem with this approach is that r is not necessarily unique, that is, more than one value may satisfy the equation. The equation for internal rate of

Table 6–2
Internal Rate of Return Calculations

				Present Value	
Year	Benefits	Costs	Discount Rate at 11.6 Percent	Benefits	Costs
1	$ 0	$100,000	0.89606	$ 0	$ 89,606
2	100,000	40,000	0.80292	80,292	32,117
3	100,000	40,000	0.71946	71,946	28,778
4	100,000	40,000	0.64468	64,468	25,787
5	0	70,000	0.57767		40,437
Total	300,000	290,000		216,706	216,725

return becomes a polynomial equation as soon as the project has more than two years of economic life (that is, when n is 2 or greater). A necessary and sufficient condition for the existence of a single positive internal rate of return, however, is an excess of undiscounted benefits over costs.[12]

The internal rate of return provides a reasonably good measure of investment potential when all alternatives are of the same order of magnitude. When the alternatives are of different scales, it is of lesser practical value, since very little is revealed about the absolute size of the net benefits in the application of this technique.

Net Benefits

Net benefits is the criterion recommended, if not used, most frequently in contemporary cost-benefit analysis. The formula for calculating the present value of net benefits is:

$$N = -C_0 + \frac{(B_1 - C_1)}{(1 + i)} + \frac{(B_2 - C_2)}{(1 + i)^2} + \ldots + \frac{(B_n - C_n)}{(1 + i)^n}$$

Two projects with equal net benefits might be regarded indifferently, however. Suppose that two projects each offered net benefits of $10,000, but one involves a present value of benefits of $2 million and a present value of costs of $1.99 million, while the other project has a present value of benefits of $100,000 and a present value of costs of $90,000. Suppose that something goes wrong, so that the calculations of costs and benefits are off by 10 percent. The first project might have a negative benefit of as much as $200,000, whereas the second would do no worse than break even.

Net benefits measure *difference,* whereas benefit/cost calculations produce a *ratio.* The results of these two techniques are not always interchangeable. The fact that the net benefits of alternative A are greater than those of alternative B does not imply that the benefit/cost ratio of A is greater than that of B. For example, suppose the benefits in alternative A have a present value of $300,000, while the costs have a present value of $100,000. The net benefit/cost ratio would be 3.0. If the present value of benefits in altertative B were $200,000 and that of costs $40,000, alternative B would have lower net benefits ($160,000), but a higher benefit/cost ratio ($200,000/$40,000 or 5.0). In addition to knowing the benefit/cost ratio for a given project or program, it also is necessary to know the size of the project or program before as much information is available as is given in the present value of net benefits.

Benefit Investment Analysis Techniques

Long-term investment decisions in the private sector focus on four basic areas:

1. *Equipment replacement:* techniques of operations research have made significant contributions in the determination of when it is more efficient (that is, more profitable) to replace existing equipment rather than repair and maintain it.
2. *Cost-saving investment:* designed essentially to increase efficiency, to replace outmoded procedures, to modernize facilities, and so forth; this form of investment often includes the acquisition of land for future expansion, and options of new sites.
3. *Expansion investment:* investments in internal and external diversification, new product lines, and so forth, often including investments in research and development.
4. *Required capital investment:* dictated by external forces such as competition or by law.

The principal objective of such investments is the maximization of profits, that is, to obtain the maximum return on stockholder's investments. Industries frequently average as much as 50 percent of their total resources in long-term investments. Much of this commitment, of course, is involved in the development of an appropriate cash flow (annual profit margin) and in routine replacement. Factors affecting investment decisions include (1) the overall philosophy of management (conservatism versus risk taking), (2) market analysis and forecasting, (3) the decisions of competition (that is, "keeping up with the Joneses"), (4) sources of funding and the cost of capital, (5) the level of working capital available, (6) the effects of inflation, (7) the degree of risk and uncertainty perceived in the marketplace, and (8) governmental policies, particularly tax and depreciation allowances.

Investment decisions in the private sector may be based on several different forms of analysis. Applying each of these different methods may yield different results (that is, different rankings of alternative investments). To illustrate how each of these techniques operates, six alternative investments may be examined, as shown in table 6–3. Each of these investment alternatives involves an initial commitment of $10,000.

The first method looks at *net cash proceeds,* that is, how much is earned back over and above the initial investment. Over a three-year period, the return on the investment varies from $10,000 in the case of alternative *A* to $18,000 in the case of alternatives *C* and *F*. Alternatives *A* and *D* both yield

Table 6–3
Benefit Investment Analysis

Alter-natives	Initial Investment	Net Cash Proceeds 1 Year	Net Cash Proceeds 2 Year	Net Cash Proceeds 3 Year	Annual Proceeds	Per Dollar Outlay	Average Depreciation	Average Income	Present Value of Return	Net Present Value
A	$10,000	$10,000	$ 0	$ 0	$10,000	1.00	$10,000	$ 0	$ 9,434	-$ 566
B	10,000	5,000	5,000	5,000	5,000	0.50	3,333	1,667	13,365	3,365
C	10,000	2,000	4,000	12,000	6,000	0.60	3,333	2,667	15,522	5,522
D	10,000	10,000	3,000	3,000	5,333	0.53	3,333	2,000	14,623	4,623
E	10,000	6,000	4,000	5,000	5,000	0.50	3,333	1,667	13,094	3,094
F	10,000	8,000	8,000	2,000	6,000	0.60	3,333	2,667	16,346	6,346
Ranking of Alternative										
A			6		1			6		6
B			5		5			4		4
C			2		2			1		2
D			3		4			3		3
E			4		5			4		5
F			1		2			1		1

$10,000 in the first year; however, *D* has the potential (not a certainty) of additional yields of $3,000 in the second and third years. Therefore, *D* is superior to *A*. Alternative *B* and *E* have a potential net return of $15,000 over the three-year period. However, *E* is superior to *B* since the first-year yield of *E* is $6,000 as compared with $5,000 for *B*. Alternatives *C* and *F* both yield a net return over three years of $18,000. However, *F* has the larger first-year return and therefore, is superior to *C*.

Which of the six alternatives is the best investment depends on what can be done with the cash proceeds—how they might be reinvested. For example, even though alternative *D* yields $2,000 less than alternative *F*, if the initial return of $10,000 from *D* can be reinvested in, say, alternative *A*, which has a quick return to an additional $10,000, then alternative *D* may be superior to alternative *F*.

A second approach to benefit investment analysis looks primarily at the *payback period*, that is, the length of time required to get back a return equal to the initial investment. This approach favors those alternatives with the shortest payback periods. Therefore, among the six alternatives in table 6–3, *A* and *D* (with one-year payback periods) would be the preferred investments. The payback period for alternative *F* is 1.25 years, for atlernatives *B* and *E*, 2.00 years, and for alternative *C*, 2.33 years.

The *proceeds per dollar of outlay* approach examines the ratio between net cash proceeds and the initial investment. This approach is similar to the first technique except that it does not consider the rate of return. Under this approach, alternatives *C* and *F* rank first (with ratios of 1:1.8), followed by alternative *D* (1:1.6), alternatives *B* and *E* (1:1.5) and finally, *A* (1:1).

The *average annual proceeds per dollar of outlay* approach tends to be biased toward those investments that yield quick returns. As shown in table 6–3, alternative *A* ranks first, although the returns from this project are only for one year (the presumption being that the monies can be reinvested). The *average income on book value* technique involves a calculation of the average depreciation on the initial investment. It is assumed that the return on the initial investment in alternative *A* depreciates $10,000 in the first year, while each of the other investments depreciates at the average rate of $3,333 per year for three years. On this basis, alternatives *C* and *F* rank first, since in each case, the average annual proceeds less depreciation (or average income) is $2,667. This approach, however, fails to take into account the timing of when these proceeds are actually received.

All of these methods have shortcomings and, therefore, are relatively limited in the analysis of long-term investments: (1) these methods fail to take proper account of the timing of proceeds; (2) unequal dollars are treated as equal; and (3) income received after the initial payback is largely ignored in these calculations. In spite of these shortcomings, however, it has been estimated that over 70 percent of the major firms in the country still use one or more (or some combination) of these techniques of benefit investment analysis, coupled with hunches and guesswork.

Discounted Cash Flow Methods

In the mid-fifties, it was found that intuitive models, developed in an era of easy profits through rapid industrial expansion, were no longer applicable to many investment decisions. Therefore, however, new tools and concepts began to be introduced in the private sector. These new methods are generally labelled *discounted cash flow* techniques. Each method uses as input data the future positive and negative cash flows of money required to produce the desired returns and those that are a consequence of the particular investment. These methods grew out of the efforts of management to get some measure of economic wisdom regarding capital investments in additional facilities, products, or processes, and the desire of design engineers for a technique of measuring the economy of design in both construction and use.

Of these more sophisticated methods, two techniques—the equivalent uniform annual net return method and the net present value method—best illustrate this approach to investment decision analysis. The *equivalent uniform annual net return method* combines all investment costs and all annual expenses into one single annual sum that is equivalent to all disbursements during the analysis period if distributed uniformly over the period. This method also includes an income or benefit factor. The formula solution indicates the amount by which the equivalent uniform annual income (or benefits) exceeds (or is less than) the equivalent uniform annual cost. This formula can be represented as follows:

$$EUANR = -I \left[\frac{i(1 + i)^n}{(1 + i)^n - 1} \right] + T \left[\frac{i}{(1 + i)^n - 1} \right] - K + R$$

whereby the initial investment (I) is multiplied times the capital recovery factor, and the terminal value (T)—the anticipated value of the facility at the end of the analysis period—is multiplied by a sinking fund factor. K represents the total uniform annual expenses of administration, operations, and maintenance. R represents the uniform annual gross income from sales revenues, receipts, or their equivalent. R is inclusive of return on investment (depreciation and net profits).

The *net present value method* determines the algebraic difference in the present worth of both outward cash flow and inward flow of income or benefits, including the factor of annual income. The formula for calculating net present value can be expressed as follows:

$$NPV = -I + \frac{T}{(1+i)^n} - K\left[\frac{(1+i)^n - 1}{i(1+i)^n}\right] + R\left[\frac{(1+i)^n - 1}{i(1+i)^n}\right]$$

whereby the present worth of the terminal value (T) is calculated, and K and R are multiplied by the present worth factor of a uniform series. (This method assumes that annual costs and returns are uniform throughout the analysis period).

To illustrate these two methods, assume that management is confronted with two alternative investment decisions. Alternative A involves an initial investment of $1.2 million and has a terminal value at the end of 10 years of $100,000. The annual administrative, operating and maintenance costs, including overhead, production, and sales expenses, for this alternative are $5 million. Alternative B requires an initial investment of $2 million and has an estimated terminal value at the end of 10 years of $180,000. The estimated annual costs are $4,855,000. Alternative A is projected to have an annual gross income from sales of $5,292,000, while alternative B is estimated to yield $5,550,000 in annual sales. The rate of interest on capital is 8 percent per annum.

Applying the formula for the equivalent uniform annual net return method, alternative A has a EUANR of $120,070, whereas alternative B has a EUANR of $359,370. Therefore, all other things being equal, alternative B is the better investment. Similarly, alternative A has a net present value of $805,660, while alternative B has a net present value of $2,411,370. It should be noted that the EUANR for any project can be converted to the NPV by multiplying by the present worth factor of a uniform series (which in the case of the above example is 6.710081).

These two investment decision techniques applied in the private sector have their counterparts in cost-benefit analysis (more often applied in the public sector). The NPV method is similar in concept to the net benefits criterion, while the EUANR method has its counterpart in the annual net benefits approach.

Limitations of Cost-Benefit Analysis

There are several limitations to the application of cost-benefit analysis. These techniques do not purport to solve all problems relating to the allocation of scarce organizational resources. Cost-benefit analysis is of limited usefulness, for example, in the evaluation of programs of relatively broad scope or in the comparison of programs with widely differing objectives. Such analysis provides only limited assistance in establishing priorities among various goals.

The basic objective of cost-benefit analysis is not merely to maximize the ratio of benefits to costs. Circumstances can exist where the equalization of benefit-cost ratios may serve a necessary condition for achieving a desired maximum goal. More often, however, other factors must be considered in selecting an appropriate cost-benefit criterion that can lead to the best decision. These factors include (1) the "time-stream" of costs and benefits and the time-preference of the organization's clientele for present as opposed to future consumption of goods, (2) limitations imposed by revenue (budgetary) constraints, and (3) the issue as to whether benefits can be quantified or measured only in a low-level optimization or an intermediate sense, that is, whether goals and objectives can be specified in sufficient detail to permit a fuller identification of direct and indirect costs and benefits.

It is virtually impossible to eliminate the need for subjective judgments in the process of making decisions for any organization. Nonetheless, a more systematic approach to cost and benefit comparison, as provided by cost-benefit analysis, and the consideration of time-preference and marginal productivity of capital investment, can contribute significantly to more rational basis for such decisions. This is particularly true when compared with the uncoordinated, haphazard, and intuitive approaches that characterize many more traditional methods. Examining expenditures in terms of programs and objectives instead of merely by spending entities, and the consideration of total benefits of expenditures for alternative programs alongside of total costs of the inputs are important contributions of cost-benefit techniques.

Cost-Effectiveness Analysis

Cost-benefit analysis often is designed to pursue efficiency, often at the expense of effectiveness. The effectiveness of a program is measured by the extent to which if implemented, some desired goal or objective will be achieved. Since there usually is more than one way to achieve a goal, the analytical task is to determine from among several alternatives the most effective program at several levels of achievement or output. The preferred alternative is the one that produces the desired level of performance for the minimum cost, or achieves the maximum level of effectiveness possible for a given level of cost. Although costs can ordinarily be expressed in monetary terms, levels of achievement usually are represented by nonmonetary indexes or measures of effectiveness. Such indexes measure the direct and indirect impacts of resource allocations.

Output Orientation

Originating in the early 1970s, the techniques of cost-effectiveness analysis are relatively new, and have not yet reached full maturity. Cost-effectiveness studies initially were applied when benefits could not be measured in units commensurable with costs. In these early applications, the output or level of effectiveness usually was taken as a given. Several alternative methods of achieving this level were then examined in the hope that the one with lower costs could be identified. These initial studies revealed many important aspects of decision making with respect to the allocation of scarce resources.

In contemporary applications, cost-effectiveness analysis provides an explicit output orientation for the evaluation of program alternatives. Particular emphasis is placed on program objectives and on the use of effectiveness measures to monitor progress toward these objectives. The extended time horizon adopted in cost-effectiveness analysis leads to a fuller recognition of the need for life-cycle costing, that is, an analysis of costs over the estimated duration of the program or project.

Cost-effectiveness analysis can be viewed as an application of the economic concept of marginal analysis. The analysis must always move from some base that represents existing capabilities and existing resource commitments. The problem is to determine the additional resources required to achieve some specified additional performance capability (the program objective), or conversely, how much additional performance capability would result from some specified additional expenditure. Therefore, incremental costs are the most relevant factors in this cost analysis. Ideally, incremental cost is the difference between two programs, one with some desired improvement and one without this improvement.

Effectiveness measures provide the other dimension to the analysis. Such measures involve a basic scoring technique for determining the status of a given program alternative relative to the level of output to be achieved from the investment of an additional increment of cost. Effectiveness measures often are expressed in relative terms, for example, percentage increase in some measure of educational attainment, percentage reduction in the incidence of a disease, or percentage reduction in unemployment. It often is desirable to array effectiveness measures along an effectiveness scale to indicate the degree of goal achievement evidenced by each program alternative.

Types of Analyses

Three supporting analyses are required under the cost-effectiveness approach:

1. *Cost-goal studies* are concerned with the identification of feasible levels of achievement.
2. *Cost-effectiveness comparisons* assist in the identification of the most effective program alternative.
3. *Cost-constraint assessments* determine the cost of employing less than the most optimal programs.

The objective of a cost-goal study is to develop a cost curve for each program alternative. This curve approximates the sensitivity of costs (inputs) to changes in the desired level of effectiveness (outputs). Costs may change in direct proportion to the level of achievement, that is, each additional increment of cost may produce the same increase in terms of desired effectiveness. However, if effectiveness increases more rapidly than costs, than the particular program alternative is operating at a level of increasing return. This is represented by a positively sloped curve that accelerates at an accelerating rate, as illustrated by the initial segment of cost curve *A* in figure 6–1. If costs increase more rapidly than effectiveness, the program alternative is operating in an area of diminishing returns (as with the upper segment of cost curve *B*).

Increasing returns do not mean that a program alternative should automatically be adopted (or expanded, if it is an ongoing program). Conversely, diminishing returns should not automatically disqualify an alternative. It is useful to know, however, that an additional commitment of, for example, $20,000 will carry one program alternative 10 percent closer to an established goal, whereas the same resources will carry another alternative only 5 percent closer.

Cost-effectiveness analysis requires a model that can relate incremental

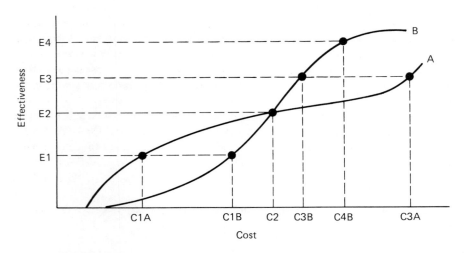

Source: Alan Walter Steiss and Gregory A. Daneke, *Performance Administration* (Lexington, Mass.: Lexington Books, 1980), p. 158. Reprinted by permission.

Figure 6–1. Cost-Effectiveness Analysis

costs to increments of effectiveness. For some types of problems, practical models can be developed with relative ease. For other problems, cost curves can be approximated from historical data. The construction of cost curves and effectiveness scales should become increasingly more sophisticated, as the input-output relationships associated with various alternatives are better understood.

Given that the cost and effectiveness for each alternative can be determined for different levels of input-output relationships, the problem remains of how to choose among these alternatives. In principle, the criterion or rule of choice should be to select the alternative that yields the greatest excess of positive impacts (attainment of objectives) over negative impacts (resources used, or costs and spillover effects that reduce effectiveness). In practice, however, this ideal criterion seldom is applied. There is no practical way to subtract dollars spent from the nonmonetary measures used to identify effectiveness.

The Optimum Envelope

Therefore, a cost-effectiveness comparison of program alternatives must be undertaken, as shown graphically in figure 6–1. Alternative A achieves the first level of effectiveness ($E1$) with a relatively modest level of cost ($C1A$), whereas nearly the level of resources ($C1B$) would be required to achieve the same level of effectiveness using alternative B. Both alternatives achieve the second level of effectiveness ($E2$) at the same level of cost ($C2$). Alternative B requires a lower level of resources ($C3B$) to achieve the third level of effectiveness. And only alternative B achieves the fourth level of effectiveness. The program cost curve of alternative A is not projected to reach this level of effectiveness.

Which of these two program alternatives is more desirable? To answer that question, it is necessary to define the *optimum envelope* formed by these two cost curves. If resources in excess of $C2$ are available, then alternative B clearly provides the better choice. However, if resources less than $C2$ are available, alternative A provides the greater effectiveness for the dollars expended.

In general, it is not possible to choose between two alternatives just on the basis of cost and effectiveness unless one program alternative dominates at all levels of effectiveness. Usually, either a desired level of effectiveness must be specified and then costs minimized for that effectiveness level. Or, a cost limit must be specified, and effectiveness maximized for that level of resource allocation.

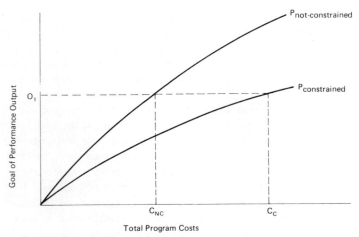

Source: Alan Walter Steiss, *Local Government Finance* (Lexington, Mass.: Lexington Books, 1975), p. 240. Reprinted by permission.

Figure 6–2. Cost-Constraint Analysis

Cost-Constraint Assessment

In practice, programs may be adopted by an organization which do not represent the most effective technically available. Among the more obvious reasons for this fact are legal constraints union rules, employer rights, community attitudes, and so forth. The purpose of a cost-constraint assessment is to examine the impact of these factors by comparing the cost of the program that could be adopted if no constraints were present with the cost of the constrained program. The assessment, shown graphically in figure 6–2, starts with the expressed goal 01, and two programs (P constrained and P not-constrained). The cost of the constraint is the difference between the program costs at the point at which 01 is achieved.

Once this cost differential is identified, decisions as to the feasibility of attempting to remove the constraint can be made. On the basis of this assessment, managers can provide decision makers with an estimate of how much would be saved through the relaxation of a given constraint. The cost of the constraint also is indicative of the amount of resources that might be committed to overcome a constraint, if such an effort were acceptable. In some cases, maintaining a constraint may be more important for social or political reasons than implementing a more effective program.

Regional Training Centers: A Case Study

The following case study illustrates the application of cost-effectiveness techniques. Assume that it is determined that some 3,000 workers in a given state become unemployed each year due to technical obsolescence. That is to say, the job for which they are trained and skilled is eliminated through automation of industrial processes. The state government has established an objective to retrain part or all of these workers to new skills through a one-year intensive training course. Through this program, it is anticipated that the workers will be employable at certain skill levels ten years earlier then if they had to attain these skills on their own. Therefore, the anticipated benefits of this program will run for ten years.

To provide this program, it is necessary to develop regional training centers, build new facilities or significantly upgrade existing facilities, hire new instructional personnel, and so forth. It is anticipated that the program will continue to operate over a ten-year period.

After considerable study, two alternatives are identified as being feasible to achieve the program objectives. Alternative A is an equipment-intensive approach, involving the extensive use of programmed learning techniques, tape libraries to upgrade basic skills in reading, use of computers, and so forth. It has only five instructors per training center and a trainee-instructor ratio of 60:1. Alternative B is a teacher-oriented approach, involving team-teaching techniques. It requires 20 instructors per training center and has a 10:1 trainee-instructor ratio. The trainee capacity at training centers for alternative A is 300 and for alternative B, 200. The costs for each system are summarized in table 6–4.

It now is possible to examine how costs and program effectiveness are related in the tests for preferredness. First, costs and benefits cannot be measured in the same units: benefits are measured in terms of the number of workers retrained and costs are measured in dollars. Since decision makers do not know the level of training they wish to support (or can afford to support given limited resources), a schedule of costs and effectiveness measures must be developed over the full range of workers to be trained (that is, 0–3,000). For convenience, it may be assumed that the costs are of a continuous nature, that is, training centers can be constructed and operated at various sizes. The training load capacities and systems costs (development,

Table 6–4
Alternative Program Costs
(*thousands of dollars*)

	Alternative A	Alternative B
Development costs	$15,000	$1,000
Investment per training center	500	400
Annual operating costs per training center	1,500	3,000

investment, and ten years of operating costs) are summarized in table 6–5. By eliminating the common denominator—number of training centers—measures of cost and effectiveness (that is, workers trained) can be combined into one chart (figure 6–3).

Nonquantifiable factors may enter into the final decision—these factors are omitted here for simplicity. It is possible to choose the best system given either a fixed budget or a specified level of benefits. The optimum envelope in indicated in figure 6–3. For all budgets under $24.2 million, alternative B is preferred because it will have a greater trainee capacity. Conversely, for all trainee loads less than 1,360, alternative B is preferred because it will cost less than alternative A. For budgets above $24.2 million or for trainee loads above 1,360, however, alternative A is preferred. For example, at a $20 million budget, alternative B has a capacity of about 1,100 trainees, while A can handle about 800 trainees. At a trainee load of 2,400, however, A would cost $31 million whereas B would cost $41.8 million.

As with other analytical techniques, the cost-effectiveness model need not be adopted in its entirety. A number of subroutines of this approach may be introduced into ongoing program analysis procedures. Particularly important are considerations developed through the techniques of cost curve analysis. As the complexity of the resource allocation problem becomes more evident, other subroutines may be adopted, depending on the availability of data and the needs and capabilities of the analysts.

Table 6–5
Training Capacity and Program Costs
(thousands of dollars)

	Centers		
	0	10	15
Alternative A			
Training Capacity	1,500	3,000	—
Program Costs			
Development	$15,000	$15,000	$15,000
Investment	—	5,000	7,500
Operations	—	15,000	22,500
Total Costs	15,000	35,000	45,000
Alternative B			
Training Capacity	1,000	2,000	3,000
Program Costs			
Development	$ 1,000	$ 1,000	1,000
Investment	—	4,000	6,000
Operations	—	30,000	45,000
Total Costs	1,000	35,000	52,000

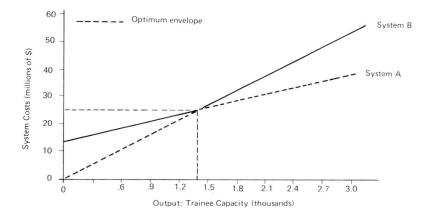

Source: Alan Walter Steiss, *Local Government Finance* (Lexington, Mass.: Lexington Books, 1975), p. 252. Reprinted by permission.
Figure 6–3. Trainee Capacity versus System Costs

Summary

It may be assumed that, in the allocation of limited fiscal resources, most organizations consider both the payoffs and pitfalls associated with various program requirements. These assessments, however, often are haphazard and uncoordinated, with little systematic effort to quantify benefits or to include all costs appropriate to particular alternatives under consideration.

Too often, organizational decision-making processes are dominated by a "money first" approach. Under this approach, only a certain predetermined amount of resources is available, and therefore, expenditures are limited to this amount. As a consequence, new program opportunities often are given lower priority, if considered at all, because ongoing program demands absorb all available resources. In other instances, an "absolute needs" approach is manifest, whereby a given set of expenditures is deemed so essential to the organization that it must be undertaken regardless of cost.

In recent years, however, there has been a significant increase in emphasis on various forms of cost-benefit and cost-effectiveness analysis. This emerging interest is due, in part, to the development of improved analytical techniques and computational capacity and, in part, to an expanding concern for more systematic budgeting techniques (discussed in further detail in the next chapter).

As with other analytical techniques, cost-benefit and cost-effectiveness models need not be adopted in their entirety. A number of subroutines may be introduced into ongoing program analysis procedures. The decision inputs that can be developed through the consideration of time-preference and marginal productivity of capital investment and the techniques of cost curve analysis are of particular importance. Examining expenditures in terms of program objectives and the evaluation of total benefits for alternative program expenditures alongside of total costs can be important derivatives of cost-benefit related techniques. The extended time horizon adopted in these analytical methods leads to fuller recognition of the need for life-cycle costing and benefits analysis. The importance of incremental costing, sunk costs, and inheritable assets also is underlined by this extended perspective. Cost-goal and cost-constraint analyses add important dimensions to the information available to the decision maker. As the complexity of the resource allocation problem becomes more evident, other subroutines may be adopted, depending on the availability of data and the needs and capabilities of the analysts.

Cost-benefit approaches emphasize the importance of quantification whenever possible, of making implicit judgmental inputs more explicit, and of minimizing the influence of prejudgments and bias. Within these limitations, cost-benefit analysis can make, and is making, important contributions to decision making, particularly within the context of strategic management.

Notes

1. Harley H. Hinrichs, "Government Decision Making and the Theory of Benefit-Cost Analysis: A Primer," in *Program Budgeting and Benefit-Cost Analysis,* edited by Harley H. Hinrichs and Graeme M. Taylor (Pacific Palisades, Calif.: Goodyear, 1969), p. 9.
2. A.R. Prest and R. Turvey, "Cost Benefit Analysis: A Survey," *The Economic Journal* (1965):583.
3. Anatol Rapoport, "What Is Information?" *ETC: A Review of General Semantics* 10 (Summer 1953):252.
4. Peter F. Drucker, *The Practice of Management* (New York: Harper and Brothers, 1954), p. 353.
5. Otto Eckstein, *Water Resource Development* (Cambridge, Mass.: Harvard University Press, 1958).
6. Herbert A. Simon, *Administrative Behavior* (New York: Free Press, 1957), p. 62.
7. Ibid., p. 65.
8. Hinrichs, "Government Decision Making," p. 13.
9. Simon Ramo, *Cure for Chaos* (New York: David McKay, 1969), p. 109.
10. Leonard Merewitz and Stephen H. Sosnick, *The Budget's New Clothes* (Chicago, Ill.: Markham, 1971), p. 85.
11. Ibid., p. 86.
12. Jack Hirschleifer, "On the Theory of Optimal Investment Decisions," in *The Management of Corporate Capital,* edited by Ezra Solomon (New York: Free Press, 1959), pp. 224–235.

7
Resource Management: Budgeting Procedures

T he traditional role of a budget is to serve as a control mechanism to ensure financial integrity, accountability, and legal compliance. The budget also can provide an important tool for management when used to ascertain operating economies and performance efficiencies. As a component of strategic planning, the budget must reflect organizational goals and objectives and the overall effectiveness of programs in meeting client needs.

It should be understood, however, that a budget does not offer any automatic or magic solutions to the problems and issues which surround the control and direction of the affairs of a complex organization. As Frederick C. Mosher has stated, "Budgeting, like other social processes, is a human undertaking, carried on by people who are subject to a wide variety of influences and motivations."[1] Strategic managers must be well aware of the limitations within which they must operate and the hazards which must be faced.

Purposes and Objectives of Budgeting

The term *budget* is commonly used to identify different aspects of financial planning. At times, the term is used to designate the financial and operating programs recommended for consideration by a governing body (such as an organization's board of directors, the city council, or an authority's executive committee). In other cases, the budget is the document approved by such bodies from which controlling appropriations, allocations, and allotments are made. It is necessary, therefore, to distinguish between a proposed and an adopted budget. A distinction also must be made in terms of the time span covered by the budget document. The current or operating budget generally covers operations for a fiscal year. The capital budget, on the other hand, represents a plan for expenditures to be incurred over a period of years to meet capital investment needs and long-term programs of operational services.

Budgeting is essentially a planning process. The annual budget cycle requires regular reviews of activities and service policies. The danger inherent in cyclical budgeting, however, is that it can result in short-run thinking and a tendency to postpone to some future budget period necessary increases in commitments or measures to generate additional resources. Failure to look beyond the current budget can result in a significant multiplication of future problems. The problem of an uncertain future must be countered by a comprehensive approach to strategic planning, by careful program analysis, and by continuous efforts to improve available techniques for projecting revenue/income potential and expenditure needs.

Organizations do not operate in a vacuum. The budget process will always be affected by economic, political, and social forces originating outside the organization, in the broader decision environment. More established organizations have built up systems of values, beliefs, and traditions that are slow to change. The budget for any current cycle will inevitably be affected by past commitments, established standards of service, existing organizational structures, and current methods of operation. Any of these factors may not be entirely satisfactory from the standpoint of effective budget making. Through budget analysis, the strategic manager may find many areas in need of improvement. However, it may not be possible to effect such improvements immediately. Budgeting must be a continuous process, and program reforms may have to be programmed over a long period of time.

Each annual budget represents only a relatively short time cycle in the long life span of the organization and its programs. An adequate budget system must provide comprehensive and effective procedural devices for controlling expenditures and thus, for establishing the price that must be paid for the services of the organization. A potential conflict exists, however, between the "fiscal watchdog" attitude adopted by some budget officials, and the more progressive service orientation necessary to provide programs geared to client needs.

Foundations for Effective Budget Preparation

An inventory of service activities should be developed and maintained along with a system of records and reports to provide information on the volume of activity and program output or performance. These records and reports provide data for the preparation of program justifications. A suggested approach to the establishment of a record and reporting system is provided in figure 7–1.

A continuous analysis of the operations of the organization is an essential tool for determining budget requirements. Budget making must be based on a constant scrutiny of services performed, operating methods, organizational structure, and the utilization of facilities. These management research activities are an integral part of the operations planning and control process (which will be discussed in further detail in a subsequent chapter).

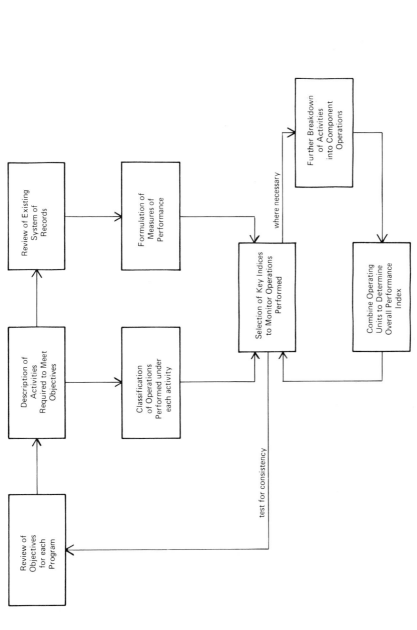

Source: Alan Walter Steiss, *Public Budgeting and Management* (Lexington, Mass.: Lexington Books, 1972), p. 176. Reprinted by permission.

Figure 7–1. Procedures for Establishing Record and Reporting System

The budget is so important to the proper functioning of any organization that its place and continuity often is assured in organic law. Such legal parameters may include the date on which the fiscal year begins, dates of budget transmittal and adoption, general scope of the budget, and responsibility and authority for budget preparation and execution. Details as to budget procedures and the specific content of the budget document, however, should be incorporated in administrative rules and regulations may be readily modified and improved.

Viewed as a process, budgeting may be described as a formalized system of communication. The extent of formalization in the process will vary with the size and complexity of the organization. However, the basic outlines of the program will be the same. Every device of communication—formal and informal—comes into play, including written instructions, schedules, forms, personal and group conferences, and so on.

The system of accounts adopted by the organization must be adequate not only for fiscal control but also for the provision of important management information. First priority should be given to the establishment of account classifications tailored to organizational needs. "Model" classification systems should be considered only as guides and must be interpreted in light of the needs of the organization and its services and activities. An accounting system, as a minimum, should include (1) comprehensive procedures for expense distribution, (2) cost-accounting procedures, (3) general ledger accounts for work in process, and (4) suspense accounts for the distribution of such expenditures as compensation insurance and retirement contributions.

The Budget Cycle

Careful scheduling is required if the management of an organization is to be given adequate time and information for sound budget decisions. Steps in the budget process must be undertaken in logical sequence in order to meet established deadlines while coordinating the required detail. Responsibility for performing each specific step should be clearly assigned. Well-designed forms should be provided to the various budget units of the organization to ensure that requests are submitted in as complete and uniform a manner as possible. (For purposes of this discussion, a budget unit is any component of an organization that is required to submit a budget request on a regular basis.) Often a budget calendar is established to set down key dates and assign responsibility for carrying out the preparation of the budget. The time intervals required for each step in the process will vary somewhat in accordance with the size of the organization, established legal requirements, and type of budget format applied.

Regardless of the format adopted, the budget cycle commonly involves four major elements: (1) executive preparation; (2) review, modification, and enactment by the governing body; (3) budget execution; and (4) postaudit and evaluation. Each of these elements are further outlined in the following section.

The Executive Budget

In most organizations, the chief executive officer has primary responsibility for the preparation of budget estimates and development of a preliminary budget document. Decisions made in connection with an annual budget often have implications far beyond the next fiscal year, however. Projections of demographic and economic characteristics of the organization's clientele are important to the development of estimates of service demand and revenue supply. Financial analysis provides an assessment of probable consequences of current organizational policies, identifies specific issues, and establishes a foundation for decisions regarding new or modified policies. Through long-range financial planning, the current budget can be placed into perspective in terms of future resources and commitments.

A budget guidance memorandum should be issued to all budget units, along with a detailed set of instructions or budget manual for completing the requisite forms and supporting information and justifications. This memorandum should outline (1) anticipated fiscal policies, (2) established goals and objectives for the organization, and (3) more specific performance expectations. Statements of client needs and demands should be presented to establish appropriate levels of program activities or services to be further structured in the submissions of each of the budget units. Budget targets may be set forth to identify preliminary revenue estimates.

The required budget forms should be completed by each budget unit to reflect the best estimate as to the appropriate assignment of resources for personnel, materials and supplies, equipment, and so forth to carry out the programs and activities within its areas of responsibility. Budget units may be called on to further refine the broad goals and objectives of the organization in order to place their specific programs into perspective. Various performance and effectiveness measures may be required as part of the budget justifications. A priority listing of all programs and a report on the current or proposed status of each program may also be required. Each budget unit may be asked to identify any major policy issues or administrative problems that should be addressed. The requirements for new organizational policies also should be outlined by the budget units.

The initial function of the central budget staff is to check submissions for completeness and accuracy. Budget unit requests are then compiled into a preliminary document to provide an overall summary of total dollar needs.

The budget staff may also prepare preliminary projections of changes in employee compensation and benefits, develop estimates of the amounts required for such items as debt service and interfund transfers, and identify any policy changes inherent in the requests of the budget units.

The chief executive must work closely with unit heads and other officials to make the necessary adjustments that will bring the total budget into line with overall financial constraints. New or modified policies may have to be examined to provide increased resources to meet justified program needs. All too often, preliminary resource estimates are taken as an absolute constraint, with the result that documented program needs are adjusted downward. Often such adjustments can have detrimental consequences for the organization.

When the budget data have been analyzed and major allocation decisions have been made, the budget document can be prepared for review by the organization's governing body. This document should provide a clear picture of both the programs to be carried out and the financial basis to support these activities. The budget document must be designed so that it can be readily understood by members of the governing body and others within and outside the organization. The enthusiasm of budget technicians for complete detail often must be curbed in the interest of clarity and simplicity. Clarity can be achieved, however, without omitting important facts. A well-constructed budget message, carefully chosen summaries, and the use of tables and charts to explain service programs and the interrelationship among various elements of proposed financial commitments are important factors in an effective budget presentation.

Action of the Governing Body

The first step in the budget review by the governing body involves consultation with the chief executive and his or her staff for detailed explanation of the proposed programs and means of financing them. The governing body should receive more than a thick document, with page after page of tables, providing little or no explanation of the services to be provided or the intent of the administration. Under such circumstances, members of the governing body may nitpick over details, and important decisions involved in setting service levels may never be faced directly. The governing body should not be concerned with minor details except as they may relate to major policies and programs.

Based on these discussions the governing body may make amendments to the expenditure portion of the budget to reflect its perspective on potential resources. The governing body may approve the budget as a whole by resolution, or it may adopt more detailed measures that list specific amounts for designated budget units by definitive categories of expense. Care must be taken, however, not to limit the ability of budget units to make adjustments during the fiscal year to meet changing conditions in the implementation of their program activities.

Budget Execution

Budget execution is both a substantive operational process and a financial process. It involves the initiation of authorized projects and programs within an established time schedule, within monetary limits, and ideally, within standard cost limits. This stage of the budget cycle covers the full fiscal year and overlaps both the formulation and review stages of the budget for the succeeding year.

Patterns of budget administration vary considerably among organizations. In some cases, budget administration consists of little more than the establishment of appropriate accounts and the recording of expenditures as they are processed for payment. Such an approach is merely a cash-flow bookkeeping process that tracks the overflow of funds in accordance with predetermined item accounts. In more advanced budgetary control systems, however, the steps in administration include (1) allocation, (2) allotment, (3) expenditure control, (4) performance monitoring, and (5) adjustments.

Allocations subdivide the budget according to organizational units, classes of expenditures, and/or programs. Allocations often are made for personal services (salaries and wages) and for operations, with further subdivisions of the operating allocations by programs, projects, or organizational units. In some cases, specific allocations are encumbered from the outset of the fiscal year and then are liquidated on an as-billed basis (legal services or other consultant fees, and indirect support payments for employee benefits, and so forth). The purpose of this encumbrance is to ensure that these monies will be available at the time needed, that is, that they will not be spent for other purposes.

Under an *allotment system,* allocations are further subdivided into time elements (for example, monthly or quarterly allotments for personal services or for some group of items in the nonpersonal service categories). An allotment system is particularly appropriate in such circumstances where commitments are contingent on some future events (such as the availability of gifts and grants or the opening of a new capital facility). Under such an approach, the portion of the budget in question may be retained in the unallocated or unallotted category until required for actual commitment.

The accounting system of the organization plays a major role in the implementation of *expenditure controls,* as will be further detailed in subsequent chapters. Budgetary accounting supplies the control mechanisms for enforcing allocation and allotment limits through periodic internal budget reports. Cost accounting and statistical reports provide a basis for developing unit costs for various workload levels and comparisons with performance and costs standards. Although much of this accounting is highly centralized, partial decentralization has taken place in some larger organizations to keep financial and cost accounting close to the operating centers of expenditures.

Mechanisms to control specific expenditures are provided to the governing body through such devices as line-item allocations, periodic budgetary reports, and the independent audit at the close of the fiscal year. In addition, the governing body may insert control conditions on the use of specific funds and/or may require prior approval for proposed transfers between major budget items.

In addition to these expenditure controls, certain supplemental management controls often are established:

1. *Position controls,* such as restrictions on the filling of vacancies, moratoria on promotions, and formula allocations of various clerical positions, may be exercised by the chief executive or personnel director.
2. *Property-management procedures* may reduce the need for new capital outlays by improving equipment care through a preventative maintenance program.
3. *Central purchasing procedures* involve quantity and quality controls, competitive bidding for nonroutine purchases, and blanket ordering.
4. *Efficiency or administrative audits* can provide valuable information regarding future operational controls that should be incorporated into ongoing procedures.
5. *Performance monitoring procedures* give specific recognition to the work actually performed in relation to that which was planned. If projected performance levels do not materialize, it may be necessary to determine alternative patterns of funding for the balance of the fiscal year.

Many departmental officials, with some justification, may consider these controls an unnecessary intrusion on their administrative responsibilities. Obviously, no competent manager wants his or her operational decisions second-guessed by budget officials who may only see the fiscal implications of such decisions. On the other hand, without the discipline of central review, expenditures may be made contrary to their justifications, thereby producing short- and long-term commitments that eventually might prove embarrassing to the organization.

Budgetary Adjustments

Most budgets require some adjustments during the fiscal year. Frequent assessments of performance and of changing conditions in the broader decision environment can point up the need for such adjustments to ensure adequate flexibility in operations. Budget units managers should take the initiative when problems come to their attention. However, the central budget staff must exercise overall responsibility for recommending any actions necessary to avoid fiscal crises, such as the lack of funds to buy critical materials or equipment.

Sufficient information should be maintained—through the accounting process and ongoing financial analysis—to anticipate requirements for formal amendments during the fiscal year. Some amendments may require immediate attention. Many can be handled more efficiently through a single omnibus amendment, usually made during the last two to three months of the fiscal year.

Estimates of the closing status of any unappropriated surplus accounts should be made during the fiscal quarter. Some accounts may be limited as to their fiscal-year carry-over, that is, unspent funds may revert back to the general account at the end of the fiscal year. Many units will attempt to zero-out such accounts as the end of the year approaches. Caution must be exercised, however, that the expenditures are eligible items of expense and will stand the test of a post audit. Year-end reversion of funds often is cited as a major shortcoming of traditional budgeting procedures. Such reversions promote year-end spending and offer no incentives for conserving resources.

Auditing the Budget

Procedures for auditing the budget at the close of the fiscal year will be discussed in further detail in a subsequent chapter. Suffice it to say that two basic types of audits can (and should) be conducted. *Internal audits* are carried out on a periodic basis (for example, quarterly or semiannually) by organization staff members in order to produce reports for internal management control purposes. The *external audit* is conducted by certified public accountants after the fiscal year has ended. This audit, normally required by good business practices, is submitted to the governing body and made available to other interested parties (such as stockholders and patrons). The governing body, in turn, reviews the audit to be sure that revenue and expenditure activities were conducted in accordance with the intentions of the budget and related financial guidelines.

Management Emphasis on Performance

Recognition that the budget can serve important management purposes in determining operating economies and performance efficiencies began to emerge in the mid-thirties. These efforts culminated in the concept of *performance budgeting,* which had its heyday in the late forties and early fifties.

Performance budgeting seldom is discussed in any detail in contemporary textbooks, being relegated for the most part to a historical footnote. Nevertheless, many attributes have survived, and to understand how the budget can be used as a more effective tool of strategic management, it is useful to explore these attributes in greater detail.

The Budget as a Work Program

Two key components distinguish performance budgeting from other budgetary approaches: (1) the identification of performance units and (2) efforts to measure performance costs.[2] A performance unit can be described as a team of workers assigned the responsibility to carry out a specific task or series of tasks, whereas performance costs are those costs directly associated with carrying out these activities.

The budget is envisioned as a series of work programs related to particular processes or functions carried out by governmental agencies or units within not-for-profit organizations. The principal focus of the performance budget is at and below the departmental level where the work-efficiency of operating units can be assessed. Work-cost data are reduced into discreet, measurable units to determine the performance efficiency of prescribed activities. In short, cost accounting techniques provide the conceptual and technical basis for the objectives of efficiency and economy.

An inability to achieve a uniform and consistent basis for identifying performance units and a reluctance to adopt accrual accounting procedures to assist in measuring performance costs were major limitations in the implementation of performance budgeting. As a consequence, many applications of performance budgeting focused only on selected components, such as activity classification systems and performance measures. These components, however, remain as major contributions to financial management procedures emerging from this period.

Budget Classification Systems

A budget classification system provides the means for organizing and facilitating comparisons among data on income and expenditures. The usefulness of a budget classification system can be judged in relation to (1) its operational character, (2) its ability to assist in decision making by bringing important fiscal questions into focus and clarifying appropriate answers, and (3) its capacity to provide information for financial reporting in accordance with generally accepted accounting principles.

The most widely used budget classification system is based on *objects of expenditure*. The principal purpose of this classification system is the control of expenditures at the agency or budget unit level. Since units within an organization tend to buy the same things, it is possible to set up a chart of accounts that is uniform through the whole of the organization, thus linking the accounting system directly with budget accounts. Object codes are three- or four-digit numbers (for example, 1100 personal services, 1200 contractual services, and 1300 supplies and materials) which can be further divided into subobject classifications (for example, 1240 travel or 1275 computing services). The four-digit format provides a large field for additional expenditure categories. The codes can be revised periodically as new areas of expenditure are encountered.

The object of expenditure budget format has two distinct advantages not possessed by other types of classifications. The first is accountability—an object classification establishes a pattern of accounts that can be controlled and audited. Each object of expenditure is subject to a separate pattern of documentation. This accounting documentation has been further facilitated by the data-processing capacity of computers. By inserting additional codes in the data field, expenditures can be tracked by appropriation, agency, program or project, and by purpose. Special funding limitations also can be specified and monitored on a continuous basis.

A second advantage of the object of expenditure approach is its use as a mechanism of management control. Deviations above a certain percentage in terms of specific object codes may require approval of the governing body. The status of existing personnel can be identified in terms of commitments to salaries and wages, and the impacts of proposed changes in personnel can also easily be determined. Since personnel requirements are closely linked with other budgetary requirements, the control of positions can be used as a lever to control the whole budget.

Building a budget on detailed object codes, however, tends to promote an incremental approach to financial decision making. If X dollars were committed to a given subobject code in the past fiscal period, the tendency is to request X plus 10 percent (or some other inflation factor) for this subobject code in the next fiscal period. Little consideration may be given to reasons why X dollars were spent, to whether these commitments were made in the most economical and efficient way, or to whether these expenditures contribute to the overall effectiveness of the organization's programs.

In short, object classifications show in great detail *what* is purchased, but not *why,* that is, the nature of organizational programs and accomplishments under those programs. To overcome this shortcoming, purchases can be organized and aggregated according to the activities they serve, not as things in themselves. *Activity classifications* seek to relate activities to the work responsibilities of distinct operating units. Activities become the basic building blocks—and performance units—of the budget. Activity classifications can provide a great deal of information about what the organization is doing and thereby help to make management more cost-conscious by providing the expenditure data needed to manage and evaluate a budget unit in terms of the efficient use of these resources.

A problem with this approach, however, is that the term *activity* can be applied under various circumstances to mean process, project, or purpose. A *process* approach, for example, would list as activities the various steps in carrying out the work program of a budget unit. A *project* approach might list the individual projects (often involving fixed assets and capital facilities) that go to make up the total activity areas of an agency. A *purpose* classification might group activities according to broad functions or by clientele groups. The confusion that could arise from mixing these approaches in a given organization should be self-evident.

Activity classifications can be refined in great detail. Such refinement, however, runs the risk of obscuring the major purposes of an organization's programs. Thus financial management may be transformed into a detailed accounting exercise not unlike that incurred in objects of expenditure classifications. As Burkhead has observed, "Nothing is gained in budgetary classification by overrefinement of detail. In fact, the overrefinement of detail is a positive evil—it detracts from the importance of programs and destroys the perspective of decision-makers."[3]

The use of activity classifications requires an accounting crosswalk to track expenditures from the more traditional categories to the chosen activity units. In the earlier days of performance budgeting, these sorts had to be carried out largely by hand. Modern computer software can facilitate the sorting of accounting data according to various categories and subcategories.

Performance Measures

The purpose of a *unit cost measure* is to aggregate all of the relevant costs associated with the delivery of a particular service and to divide these costs by the total units of service provided. The unit cost for the administration of a Rubella immunization program, for example, would include the salary costs of the medical personnel involved, the cost of the vaccine, other supplies and equipment required, and so forth. These costs may vary with the number of children innoculated (presumably there is some economy of scale as the size of the program increases) and with the method of delivery (for example, through public health clinics, in the schools, or by private practitioners). As the "hard-to-reach" cases are encountered, however, unit costs may increase.

Workload measures, a second area of performance measurement, relate to the volume of work performed during some time period. In a public welfare department, for example, it may be possible to determine the number of cases in various categories that can be handled by a case worker daily, weekly, or annually. With this information and an estimate of the total number of cases to be processed, the department head could calculate the manpower required during any fiscal period. Other common workload measures include number of customers served, tons of trash collected, number of children vaccinated, number of inspections made, number of library books circulated, and number of emergency calls responded to. Workload measures serve as basic budget-building information, and retrospectively, can often provide an indication of the adequacy of previous resource allocation decisions.

Workload measures represent *output measures* in that, in the aggregate, they indicate the volume of goods and/or services delivered by a program or activity. Unit cost measures, on the other hand, represent an important category of *input measures,* that is, data which indicate the resources employed to operate a program. When workload or output measures are related to unit costs or input measures, the resulting index often is called a *performance measure.*

Such measures often are used as indicators of operating efficiency, for example, the cost per patient-day of hospital service, the number of cases successfully prosecuted per law enforcement officer, or the response time involved in providing some public service. As may be seen from these examples, not all performance measures are expressed in cost terms. Performance measures provide basic management information on program economics, that is, such measures reveal the relationship between initial resource allocations (inputs) and the delivery of services (outputs).

Productivity measures represent a special class of performance measures that deal more directly with the production process—with the conversion of various input factors (for example, capital and labor) into direct outputs (goods and services). In private sector applications, productivity measures usually are expressed in terms of the ratio of physical units of output (for example, number of widgets produced) to physical units of inputs (for example, raw materials, labor, and energy). Unit cost measures are expressed as the ratio of current dollars of input per physical unit (or constant dollar) of output. And workload measures are expressed as tasks per unit of time. All three of these measurements can be termed *efficiency measures.*

An overemphasis on performance measures in administrative decision making can result in pseudoefficiency, however. Performance measures can be overstated. Or organizations may resort to "creaming"—doing the easy assignments first and deferring or neglecting the more difficult ones—in order to meet such measures of efficiency. For example, if a forensic laboratory is evaluated in terms of the number of tests performed, priority might be given to the relatively simple tests, leaving the more involved ones until the "volume" tests have been completed. Such problems suggest the need for careful review of performance data by disinterested third parties (such as internal auditors).

Performance budgeting introduced a broader use of program information in the development of budget documents and the subsequent accounting for expenditures. Although seldom practiced today in its "pure" form, many characteristics of performance budgeting have survived. Performance measures—workload and unit cost measures—and the concept of performance levels or levels of service have been incorporated into many contemporary financial management applications which seek greater efficiency and economy in the allocation of limited resources. The focus on cost-efficiency, a hallmark of performance budgeting, has its parallel emphasis in current budget and accounting formats. Cost accounting systems also are beginning to receive wider application in government and nonprofit organizations, particularly in support of the techniques of cost-benefit and cost-effectiveness analysis.[4] The basic techniques of cost accounting are discussed in further detail in a subsequent chapter.

Service Delivery Accountability

For over sixty years, budget reformers have criticized the incremental aspects of the financial management process as arbitrary and irrational. They have pointed to the lack of coordination and the neglect of important values in traditional budget-building procedures, suggesting that incremental budgeting produces only small changes in the status quo. *Incrementalism* involves an examination of differences between budget appropriations for the previous year and requests for the next fiscal year. Since the results from previous allocations are accepted as the primary decision criteria in incremental budgeting, existing programs are continued into the future without being subjected to intensive reexamination. A comprehensive analysis of previously allocated resources—the *budget base*—seldom is an integral part of the incremental approach. Therefore, incremental budgeting is suspect in its ability to allocate scarce fiscal resources in the most efficient, economical, and effective manner. As E. Hilton Young observed in 1924:

> It must be a temptation to one drawing up an estimate to save himself trouble by taking last year's estimate for granted, adding something to any item for which an increase expenditure is foreseen. Nothing could be easier or more wasteful and extravagant. It is in that way an obsolete expenditure is enabled to make its appearance year after year, long after reason for it has ceased to be.[5]

Service Level Analysis

The same sentiments expressed by Young over sixty years ago have been reiterated in recent years by critics of the traditional incremental approach to financial management. New procedures have been proposed to promote greater rationality, comprehensiveness, and accountability—procedures by which every program, new and old, must compete equally for available budget dollars. Rather than reviewing only the incremental adjustments over previous levels of funding/expenditures, the budget is analyzed in its entirety. In this way, inefficient and obsolete programs can be revised or eliminated, thereby freeing more resources for new or higher priority programs. This more comprehensive budget format sometimes is referred to as a "zero-base" approach because no incrementally established budget base is accepted as permanent.

Current applications of the zero-base approach have taken a somewhat more modest and more realistic approach as compared to earlier efforts of zero-base budgeting in the mid-sixties. The detailed analysis of programs to the zero base has been replaced by the concept of *levels of effort*. Zero-base budgeting requires agencies "to examine their budgets below the base; the base being their current level of expenditure. . . . Zero-base budgeting re-quires each agency to specify—on paper—as part of its regular policy sub-mission—possibilities for spending less money than the current year."[6]

While receiving the greatest publicity at the federal and state levels, the techniques of zero-base analysis may have more significant potential in appli-cation in local government and nonprofit organizations. In such applications, "decision packages" are more readily identified and managed. Many have argued, however, that zero-base budgeting is a budgetary fad and have pre-dicted its rapid demise following a rather lackluster performance at the national level in the late seventies. As with performance budgeting, however, a number of aspects of zero-base budgeting are likely to survive and become amalgamated into other budgetary approaches. One such aspect is the con-cept of *service level analysis*.

Traditional budgeting procedures tend to focus attention on proposed dollar increases in the budget. Under service level analysis, attention is drawn to considerations of the elements of the budget base along with proposed changes in the level of services delivered. Rather than involving any radical departures from established financial management methods, service level analysis embodies a long accepted principal of building the budget on the basis of a sound appraisal of needs matched against the limitations of re-sources.

Service level analysis is applicable to all *actionable* programs or activities, that is, those in which there is some discretion as to the courses of action pursued. Although so-called actionable or discretionary programs may make up only a portion of the total budget (less than 25 percent, according to some estimates[7]), they often represent activities that are more difficult to analyze and plan. Thus, more effective management of these components through service level analysis can greatly affect the entire budget.

Unfortunately, there may be some confusion between fixed expenditures and essential levels of service. Local governments, for example, may have relatively little choice about the funding of essential service levels, and such service levels may comprise a major portion of the annual budget. However, one of the basic objectives of service level analysis is the identification of these essential service levels so that a jurisdiction can maintain and deliver—and be held accountable for—such programs in a more efficient and effective manner. Labeling a public service as essential is not the same thing as defining its supporting expenditures as fixed. Essential services can be provided more efficiently (at less cost) or more effectively (with greater benefits). With experience, categories of expenditures excluded from service level analysis should be reduced significantly relative to the total budget.

Components of Service Level Analysis

While the terminology may vary from application to application, there are three basic components to a service level analysis:

1. *Identification of budget units:* the designation of the basic building block within the organizational structure responsible for decision making and an examination of goals and objectives, current purposes and methods of operation, ways of measuring performance and effectiveness, and relations with other budget units.
2. *Decision package analysis:* the identification of alternative ways of providing essential services and the justification of various levels of service at which each budget unit might operate.
3. *Priority ranking and evaluation:* the arrangement of all levels of service in descending order of importance and the determination of a funding cutoff point.

The linkages between these analytical components are shown in figure 7–2.

It is important that budget units be of such a size that their data needs can be served adequately by the available accounting system. The identification of appropriate budget units may be a fairly time-consuming effort initially, requiring considerable thought and organizational analysis. It is unlikely, however, that budget units will change dramatically from one year to the next. Consequently, the identification of budget units generally is a one-time task, requiring only minor adjustments in subsequent years as new program responsibilities are assumed or major program revisions are initiated.

A decision package represents a discrete set of services, activities, and resources application to the performance of a given operation or the accomplishment of a program goal. A decision package should describe the set of activities in such a way that management can (1) evaluate and rank it against other activities competing for limited resources, and (2) decide whether to approve or disapprove it.[8] Decision packages may involve alternative

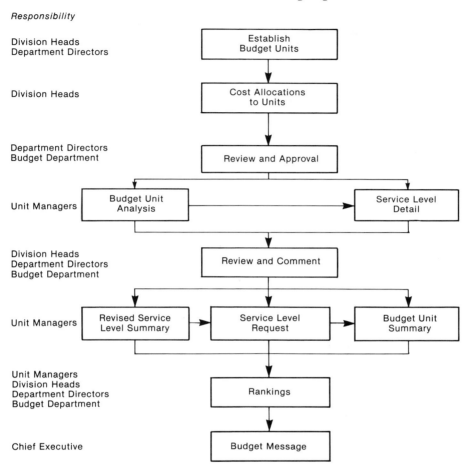

Figure 7–2. Flow Chart for Service Level Analysis

methods for delivering a service (for example, contracting out part of the activities involved versus carrying out these functions in-house). Or they may be alternative approaches which make use of more or less of the same basic resource inputs (for example, full-time salaried personnel versus part-time wage personnel hired on an "as needed" basis).

Figure 7–3 illustrates a summary sheet for the service level analysis of the rescue squad/ambulance service in the fictitious city of Rurbania. Three decision packages are identified: (1) the current approach, involving free, around-the-clock ambulance service provided as part of the operations of the fire department; (2) a contractual option frequently used in the past in smaller communities, involving the local mortuary; and (3) a contractual option relying on the ambulance service of the city-county hospital.

FUND: General   **DEPARTMENT PROGRAM:** Fire Safety   **DIVISION/ELEMENT:** Operations

Goals and Objectives
Reduce and eliminate complications due to injury or other medical need because individuals cannot be transported rapidly and adequately to medical facilities.
Provide free ambulance service to those who cannot pay for medical transportation.

Current Operations and Resources
Free ambulance service provided to all people in the city. Calls for emergency transportation are dispatched over the fire emergency communications network. Vehicle responds to scene of need. One vehicle, 4 drivers and 2 paramedics provide around-the-clock service 365 days per year.

Alternative Methods of Operation
Contract with Diggers Mortuary—save about $10,000 per year but run risk of not having dedicated vehicle.
Contract with city-County Hospital—hospital ambulance sometimes dispatched to remote parts of county or to other medical facilities outside of county.

Critical Linkages
Fire Emergency Communications—receive dispatch services

City Garage—routine maintenance and repairs

Service Level Impact Summary
Rescue Squad/Ambulance Service

1. 10-minute response time; no medical or first aid assistance
2. 7-minute response time; no medical or first-aid assistance
3. Add medical assistance and reduce complications due to no first aid
4. Paramedic services provided around-the-clock

Service Level Summary	Service Level		Cumulative		Cumulative Percent		Cumulative Program Measures				
							a	b	c	d	
Service Level Title	Gr. Total	Pos.	Gr. Total	Pos.	Gr. Total	Pos.	Average Number of Calls Per Year	Average Response Time	Average Turnaround Time	Number of Responses greater than 10 minutes	
1. Fire Operations/ Volunteer Service	$ 5,825	0	$ 5,825	0	8.6%	0%	125	10	25	25	
2. Fire Operations/ Assigned Drivers	$31,004	3	$ 36,829	3	54.7%	50%	125	7	19	15	
3. Add Paramedic Team	$30,534	3	$ 67,363	6	100.0%	100%	125	5	15	10	
4. Add 2nd Paramedic Team	$18,320	2	$ 85,683	8	127.2%	133%	125	5	15	7	
5. Add 2nd Ambulance Unit	$43,361	4	$129,044	12	191.6%	200%	250	3	10	0	

Figure 7–3. Summary Sheet for Service Level Analysis

For some essential services, only one decision package may be readily evident; the level of investment from prior budget years may be such that a continuation of the current approach may be the only feasible decision. However, such prior program investments, whether in dollar terms or in terms of other administrative (or psychological) commitments, should not preclude a search for alternative decision packages. Maintaining an existing program simply because it represents the way business has always been done is one of the underlying sources of waste and inefficiency in organizational operations.

Minimum Service Levels

After a decision package is chosen, a minimum level of service tor each package should be identified. By definition, below this minimum level, the maintenance of an existing program or the initiation of a new program would not be feasible. Minimum service levels include only the most essential elements or activities within chosen decision packages. These elements provide the highest priority services or meet the most critical needs of the organization. The minimum service level also defines the minimum level of funding for each package. The minimum service level shown in Figure 7–3 would involve the operation of the rescue squad/ambulance service strictly on a volunteer basis.

It often is difficult to get program personnel to think in such terms, that is, to identify a level of service/funding below the present level of support. In such cases, a percentage of the current level may be arbitrarily set as the minimum level. Sixty-five to eighty percent of the current appropriation frequently is used, that is, the budget unit manager is asked to identify the level of service that could be provided at this reduced funding level (and what current activities would have to be sacrificed to accommodate this funding level).

Additional levels of service should then be identified. Each succeeding level should expand the services available, step-by-step, until the level of service is back to and even above current service standards. Each level of service must be analyzed in terms of the specific quantities and qualities of work to be performed (and services to be provided). Appropriate costs should be assigned to each level. Potential service impacts should be described. And the importance of each level should be justified (in terms of program goals). Several levels of service may be identified between the minimum or survival level and the current level—two or three in smaller units, perhaps four or more for larger units.

The current level of service in figure 7–3 is level #3, involving four drivers and a two-person paramedic team (identified by the 100 percent of service designation). Thus two service levels are shown below the current level, and two levels are indicated above the current level. The addition of a second paramedic team is involved in the level above current services, while a second ambulance unit (requiring four additional drivers) is the next projected level.

A summary for each budget unit should reflect all the resources required to deliver each level of service, including detailed costs from all funding sources and a summary of personnel, equipment, and other major resource requirements. At this point, the mechanisms of the object-of-expenditure format can be reintroduced. In effect, once the detailed cost data have been established for the minimum level of service, these costs are then built upon in a cumulative fashion for each successive level. It is not necessary to prepare a separate and distinct object-of-expenditure budget for each service level. In exceptional cases, where decision packages present distinctive service delivery alternatives (for example, a labor-intensive versus a capital-intensive approach), separate budget summaries may be necessary.

Ranking Service Levels

The difference between formulating levels of service and ranking them is similar to the distinction between efficiency and effectiveness. Peter Drucker has defined *efficiency* as "doing things right" and *effectiveness* as "doing the right things."[9] The formulation of levels of service, in essence, involves a determination of how to do things right. Deciding to do the right things is the objective of the ranking process.

Before ranking can begin, a set of criteria must be established on which to base these decisions. Criteria should address such questions as: Is the program or service legally required? Does the organization possess the necessary technical skills to implement the activities? Does the proposed approach have a previous record of success? Will lower-level management accept and execute the program? Will the service delivery be cost-effective? Can the organization afford not to implement the proposed program?

In each successive review, ranking establishes an order of priority for each service level. Highest priority (most important) service levels are ranked until all levels have been included. This process of ranking or prioritizing should be quite familiar to those municipalities with established procedures for capital improvements programming (CIP). It is merely the CIP priority system applied to an analysis of the operating budget.

It is likely that more service levels will be presented than can be funded from available revenues. Therefore, three alternatives can be employed, either singularly or in concert, to bring projected revenue and proposed expenditures in balance:

1. Funds can be withheld from the lowest priority service levels.
2. Efforts can be made to reduce the cost of providing one or more levels of service.
3. Resources can be increased (for example, by increasing service fees, raising taxes, or liquidating assets).

The final priority list can be used to allocate funds to the service levels in order of priority until anticipated resources are exhausted. At this point, a funding cut-off line is drawn, and those services below this line are not funded. Unfunded service levels should be examined, and if deemed necessary to the well-being of the organization, the other two alternatives should be explored.

Driving Accountability Deeper into the Organization

An examination of the consequences of various service levels is important in any organization, especially when budget requests must be balanced within relatively fixed fiscal resources. The ranking techniques used in service level analysis assures that high priority activities will be funded.

Without a ranking process, budgeting is little more than a juggling act, trying to find the proper pieces in a hit-and-miss fashion that will add up to an acceptable whole. Unable to discern which programs or activities are of lower priority and, therefore, can be deferred or eliminated, decision makers often are forced to make across-the-board cuts. Service level analysis minimizes this need by creating a definitive priority listing.

Service level analysis also can be helpful in driving accountability for budgeting and budget execution deeper into the organization. From the outset, these analytical techniques require the involvement of program managers, thus tapping a larger reservoir of program knowledge and analytical skills. Direct involvement of program managers in budget making, in turn, often increases their concern for the proper implementation of organizational policies and programs. Thus, service level analysis helps to facilitate the transformation of policies into plans, and plans into action.

First and foremost, service level analysis, like zero-base budgeting, in which it is frequently applied, is an attack on budgetary incrementalism. Service level analysis goes beyond an examination of new programs and incremental changes to existing programs. It involves a close scrutiny of all activities, old and new. In this sense, service level analysis provides a mechanism of management control—a mechanism for increased accountability—seeking to eliminate unnecessary spending which may be the consequence of obsolete, inefficient programs or duplications of effort. Organizational resources are thus channeled to more important demands, thereby increasing overall efficiency.

Planning and Budgeting

The budget offers an opportunity to reevaluate the broad goals and objectives of an organization on a regular cycle. It also affords a basis on which to compare programs and their costs in light of these longer-range goals. The budget document can provide a common terminology for describing the plans and programs that relate to diverse operations of an organization. The planning potential within the budgetary process, however, has largely been overshadowed by the focus of traditional budgeting and accounting procedures on fiscal controls.

Planning-Programming-Budgeting Systems

The object-of-expenditure budget sought to control expenditures at the agency level. Performance budgeting provided mechanisms for assessing efficiency at the activity level. In the mid-sixties, the Planning-Programming-Budgeting System (PPBS) was introduced at the federal level to provide a broader basis for policy analysis and decision making within the context of a central review by the chief executive and legislative body. As shown in table 7–1, PPBS represents a "top-down" budget format, with decisions and directives flowing from the policy levels to the operating levels of the organization. As Schick has observed:

> PPB reverse the information and decisional flow. Before the call for estimates is issued, top policy has to be made, and this policy constrains the estimates prepared below. For each lower level, the relevant policy instructions are issued by the superior level prior to the preparation of estimates. Accordingly, the critical decisional process—that of deciding on purpose and plans—has a downward and disaggregative flow.[10]

PPBS was received with enthusiasm by the proponents of a more rational and comprehensive approach to financial planning and fiscal control. It was greeted with great skepticism, however, by many who had survived earlier experiments with performance and program budgeting.

Unfortunately, PPBS was never fully integrated with the "bottom-up" informational flow that characterizes more traditional accounting and budget formats. Consequently, operating agencies often were left on the periphery of the process. These agencies were required to provide new responses to policy directives (for example, measures of effectiveness). However, they had little understanding or appreciation of how these responses would impact their resource allocations.

Table 7–1
Basic Differences among Budget Orientations

Characteristic	Objects of Expenditure	Performance Budget	PPBS/Program Budget
Control responsibility	Central	Operating	Operating
Management responsibility	Dispersed	Central	Supervisory
Planning responsibility	Dispersed	Dispersed	Central
Role of budget agency	Fiduciary	Efficiency	Policy
Decision/information flow	Bottom-up aggregative	Bottom-up aggregative	Top-down disaggregative
Information focus	Objects	Activities	Programs
Decision basis	Incremental	Incremental	Programmatic
Key budget stage	Execution	Preparation	Analysis
Basic personnel skills	Accounting	Administration	Economics
Appropriation/organization linkages	Direct	Activity-based	Across-the-board

Source: Adapted from Allan Schick, "The Road to PPB: The Stages of Budget Reform," in *Planning Programming Budgeting: A Systems Approach to Management,* edited by Fremont J. Lyden and Ernest G. Miller (Chicago: Ill.: Markham, 1968), p. 50.

Operating in a realm of uncertainty, line personnel tended to be suspicious of the consequences of PPBS. These suspicions were reinforced by an emphasis in PPBS on across-the-board program structures which carried the threat of reorganization. The pendulum had swung to the opposite extreme from the focus of traditional financial management practices. And many agencies were totally unprepared for (and unwilling to participate in) the transition.

By the early seventies, even the proponents of PPBS were eulogizing its demise. PPBS had attempted to go too far, too fast in reforming the budget process. The emphasis on long-range planning to the near exclusion of the management planning and control functions proved disorienting to both operating agencies and policy makers. The latter group often was unable to fully absorb the implications of the more abstract information about broad organizational programs.

Program Budgeting

Many localities and organizations that experimented with PPBS in the sixties and early seventies more recently have adopted (and adapted) the techniques of program budgeting as a more realistic compromise to achieve a more systematic and comprehensive approach to budget making, the planning orientation. Program budgeting offers considerably more flexibility through which the underlying planning framework can be combined with the basic functions of management and control. Therefore, program budgeting holds the potential of a more appropriate interface between long-range planning and decision making and the day-to-day operations of complex organizations. Program budgeting also provides a foundation for a multipurpose accounting system that is more fully attuned to the basic goals of greater accountability, efficiency, and effectiveness.

As noted previously, programs form the fundamental building blocks for strategic planning. In the terminology often adopted by program budget guidelines, a program is a distinct organization of resources directed toward a specific objective of either (a) eliminating, containing, or preventing a problem; (b) creating, improving, or maintaining a condition affecting the organization or its clientele; or (c) supporting or controlling other identifiable programs. A program is concerned with a time-span of expenditures; it extends beyond the current fiscal period.

Programs may be factored or subdivided into component parts—for example, subprograms and program elements. More specific, measurable objectives, activities, and outputs, in turn, can be associated with these components. Resources provided for subprograms often are interchangeable for the maximum accomplishment of program objectives. That is to say, given a budget target at the program level, an organization must determine how to distribute the financial and personnel resources available among the component subprograms to achieve an optimal output.

Precision in the identification of goals and objectives is a prerequisite to sound analysis of financial commitments. In identifying program objectives, an effort should be made to specify the result to be accomplished within a specific time period. Program objectives must be consistent with the resources available (or anticipated). As has been pointed out, the formulation of precise, qualitative statements of objectives often is a difficult undertaking. The tendency is to describe what the organization does, instead of addressing the question of why these activities are appropriate to achieve the long-range goals of the organization.

The activities of the organization should be grouped according to the program objectives to which they contribute or relate. Each separate activity cluster thus identified serves as a program element. It is at this level that the detailed object codes identifying resource inputs often reenter the process. To be effective, however, program elements must be more than merely a regrouping of traditional objects of expenditures in pseudoprogrammatic terms.

To avoid this pitfall, specific objectives must be described—*how* and *where* specific resources (personnel, equipment, materials, capital expenditures, and so forth) will be used. These statements, in turn, should be related to performance measures. Such measures provide the mechanisms to determine the success (or lack thereof) and the efficiency of a program in achieving agreed-upon objectives. These measures may be equated to costs or inputs.

These efficiency standards can also be used to determine the adequacy of current or proposed funding levels by asking such questions as:

> What combination of inputs can most appropriately be applied to achieve the desired level of outputs?
>
> How much additional resources will be needed to attain this level?
>
> If the limitations of available resources prohibit the attainment of this tentative level, what estimated level could be achieved within the budget constraints?

Appropriate measures of efficiency and effectiveness provide a base line against which to test the notion of adequacy. In the absence of such measures, the traditional least-cost compromise is likely to prevail.

Program Analysis

The systematic analysis of program alternative is a cornerstone of more effective resource management. The same dollars spent on different program objectives (or on alternative approaches to the same program objective) may yield greatly varied results. In any organization, the best policy is to spend resources where they can produce the greatest net benefits. Programs should be selected through a systematic analysis of associated costs and benefits. Program analysis may be undertaken as a precursor to budget preparation or as a continuous process to ascertain optimal expenditure patterns and fiscal policy recommendations.

To undertake program analysis, explicit output measures must be identified and quantified. This task frequently is a difficult one, particularly for organizations more accustomed to measuring activity levels in terms of inputs rather than the outputs produced. As Krueckeberg and Silvers have observed, considerable resistance may be offered to the formulation of output measures.

> After all, it is not difficult to spend budgetary money and, hence, . . . performance, when measured in terms of "number of new hospital beds installed" or "new teachers hired," is much easier to define than performance measures such as "number of low income persons made healthy" or "low income persons successfully trained."[11]

Program analysis seeks to (1) determine whether or not a particular program or proposal is justified, (2) rank various program alternatives appropriate to a given set of objectives, and (3) ascertain the optimal course(s) of action to attain such objectives. More traditional forms of evaluation tend to be short-range and narrow in scope. In contrast, program analysis operates within an extended time horizon. Insofar as possible, such analyses include explicit consideration of both direct and indirect cost factors involved in the allocation of resources.

Cognizance must be taken of the feedback from, and subsequent revisions in, the programs that have been formulated to meet agreed-upon objectives. Thus, programming must be an iterative process, involving continuous refinement and modification as dictated by changing circumstances in program delivery. The probability that program revisions will be required increases significantly as the time-span of decisions increases.

Multiyear Program Plans

In practice, the time range of programs formulated under a program budget is between five and ten years. Multiyear program plans often are developed to identify the anticipated outputs of services and facilities according to the objectives outlined in the strategic planning stage. Such plans indicate what accomplishments can be expected from a given commitment of resources. This approach closely approximates procedures used in the formulation of a six-year capital improvements program. As Howard has observed, "Increasing the time horizon used in projecting operating costs would reduce the difficulties that arise when operating costs are projected for one length of time but a program's capital aspects are estimated for another."[12]

Program costs, obtained from the organization's accounting system, are projected to match revenue projections. Through such procedures, it is possible to determine the adequacy of revenue sources to support proposed programs. It also is possible to identify future cost commitments generated by current programs. Once the budget is framed in program terms, total costs can be disaggregated by type of inputs (for example, salaries and wages, materials and supplies, and equipment). In short, multiyear program and financial plans serve as the critical link between objectives and outputs, on the one hand, and resource inputs on the other. When these budget costs and outputs are included as a part of the accounting records, "real-time" comparisons can be made between budgeted costs and outputs and actual costs and output.

Program Evaluation

Once programs are implemented, evaluation techniques should be applied to determine needed improvements and modifications. While program analysis tends to be prospective, program evaluation focuses on the actual performance of ongoing or recently completed activities. It is not completely retrospective, however, for the purposes of evaluation often are to (a) suggest changes in resource allocations, (b) improve current operations, or (c) plan future activities. Program evaluation seeks to measure the overall success of the selected approach and to identify areas where improvements might be made to more fully realize the projected program benefits. As Quade points out, the monitoring and evaluation of on-line programs and activities may pose some particular problems for the analyst:

> The key element that leads us to distinguish evaluation from say, the cost-effectiveness or cost-benefit of a proposed program is that the latter do not have to cope with an activity that is ongoing and thus the people participating in or being affected by the activity. People interact with an evaluation in ways that must be taken into account by the analyst.[13]

In short, program analysis and program evaluation represent an iterative cycle: analysis precedes program commitments, and evaluation assesses the impacts and effectiveness of these decisions and commitments.

The output of many organizational activities may be difficult to define and measure in direct terms. As a consequence, secondary measures of effectiveness—*surrogates*—often must be used to test alternative approaches and to evaluate costs. For example, the total direct benefits to be realized from a program that reduces the incidence of dropouts from high school may be difficult to measure. However, a surrogate measure would be the difference in lifetime earnings that individuals who complete a high school education can anticipate over those individuals who drop out. Such figures are available in terms of national averages and can be applied as a rough measure of benefits to be derived.

Summary

Planning, programming, and budgeting are different but complementary activities in the strategic management process. As such, they should be consistently related and fully coordinated with one another. Programming involves the ordering of proposed activities and projects based on some schedule of priorities. Budgeting entails the assignment of costs to the implementation of these priorities over a reasonable time period. Planning points up needs; programming provides a basis for determining the sequence in which these needs can be met most effectively. These processes seek ever-increasing precision in the identification of relationships between inputs (resources) and outputs (accomplishments).

Contemporary resource management activities are both information-demanding and information-producing. As the preceding discussions should clearly demonstrate, the information input and output requirements of program budgeting differs significantly from those associated with more traditional budget practices. Program budgeting can provide important managerial feedback—soundings, scanning, and evaluations of changing conditions resulting from previous program decisions and actions. This feedback is strengthened significantly by the adoption of managerial accounting procedures, as described in chapter 10.

Such procedures also generate information "feedforward," which is intended to provide a basis for more informed decisions and actions over a range of time periods, locations, and perspectives. Feedforward information emerges from such components as projections and forecasts; goals, objectives, and targets to be achieved; program analyses and evaluations; and the projections of outcomes and impacts of alternative programs.

Notes

1. Frederick C. Mosher, *Program Budgeting: Theory and Practice* (Chicago, Ill.: Public Administration Service, 1954), p. 5.

2. Jesse Burkhead, *Government Budgeting* (New York: John Wiley & Sons, 1956), pp. 153–155.

3. Ibid., p. 149.

4. Ernest Enke, "The Accounting Precondition of PPB," *Management Accounting* 53 (January 1972):33–37.

5. Cited in Aaron Wildavsky and Arthur Hammann, "Comprehensive Versus Incremental Budgeting in the Department of Agriculture," *Administrative Science Quarterly* (December 1965), p. 321.

6. Allan Schick, "Putting It All Together," *Sunset, Zero-Base Budgeting and Program Evaluation* (proceedings of a Joint Legislative Audit and Review Commission conference on legislative oversight, Richmond, Va., 1977), p. 41.

7. Ibid., p. 17.

8. Peter A. Pyhrr, *Zero-Base Budgeting* (New York: John Wiley & Sons, 1973), p. 6.

9. Peter F. Drucker, "The Effective Decision," *Harvard Business Review* 45 (January-February 1967), p. 95.

10. Allan Schick, "The Road to PPB: The Stages of Budget Reform," in *Planning Programming Budgeting: A Systems Approach to Management,* edited by Fremont J. Lyden and Ernest G. Miller (Chicago: Markham, 1968), p. 42.

11. Donald A. Krueckeberg and Arthur L. Silvers, *Urban Planning Analysis* (New York: John Wiley & Sons, 1974), p. 198.

12. S. Kenneth Howard, *Changing State Budgeting* (Lexington, Ky.: Council of State Governments, 1973), p. 250.

13. E.S. Quade, *Analysis for Public Decisions* (New York: American Elsevier, 1975), p. 224.

8
Information for Strategic Management

E ffective planning and control in any organization requires relevant management information. The timely flow of information (communications) is vital to the decision-making and management processes. Information is the raw material of intelligence that triggers the recognition that decisions need to be made. Timely and accurate information is essential to understanding the circumstances surrounding any issue and to evaluate alternative courses of action to resolve any problem. In this sense, information is incremental knowledge that reduces the degree of uncertainty in a particular problem situation.

Management Information Systems

Although vast amounts of facts, numbers, and other data may be processed in any organization, what constitutes management information depends on the problem at hand and the particular frame of reference of the manager. Miscellaneous accounting data, for example, can provide information when arrayed appropriately in balance sheets and financial statements. Regardless of how elaborately processed, traditional accounting data may be relatively meaningless if the objective is an evaluation of the effectiveness of a new program. Thus, to achieve better management decisions, the information available must be both timely and pertinent.

The Objectives of an MIS

A management information system (MIS) is first and foremost a process by which information is organized and communicated in a timely fashion to resolve management problems. The information maintained in such a system is determined by what the information will be used for. Traditionally, management information systems have been developed as tools for operational management. There has been less emphasis on the use of information systems in strategic management. Strategic decisions differ from operational decisions, and therefore, the information necessary for strategic management varies from the more traditional MIS used for operational control.

As a concept, MIS often is vaguely described and broadly misunderstood. Some people confuse MIS with an electronic data-processing system, thinking that the all-knowing computer will provide the answers to complex problems if and when the manager simply learns to press the right buttons. Many management information systems make effective use of modern data- and word-processing equipment. However, an MIS is much more than an electronic marvel to direct and control the destiny of complex organizations.

Computers *can* be an important asset to the strategic manager. Through their ability to store, retrieve, and carry out rapid computations on data, computers have made possible the collection and dissemination of greater quantities of information more quickly and economically. Computers can help to achieve better management information if used to process properly designed information flows. Computers are not the automatic answer to the need for better information, however. In fact, undue preoccupation with how data will be processed and with the characteristics of the hardware often can inhibit the design of an effective MIS.

Information systems make use of the computer's capacity to store and retrieve vast amounts of data. Thus, an MIS is composed of data bases and the software packages (computer programs) required to manage them. A data base is a collection of structured and related information stored in the computer system. Different software packages permit easy access and management of these data, along with the tools necessary to generate reports. Together, these capabilities make up a data base management system (DBMS). Bassler defines a DBMS as

> a software system that provides for a means of representing data, procedures for making changes in these data (adding to, subtracting from, and modifying), a method for making inquiries of the data base and to process these raw data to produce information, and to provide all the necessary internal management functions to minimize the user effort to make the system responsive.[1]

An MIS goes beyond the objectives of centralized data collection and retrieval, however. As Kennevan suggests, an MIS is

> an organized method of providing past, present, and projection information relating to internal operations and external intelligence. It supports the planning, control and operational functions of an organization by furnishing information in the proper time frame to assist in the decision-making process.[2]

An MIS must be flexible and adaptive. It must be assumed that deficiencies will be accommodated as the system evolves. Procedures should be developed to detect these deficiencies and to correct the system so as to eliminate or reduce them. Managers, as well as information specialists and operations researchers, should participate in each phase of the design of an MIS.

Designing an MIS

The design of an MIS should begin with an identification of the important types of strategic, managerial, and operational decisions required by the organization. This study should define relationships among decisions, as well as determine the flow of decisions. Such a decision-flow analysis often reveals important decisions that are being made by default, for example, where past decisions are still binding, even though they are no longer applicable to current problems and procedures. This analysis also may uncover situations in which interdependent decisions are being made independently. The analysis of decision flows frequently identifies areas in which changes should be made in (a) the responsibilities of management, (b) the organizational structure, or (c) measures of performance. Such changes are necessary to correct information deficiencies.

The next step in the design of an MIS involves an analysis of the information requirement of the major classes of decisions. Ackoff has suggested that organizational decisions can be grouped into three types: (1) decisions for which adequate models exist or can be developed and from which optimal solutions can be derived; (2) decisions for which models can be constructed but from which optimal solutions cannot be readily extracted; and (3) decisions for which adequate models cannot be constructed.[3]

In the first case, the decision model should have the capacity to identify what information is required and relevant. The decision process should be readily incorporated into the MIS (thereby converting it, at least partially, to a control system). In the second case, the model may specify what information is required. However, a further search process may be necessary, including the examination of alternative approaches, to fully explicate these information requirements.

In the third situation, further research is required to determine *what* information is relevant and *how* this information can be organized to address the decision situation. Through such research, it may be possible to make implicit models used by decision makers more explicit and in so doing, treat such models as type-2 decision situations.

It is appropriate in each of these categories to provide feedback by comparing actual decision outcomes with those predicted by the models. It is important that the MIS have the capacity not only to answer questions that might be addressed to it, but also to report any deviations from expectations (that is, actual decision outcomes that differ from those predicted). Each decision made, along with its predicted outcome, should become an input to a management control system.[4]

Once the information to be collected for particular decision situations is identified, an MIS can be developed to assist in the strategic management process. A useful information system should include a data base management system (DBMS) with (a) a high-level, interactive query language facility; (b) an interactive financial modeling package that permits "what if" calculations to be made; (c) a package that supports modeling and simulation; (d) a statistical analysis package; (e) word-processing software; and possibly, (f) customized software related to specialized management needs.

In the past, the use of such systems—with collections of extensive and often expensive software packages—have been limited to large mainframe computers. This limitation is one major reason why management information systems have been used mainly for operational decisions and not for strategic management decisions.

With the further miniaturization and mass production of computer systems, however, the cost of mainframe type capabilities has decreased dramatically. Through the introduction of more and more powerful desktop computers for home and business, the power of the computer is now more readily available to managers and planners in most organizations.

With the advent of smaller hardware systems has come major breakthroughs in software support. These software packages, such as word-processing systems, spreadsheets, and micro-databases, are useful and affordable. Some hardware producers have combined several of these packages into decision support systems (DSS), such as the popular Lotus 1–2–3, which combine spreadsheets, word processing, a DBMS, and reporting functions. These systems can be very useful to the strategic manager.

The building and use of an MIS for strategic management depends on the collection and manipulation of the correct type of data. With this in mind, some examples can be given as to how an MIS can be integrated with the basic components of strategic management. For these examples, the MIS will be viewed as being a combination of a DBMS, modeling, and other computational and word-processing software.

An MIS for Strategic Management

The basic components of an MIS applicable to the information needs of strategic management are illustrated in figure 8–1. Three specific data areas provide inputs for the formulations of strategic decisions: (1) *environmental intelligence,* data about the broader environment of which the organization is a part, including assessments of client needs; (2) *autointelligence,* data about the component elements of the particular organization, including an evalua-

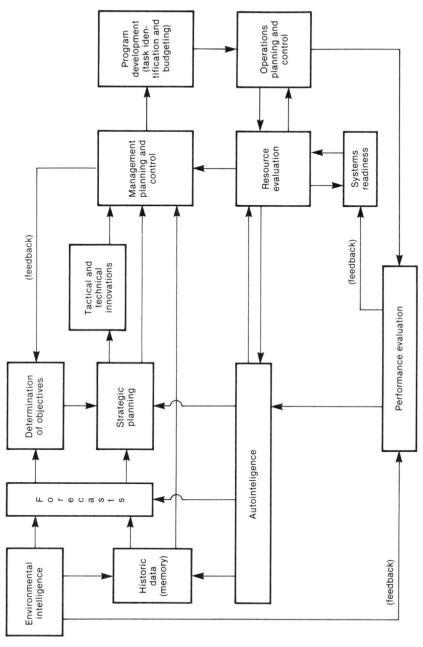

Source: Alan Walter Steiss, *Management Control in Government* (Lexington, Mass.: Lexington Books, 1982), p. 127. Reprinted by permission.

Figure 8–1. Basic Components of an MIS

tion of organizational resources and its capacity to respond to client needs; and (3) *historic data,* which bring together and analyze the lessons of past experience. Much of the environmental and internal data may not be applicable to more immediate decision situations. These data are stored in the memory banks of the organization, to be retrieved when particular decision situations arise or when a broader assessment of the overall goals and objectives of the organization is appropriate.

Basic research and analysis are essential to effective strategic management. Data must be collected and stored for future use and reference. Data can be generated externally (for example, macro-trend analyses and census data) or internally (for example, accounting and other financial management data). Basic analysis can be carried out using various modeling programs available in a well-constructed MIS, and the results can be stored in the data base for reference and updating. Under the category of modeling and computational software are those packages that perform functions in the areas of trend analysis, systems analysis, operations research, and management science. The diagnosis of trends can be aided, in part, by the modeling and simulation programs and statistical analysis packages. This aspect of strategic management can be facilitated by programs that perform functions related to operations research, such as network analysis.

Forecasts of the probable outcomes of events can be developed on these data foundations. Forecasting is the first and fundamental step in strategic planning. Probable happenings are outlined by assuming the continuance of existing trends into hypothetical futures. These probabilistic forecasts provide important inputs in determining organizational objectives—an initial impetus for strategic management.

Computer-based data have not been used extensively in the formulation of goals and objectives. However, an MIS can aid in the development and evaluation of such statements.[5] Objectives can be written so as to take fuller advantage of available information in the system. Additionally, written objectives can be stored, permitting easy access, change, and output.

Once objectives have been determined (at least in a preliminary fashion), and with further inputs from autointelligence, the strategic planning process can begin to suggest possible directions that the organization can take in response to client needs in the broader environment. Strategic management can provide two important initiatives in this regard: (1) the search for possible new courses of action to improve the overall performance of the organization; and (2) a framework for resource management and control.

The same system components used in the basic research and analysis phase can be applied in the formulation and analysis of alternatives. However, this phase of the strategic management process must build on the basic analyses previously carried out and therefore, can make significant use of the effective storage and query capabilities of the DBMS. The results of previous decisions and program actions are combined through policy and resource recommendations. In this capacity, the MIS can be useful in the storage and retrieval of needed information and in report generation.

Tactical and technical innovations must be sought to improve the overall responsiveness of the organization (in the private sector, these innovations also improve the competitive position of the organization). Various "what if" scenarios may be tested through the analytical subroutines contained within the MIS.

Resource management plans translate the overall intent of strategic plans into more specific programs and activities. As outlined in previous chapters, these management plans are both information demanding and information producing. The budget process provides important managerial feedback in terms of evaluations of prior program decisions and actions. Feedforward information emerges from the various projections and forecasts that are required by financial analysis and budgeting processes.

Management control activities draw on the memory banks of the organization in search of programmed decisions—decisions that have worked successfully in the past. Timely resource evaluations also provide important inputs into the management control process. These evaluations include information regarding the current fiscal status of the organization (accounting data), as well as the overall response capacity of other organizational resources (systems readiness). The resource management and control processes should provide critical feedback to the further refinement of objectives. In some cases, this feedback will require a recycling of the strategic management process before proceeding to the next phase.

Program development involves the activities of task identification and budgeting. Specific operations are detailed within the framework provided by the strategic plan and resource management decisions. Responsibilities for carrying out these operations are assigned, as are the resources required by these operations. Specific operations may be further detailed through operations planning and control, which may include such programming techniques as Program Evaluation Review Technique (PERT) and Critical Path Method (CPM). These programming and scheduling procedures usually require further information regarding resource capabilities. They also may precipitate a recycling of the resource management process.

The final component of the MIS involves the information derived from performance evaluation. Some writers view performance evaluation as a separate process outside the management information system. Others recognize the importance of incorporating the data and information developed through such evaluations by referring to a *management information and program evaluation system* (MIPES).[6] Performance evaluation draws data from the broader environment regarding the efficiency and effectiveness with which client needs are met, problems are solved, opportunities are realized, and so forth.

Such evaluations provide feedback as well as new inputs into autointelligence and feedback in terms of systems readiness. A basic problem of organizations today, in both the public and private sectors, is achieving an appropriate balance in programs and decisions to ensure systems readiness. Systems readiness defines the response capacity of the organization in the short-, mid-, and long-range futures. Sufficient flexibility is required to meet a wide range of possible competitive actions. The development and maintenance of an MIS that includes the basic components outlined herein can contribute significantly to meeting this challenge.

Feedback is a basic requirement of any MIS. Feedback must be obtained on the output of the organization in terms of quality (effectiveness), quantity (efficiency of service levels), cost, and so on. Programs must be monitored to maintain process control. Evaluations of resources (inputs) provide feedback at the earliest stages of program implementation.

Feedback data must be collected and analyzed at various stages in the implementation of programs and the maintenance of ongoing operations. These analyses involve processing data, developing information, and comparing actual results with plans and expectations. Many decisions based on feedback are made within the management control system. Routine adjustments may be programmed into the set of ongoing procedures, and instructions can be provided to those individuals who must carry out specific tasks. Feedback from the operating systems provides an information flow within the management control procedures to initiate and implement program changes in a more timely basis. Thus, procedures are modified and files updated simultaneously with routine decision making and program adjustments.

Summary and exception reports may be generated by the MIS and become part of higher-level reviews and evaluations. These evaluations, in turn, may lead to adaptations or innovations of goals and objectives. Subsequent strategic management activities should reflect such feedback, and the entire process is recycled.

Strategic managers must seek out data and information that will permit actions to be taken before problems reach crisis proportions. Historic data provided by conventional accounting systems (even when the time lag is only a few weeks) may be insufficient to meet these decision needs. Resource evaluations on the input side and resource monitoring as programs or projects progress can provide the more timely information required to anticipate rather than merely to react to problems.

An information system appropriate for strategic management must use feedforward as well as control based on feedback. Feedforward anticipates lags in feedback systems by monitoring inputs and predicting their effects on output variables. In so doing, action can be taken to change inputs and, thereby, to bring the outputs into equilibrium with desired results *before* the measurement of outputs discloses a deviation from accepted standards.

In time, an organization "learns" through the processes of planning, implementation, and feedback.[7] Approaches to decision making and the propensity to select certain means and ends change as the value system of the organization evolves. A basic objective of strategic management is to guide this evolution along more effective lines. And a management information system can provide critical signposts, both to mark the progress and to point the way in this process.

Decision-Support Systems

Decision-support systems (DSS), like management information systems before them (and electronic data processing systems that preceded MIS), represent a new stage in the "computer revolution." These emerging systems are supported partly by technological advances and partly by a long-standing conviction that such capabilities are possible. At least for the time being, however, the long-term potentials of DSS have been clouded, to a considerable extent, by industry hype.

DSS Defined

Advances in technology are represented by more powerful and more user-friendly capabilities for data retrieval, database management, modeling, and graphics. These capabilities afford nontechnical users an opportunity for relatively effective, *ad hoc* use of computers to support a variety of management-related functions.

The conviction reflects a grand vision that computers are capable of doing more than merely automating routine tasks (EDP) or supplying regularly scheduled reports in predetermined, standardized formats (MIS). The ultimate mission of the computer, according to the proponents of DSS, should be to interact effectively with management so as to influence decisions on a day-to-day basis.

DSS is being promoted by segments of the computer software industry as a revolutionary new product that will save "megabucks" for many types of organizations. Software packages currently being offered do incorporate powerful technical tools that may make it possible to realize the potential suggested by computerized decision support. There are no easy solutions here, however—no magic that will instantaneously create the kind of man-machine interface necessary for true decision support. As one manager of a DSS service in the field of investment banking has observed, "DSS is a philosophy. It provides users with an effective way to get information without intermediaries. It's software, it's support, and it's an organization that coaches the user as he continually changes and improves his decision-making models."[8]

The effective implementation of a decision support system requires that consideration be given to several important organizational issues. DSS represents a major break with tradition—a tradition that has seen individuals and groups as participants in the decision-making process based upon access to certain data and information.

> The distribution of . . . information . . . may have a significant bearing on authority relations in any given situation. The participation (and relative influence) of an individual is conditioned, in part, by how much he knows. As a consequence, the withholding of information and the jealous guarding of informational resources are strategies frequently employed to gain greater influence in decision-making situations.[9]

Armed with user-friendly technology, managers are laying stronger claim to available data and information, with or without the blessings of those in the organization who are responsible for the gathering and recording of this information.

A primary objective of DSS is to provide decision support for problems within an organization that are continually changing—problems that often have more than one right answer. Many computer professionals do not feel comfortable with such relatively unstructured problems. The more conventional methods of programming seek to freeze the specifications of a problem as soon as possible, so that the programmer can work on a solution (the system) in relative isolation from the problem.

Decision-support systems, however, must be built on an iterative approach which may never have the problem specifications frozen. As Ralph H. Sprague has noted,

> If I were to try to build the system the old way, I would go to the decision-maker and ask him what his requirements are. The problem is, he won't know. You ask him what information he needs—again, he won't know. Now, by contrast, the iterative approach says, "OK, give me a small problem, and I'll help you in the process of using and changing the system as your requirements grow and evolve over time."[10]

Management problems also are often relatively short-lived. Therefore, more traditional methods of building relatively large management information systems to deal with such problems may result in the delivery of too much, too late. An elaborate data base which provides inputs into a sophisticated simulation model requires substantial resource commitments to develop and maintain. If the problems that management must address keep changing, the response time of the MIS may be too long to provide useful answers.

The actual impacts of a DSS on an organization often are not self-evident. The relationship between decision support and decision making cannot be considered clear-cut. As Steven L. Alter has stated:

The development of modeling and data-retrieval technologies is not inexpensive, and the immediate benefits are not always clear. The justification for much of the initial work is necessarily based on pure faith. It is difficult to quantify the benefits from such efforts, even after they have attained momentum: What is a good decision worth?[11]

In light of such uncertain payoffs, it is not surprising that much of the pioneering work in decision support research has been dedicated to understanding just how managers go about making decisions. We have just begun to scratch the surface in our understanding of the intricacies of human decision making. However, current research does suggest that DSS can make an important contribution in making improvements in the decision-making process. Studies have shown that decision-support systems have led to better communications among managers. These improvements in communications, in turn, have contributed to a more unified approach to problem solving by providing a broader consensus as to goals and objectives and the underlying assumptions concerning problems confronting the organization.

The Right Problems/People/Tools/Process

Certain basic conditions must be met if a DSS is to have the desired impact on the decision-making process of an organization: (a) the right problems must be addressed; (b) the right people must participate in the development of the decision support system; (c) the right tools must be used; and (d) the process must evolve as decision situations and technology change.[12] In attempting to meet these conditions, conflicting interests must be balanced in terms of the available technology, the costs of systems development and maintenance, and the ever-present organizational issues of data "ownership" and inherent prerogatives to participate in the decision-making process.

> Individuals are brought into the system because of the need for special skills and information. Initially, at least, such participation is merely in an advisory capacity and involves neither claims nor actual authority or responsibility for the decisions made . . . the line between advisory and prerogative-based participation often becomes blurred and, over time, advisory participants often become "prerogative" participants. Further, they come to expect this relationship to exist in any decision-making situation in which their technical expertise may be required.[13]

The Right Problems. Should the DSS be designed as a flexible system with wide-ranging applications, or should it be geared to address well-defined, specific problems? Sprague and Carlson assert that:

> Because of the variety of decision-making processes, a DSS is more likely to be useful and cost-effective if it supports multiple processes. If a specific DSS

is designed for only one type of decision, any change in the decision requires a change in the DSS to accommodate changes in the information-processing requirements.[14]

On the other hand, since decision support often is difficult to cost-justify, the DSS should address, at the very least, the specific problem situations which the top officials of the organization deem to be most important. The development of DSS should be demand-driven rather than supply-generated. That is to say, the demand for decision support must come from top-level management rather than being generated on the basis of available data.

The Right People. Participants in the development of the DSS must have a general understanding of management principles, as well as the technical skills to solve problems as they arise. As many studies have shown, such individuals are exceedingly rare, and this may impose a definite limit on how far a given organization can go with decision support.

Lacking an appreciation for technical considerations, management can be "sold" on the purchase of extensive hardware or software systems which may have very little immediate use in the decision-making process of the organization. On the other hand, management can be unduly influenced by cost considerations regarding equipment purchases which may not serve the real decision needs of the organization.

The Right Tools. An effective way to reduce the burden on technical experts is to bring in technical tools that are as user-friendly as possible. Recent developments in artificial intelligence are on the frontier of user-friendliness. Artificial intelligence is distinguished from conventional computer intelligence by its ability to understand natural English, so that users need not learn special languages or elaborate sets of commands in order to use the system.

There is a price to be paid for such friendly systems, however, beyond the purchase cost of the software. The easier a system is to use and the more comprehensive it is, the heavier the load it tends to place on computer hardware in terms of machine cycles. Often a separate computer may be required to support the DSS. As an alternative, some companies are switching from large mainframe systems to the use of microsystems, supported by PC hardware. Such microsystems are much slower in terms of processing time. However, the hardware costs, when compared to the operation and maintenance costs of a typical mainframe, can represent a significant trade-off.

This approach is not without its own risks, however. While desktop, personal computers can provide the strategic manager with a significant analytical tool, the decentralization of computational capacity exacerbates the need to manage information more carefully. With the proliferation of micros, it is possible that the organization will miss out totally on one of the primary advantages afforded by DSS—more effective communications and the sharing of assumptions regarding problems confronting the organization. A shared resource on a mainframe system encourages and supports such communications; distributing the resource among micros might not.

The Right Process. From the purist's point of view, a DSS is a dynamic mechanism, capable of continual evolution in new and often unanticipated ways as problems evolve. Needless to say, such an evolution can put considerable stress on an organization. And this stress, in turn, can stymie the momentum in support of DSS. This problem often arises when procedures and controls have to be considered to bring the demands placed on the DSS into manageable bounds. It is important, particularly during the early stages of development, that user support stay ahead of user demands. Often the tendency is to spread access to the system as broadly as possible—to promote the adoption of the software by providing hardware to as many people in the organization as possible. When the communication links become overloaded, however, and users incur significant delays in response time (or difficulties in logging on to the system), then users frequently abandon the system and return to their prior approaches to making decisions.

Since DSS is a process, many argue that it is inconsistent to think of it as a deliverable product. Nevertheless, some users want it to be a product. They do not want to have to learn new commands every few weeks in order to access the system. For these users, who may well be in the majority in any organization, it may be appropriate to provide a DSS as a relatively stable product. Major changes in language or in presentation formats may be very disconcerting to those users who view the system as a tool and not as a vocation. At the same time, a select group of users might be treated as iconoclasts, by being exposed to the latest versions of software as they become available. As more is known about the system, it may be perfectly natural for a DSS to stabilize. As Alter suggests, "What's referred to as a management information system might very well be able to support decisions if it's designed well."[15]

Large-scale management information systems often require many months of formal planning, review, and development before they begin to offer the pay-offs initially promised. The conventional wisdom concerning DSS is to eschew the more formal systems analysis and design procedures, so as to avoid inhibiting the process of managerial learning and systems evolution. In short, the development process of an MIS often is viewed as unwieldy from the standpoint of getting useful decision-support systems designed and built quickly. As Moore and Chang point out, however:

> The unfortunate side effect of this is that informal and ad-hoc design approaches, so desirable from a design and implementation standpoint, highly personalize the DSS design process and the DSS itself, thereby sub-

jecting the DSS designers and users to greater buffering, whipsawing, and other organizational turmoil.[16]

For all the risks, uncertainties, and conflicts it poses, the prospect of computerized decision support is nevertheless an exciting one. However, no matter how good the system, a DSS will not miraculously transform bad decision makers into good ones. As yet, science has been unable to tell us what makes great decision makers. Reasonable assumptions are that they are meticulous about facts as well as intuitive; that they have a feel for the big picture; and that they can distinguish between genuine merit and unreasonable bias. The fundamental objective of a DSS is to enhance these attributes of good decision making and not to devalue them by substituting quantity of data for quality of information.

Summary

Management information and decision support systems have the potential of serving as the foundation for effective strategic management. MIS and DSS often are vaguely described and broadly misunderstood, however. Some people think that the all-knowing computer will provide the right answers to complex problems if and when the manager simply learns to press the right buttons. Most management information and decision-support systems do make effective use of modern data- and word-processing equipment. However, these systems are much more than mere electronic devices to direct and control complex organizations. First and foremost, they involve processes by which information is organized and communicated in a timely fashion to resolve management problems. The development of such systems must begin with an appreciation of these problems. Many managerial decisions require information inputs that cannot be computerized. Thus, management information and decision-support systems must be designed to include explicit attention to nonquantifiable inputs as well as to those that may result from computerized data-processing applications.

Hardware should be the last matter to be considered when thinking about an MIS. It is first necessary to decide what kind of information is needed—how soon, how much, and how often. The kind of equipment that will best serve these needs is a secondary, although important, consideration. Many wrong notions about data processing can be dispelled by concentrating first on the information and communication requirements and by consequently shrinking to more realistic size the plans for the computer hardware.

Large, centralized data-processing centers are not a prerequisite to, or concomitant of, an MIS or DDS. The desirability of large computers depends more on the size and nature of the organization than on the purposes of the

MIS. Many excellent systems are serviced by relatively simple, local data-processing operations, tailored to the particular needs of the users. In the late 1960s and early 1970s, many organizations were sold on the notion that bigger is better, only to find that, with the rapid changes in computer technology, they were saddled with a "dinosaur" that consumed vast quantities of resources but could not serve the expanding needs of particular users.

Notes

1. Richard A. Bassler, "Data Bases, MIS and Data Base Management Systems," in *Computer Science and Public Administration,* compiled by Richard A. Bassler and Norman L. Enger (Alexandria, Va.: College Readings, 1976), p. 203.

2. Walter J. Kennevan, "Management Information Systems," in *Management of Information Handling Systems,* edited by Paul W. Howerton (Roselle Park, N.J.: Hayden, 1974).

3. Russell L. Ackoff, "Management Misinformation Systems," in *Computers and Management in a Changing Society,* edited by Donald H. Sanders and Stanley J. Birkin (New York: McGraw-Hill, 1980), p. 44.

4. Ibid., p. 45.

5. Sujata S. Pathapati, "A Systematic Approach to Intent Analysis to Aid the Strategic Planning Process" (Ph.D. dissertation, Virginia Polytechnic Institute and State University, 1984).

6. For a further discussion of the concepts of MIPES, see Alan Walter Steiss, *Public Budgeting and Management* (Lexington, Mass.: Lexington Books, 1972), chap. 10.

7. Richard M. Cyert and James G. March, *A Behavioral Theory of the Firm* (Englewood Cliffs, N.J.: Prentice-Hall, 1963), p. 123.

8. Samuel Solomon, as cited in Martin Lasden, "Computer-Aided Decision-Making," *Computer Decisions* 14:11 (November 1982):157.

9. Steiss, *Public Budgeting and Management,* p. 79.

10. Ralph H. Sprague, as cited in "Computer-Aided Decision-Making," Lasden, p. 158.

11. Steven L. Alter, *Decision Support Systems: Current Practices and Continuing Challenges* (Boston, Mass.: Addison-Wesley, 1980), p. 2.

12. Lasden, "Computer-Aided Decision-Making," pp. 160, 162, 168.

13. Steiss, *Public Budgeting and Management,* pp. 79–80.

14. Ralph Sprague and Eric Carlson, *Building Effective Decision Support Systems* (New York: Prentice-Hall, 1982), p. 14.

15. Alter, *Decision Support Systems,* p. 3.

16. Jeffery Moore and Michael Chang, in *Building Decision-Support Systems,* edited by John L. Bennett (Boston, Mass.: Addison-Wesley, 1983), p. 160.

9
Management Control

S
ome form of management control has been applied for as long as formal organizations have existed. Only in the past fifty years, however, have more comprehensive procedures to direct and control the activities of complex organizations become a primary focus of management. The more recent emphasis on accountability, both in the public and private sector, has made the adoption (and adaptation) of more effective management control techniques all the more imperative.

Definitions of Management Control

The importance of initiating corrective action when errors or deviations were discovered served as the emphasis of early definitions of management control. Henry Fayol, in one of the better-known definitions, suggests that, "Control consists of verifying whether everything occurs in conformity with the plan adopted, the instructions issued, and the principles established. It has for an object to point out weaknesses and errors in order to rectify and prevent recurrence."[1] Current definitions, however, emphasize more positive aspects of control (rather than merely after-the-fact corrective actions). Robert Mockler suggests that management control is

> a systematic effort to set performance standards consistent with planning objectives, to design information feedback systems, to compare actual performance with these predetermined standards, to determine whether there are any deviations and to measure their significance, and to take any action required to assure that all corporate resources are being used in the most effective and efficient way possible in achieving corporate objectives.[2]

Four Fundamental Elements of Management Control

Management textbooks written for use in the private sector tend to emphasize overall financial controls and, in particular, the controls provided through accounting systems. In a widely cited text on management accounting, Robert Anthony and Glenn Welsch expanded this focus by suggesting that management control serves as the centerpiece in a hierarchy bounded by strategic planning ("the process of deciding on the goals of the organization and the strategies that are to be used in attaining these goals") and operational control ("the process of assuring that specific tasks are carried out effectively and efficiently").[3]

Taken in this context, management controls can provide the tools for determining whether an organization is proceeding toward established objectives and can alert decision makers when actual performance deviates from planned performance. These procedures also can assist in the identification of the magnitude of the deviation and appropriate corrective action to bring the activities back on course.

Management control involves four interrelated activities, as shown schematically in figure 9–1. A set of standards must first be established against which planned activities can be evaluated as they are carried out. Monitoring devices measure the performance of individuals, activities, and/or programs within the organization. The measurements thus obtained are then compared with the standards to determine whether the current state of affairs approximates the planned state. Finally, action devices must be applied to correct any significant deviations. Corrective action may involve bringing performance in line with plans or modifying plans to more closely reflect performance.

Mockler has elaborated upon the four steps of the management control process as follows, suggesting that this process closely parallels the processes of problem solving or decision making:

1. Diagnose the situation in order to define the control problem and the method for dealing with it.
2. Examine the control problem and review the facts in order to find the key factors affecting the problem and its solution.
3. Develop and evaluate alternative controls to determine the best tools, techniques, or system, and how they can best be put into operation.
4. Exercise control by comparing actual performance against established standards, determining signficant deviations (including checking the accuracy of standards and performance data), and taking action as necessary.[4]

Mockler suggests that problem diagnosis should result in simple statements of (a) the specific kind and level of control situations to be dealt with, (b) the objective and scope of the control effort, (c) the methods to be used in solving the problem, and (d) the organization unit to carry out the control efforts. Principal areas under step two include (a) planning factors, such as important premises, goals, objectives, major policies and implementation plans; (b) specific characteristics of the operation or decision for which the control tools are being created; (c) the purpose for which the controls are being developed, including who will use them and the kinds of decisions which will be made based on the control system; and (d) the nature of the standards or criteria agains which performance will be measured.

The tools and techniques of control might include an overall financial management system, cost accounting controls, specific operating controls, a management information system, reporting forms to facilitate information feedback, mathematical and analytical models, and so forth. Mockler suggests that existing controls should be included as one of the alternatives to be explored under step three.

The terminology of systems theory has found broad application in recent definitions of management control. Kast and Rosenzweig, for example, draw analogies to homeostasis and dynamic equilibrium. They cite the fact that the modern term cybernetics is derived from the ancient Greek word *kybernetike,* literally meaning helmsmanship.[5] Albanese discusses the differences between closed- and open-loop control processes, suggesting that most management controls are open-loop, requiring human intervention for maintenance purposes.[6] Gannon contrasts the notions of feedback and feedforward as applied to management control. Since feedforward systems are more difficult to establish and maintain, he concluded that control based on feedback is much more common.[7]

What Can Managers Control?

It has been said that managers manage people rather than things. In other words, by managing people, managers indirectly manage all other factors that enter into performance—materials, supplies, equipment, and the finan-

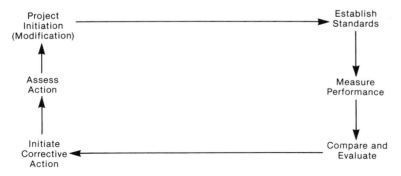

Figure 9–1. A Corrective Model for Management Control

cial resources necessary to support these factors. Managers also manage information; this is an important factor often overlooked in listing the tangible factors of performance. Managers seldom deal directly with a problem situation. Rather, they deal almost exclusively with information about the problem. In turn, managers must make decisions that best satisfy not actual conditions but, rather, information about those conditions.

Four aspects of performance that can be controlled include (1) quantity, (2) quality, (3) time, and (4) cost. These four controllable aspects, in turn, can be related to the major functions of an organization. Controls can be applied to human and nonhuman factors of performance. The quality of employee performance, for example, might be controlled by written job instructions, policies that assure consistent job behavior, training programs designed to increase skill levels, salary plans that reward quality, and so forth. Inventory system procedures, on the other hand, provide the control of the quantity of things.

Vilfredo Pareto, an Italian economist and sociologist writing at the turn of the century, formulated a law that has interesting application in controlling quantity and cost. Pareto's law states that "the significant elements in a specified group usually constitute a relatively small portion of the total items in the group."[8] For example, a university may have over five hundred sponsored projects in force at any one time. Of these projects, less than 10 percent may generate 80 percent of the problems that require the attention of central administration. When Pareto's law applies, the manager should identify the significant elements in the total set and concentrate control efforts on those elements. In effect, Pareto's law supports the notion of management by exception.

Peter Drucker reflects the basic notion of Pareto's law in his concept of *cost points*.[9] A cost point is an activity in a manager's area of responsibility that accounts for a significant portion of total cost. Drucker suggests that major cost points fall into four major categories: (1) *productive costs* contribute directly to the value of the product or service; (2) *support costs* provide no direct client value but are necessary to support production; (3) *policing costs* are aimed at preventing things from going wrong; and (4) *waste* or the cost of efforts that produce no productive, support, or policing results.

A guiding principle in applying controls to any of these cost points is that the marginal cost of the last control expenditure should be at least equal to the marginal benefits achieved. The costs and benefits of management controls, however, should not be considered simply in financial terms. Costs of controlling organizational activities can also take the form of lost time, negative attitudes, lowered job expectations, dysfunctional job behavior, adverse client relations, and so forth. Benefits can take many forms, such as time and cost savings, improved morale, higher job expectations, improved client and public relations, quality improvements, and so forth.

Controls have no value in themselves. As with organizational plans, the value of controls is instrumental to goal achievement. In practice, however, controls often are imbued with some intrinsic value, so that, long after they serve any useful purpose, controls may be retained "for their own value." As with plans that are obsolete, inappropriate controls can severely hinder goal achievement.

It often is difficult for managers to determine the most appropriate amounts and kinds of controls to use in their areas of responsibility. Too much control can stifle initiative and encourage behavior designed to beat the system. Too little control increases the probability that desired results will not be achieved.

Financial versus Nonfinancial Controls

A systematic network of financial controls extends into every operating area. Such a network is important in monitoring costs, assessing the effectiveness of performance (profits or benefits achieved), and evaluating the use of assets. Financial controls are essential to organizational survival, and as a consequence, accounting and finance departments traditionally have served as the locus of the control function in most organizations.

The concept of management control is much broader, however. It is a functional process which must make use of a variety of control mechanisms, not just accounting and financial tools. Management controls operate in many different situations at all levels of an organization. Managers of operating units have always found it necessary to develop and maintain various nonfinancial controls applicable to their particular areas of responsibility.

Nonfinancial controls are designed to monitor critical activities in various program areas—activities that affect performance efficiency, economy, and effectiveness. From an operating manager's viewpoint, such nonfinancial controls may be far more relevant and immediately useful than traditional financial controls. These controls often must be tailored to particular areas of responsibility. Many large organizations have established systems development units to assist in the formulation of appropriate operating controls. Systems analysts, trained to examine total information networks for control, can provide professional insights to aid the operating managers in developing appropriate networks of controls.

Types of Controls

Management controls can be classified as either organizational or operational.[10] Organizational controls are used to evaluate the overall performance of an organization or a significant part thereof. In the private sector, management standards such as profitability, ratio of assets to liabilities, and sales growth provide a broad basis on which to assess the overall performance of an organization. Standards applicable to activities in the public sector, in recent years, have been detailed in terms of measures of effectiveness. When an organization fails to meet such broad standards, the remedies may be equally broad. They may include the recasting of goals and objectives, a reformulation of plans and programs, changes in organizational structure, and improved internal and external communications.

Operational controls measure day-to-day performance by providing comparisons with various standards to determine areas that require more immediate corrective action. While organizational controls may be rather broadly based, operational controls are very specific and situation-oriented. Such measures most frequently focus on issues of efficiency and economy. Measures such as productivity ratios, workload measures, and unit costs are examples of such performance measures.

Five different approaches to control have been suggested by Rowe, Mason, and Dickel.[11] They can be categorized as follows:

1. Controls may be based on past performance, historic data, or performance meaurement.
2. Performance management controls focus on goal congruence and organizational effectiveness and emphasize behavioral aspects of control.
3. Real-time controls use computers to provide information that is as current as possible.
4. Adaptive controls attempt to respond to the required changes in an effective manner through adjustments in ongoing policies and procedures.
5. Strategic controls anticipate potential deviations from desired outcomes and develop ways to minimize them.

Since performance management is based largely on historic data regarding past performances, the first two categories can be considered together. Traditional methods of control, for the most part, measure results after the fact. With some time delay, such measures provide management with information as to how well operational objectives have been achieved. As a consequence of the time lag between the emergence and actual detection of specific problems, however, corrections may not be possible. Rather, emphasis may be placed on trying to keep the same problems from occurring again.[12]

Financial and budgetary controls are good examples of such after-the-fact techniques. When financial statements are prepared, they provide a snapshot of how the organization or program has been doing in a preceding fiscal period. Such statements may point out areas in which future corrective action is needed. It often is too late, however, to resolve the specific problems that have been identified. As the time lag between occurrence and reporting increases, the overall effectiveness of such management controls is significantly diminished.

Successful programs in performance management seem to have three elements in common: (1) top management is involved and supports the program, (2) objectives are specific and are set with the participation of various levels of management, and (3) feedback is concrete and periodic. Performance management uses the following techniques for measuring performance:

1. Measures which rely on observable behavior and use anchored rating scales, that is, scales in which the base level of acceptable performance is clearly identified.
2. Objective measures which focus on outcomes rather than on the process of achieving results, that is, the ends and not the means are subjected to measurement.
3. Evaluation techniques which rely on the experience and judgment of individuals conducting the performance appraisal.

Measures such as cohesiveness, responsiveness, adaptability, or effectiveness provide important insights into the organization's performance.

Behavioral measures are most useful where the work is well defined and the individual's expectations can be taken into account. Where tasks can be defined in specific terms, such as by operational objectives, direct measurement of output may be most appropriate. Subjective or judgmental evaluation may be required where the tasks cannot be easily defined or where no direct measures are possible.

In the past, the emphasis in performance management has been on a closed-loop feedback approach.[13] Organizational objectives may not have been clear, however, making accomplishments difficult to measure in unambiguous, quantitative terms. Feedback information often is not relevant or usable. As a consequence, increased emphasis is being placed on other behaviorally oriented systems such as management by objectives (MBO).

Management by objectives foregoes more rigid and formal processes of traditional administration for a more open, fluid, and democratic approach. Employees at each level within the organization are asked to participate in the formulation of objectives, which are then integrated with broader organizational objectives. The basic purpose of the MBO cycle is to make personnel aware not only of what they do, but why they do it—how their activities relate to organizational goals and objectives.

The techniques of participative management predate the concept of MBO. As Peter Drucker has observed, the objective of MBO is not merely employee participation but employee commitment.[14] It is assumed under MBO that by involving employees in the formulation of objectives, they will become more committed to those objectives. It also is assumed that greater performance and productivity will result from making employees more aware of their role within the organization.

MBO builds on the notion that the traditional incentives of money, job security, promotion, and other status symbols often are insufficient responses to the many needs of individual employees. Thus, it is assumed under MBO that work can provide a source of commitment and satisfaction to the individual, and thereby, employees can be motivated to meet needs at a higher level than those of more immediate economic gratification.

The mechanisms provided for review and evaluation of performance are a major aspect of MBO. Based on Drucker's concept of self-control, employees are given the responsibility for evaluating the results of their own performance in meeting previously agreed-upon objectives. They also have the corresponding responsibility for making the necessary adjustments suggested by such evaluations. Thus, management must delegate the authority as well as the responsibility to achieve individual objectives. An often-heard complaint in complex organizations is that authority is not commensurate with responsibility. Although MBO does not address this complaint explicitly, its assumptions necessarily strive to correct this situation.

Modern management information systems, supported by the data processing and analysis capabilities of computers, have made possible other forms of management control that can be used to anticipate problems and make adjustments often before their impact is fully upon the organization. Concurrent or real-time controls, for example, measure deviations from standards more or less as they occur. Such controls permit a program to be carried out within established tolerance as it moves through time. The quality control chart used in production operations is an example of concurrent control techniques in the private sector. Statistical samples of the product are taken periodically and measured for their adherence to some quality standards. If the samples begin to fall outside the established quality limits, corrective action can be taken before additional items are produced.

Computers have made real-time control devices both possible and practical. The computerized inventory control systems used by some retail establishments, such as large department stores and supermarkets, provides an example of real-time controls made possible by computer technology. Inventory records are continually updated as items purchased are recorded at the check-out registers.

Adaptive controls have been used principally at the operating level. Some efforts have been made, however, to use this approach to modify various aspects of the internal structure and processes of organizations to match changing requirements in the external environment. These efforts have given rise to the development of *predictive controls techniques* designed to anticipate and identify problems before they happen. An obvious approach is to anticipate deviations, as is done in statistical quality control. For example, if an expenditure is proposed, the possibility that it might exceed the budget should be ascertained ahead of time rather than after the fact. Such controls are related to the planning process and generally involve various forecasting and projection techniques.

A strategic control system permits changes to be made in both the desired objectives and the control approach. Donald Harvey defines strategic control as

> the managerial function that ensures that actual organizational actions correspond to planned actions. Two aspects are important: First, control and review should take place at many stages of the implementation process; and second, control is closely related to other managerial functions—goal-setting, planning, and decision making. It is an interrelated function, rather than a separate activity.[15]

Complex organizations often require large amounts of data to achieve effective management control. Continuous monitoring of activities is required for appropriate corrective action to be taken on a timely basis to achieve the desired objectives. Thus, a simulation model may be required to provide strategic information to support the decision system. Objectives often are based on estimates, and therefore, considerable uncertainty may exist about the validity of these objectives. Estimates are based on experience, comparable work, or some arbitrarily determined standard. As a consequence, it may be inappropriate to use the estimate (the objective) as a rigid basis for measuring performance. It is precisely because of rapid and often unpredictable change that strategic controls are needed to determine the appropriate corrective action.

Strategic, predictive, concurrent, and after-the-fact controls are all valuable to managers. Together they can provide a clearer picture of where the organization or program is and where it should be. A proper balance among these various types of controls can vastly improve the effectiveness of any organization. Historically, however, most organizations have relied largely on after-the-fact control measures.

The Need to Integrate Planning and Control

Planning is a prerequisite for effective management, whether in the private or public sector. The links between planning and control are recognized explicitly in the definitions of several contemporary authors. Kast and Rosenzweig, for example, define organizational control as

> the phase of the managerial process concerned with maintaining organizational activity within allowable limits, as measured from expectations. Organizational control is inextricably intertwined with planning. Plans provide the framework against which the control process works. On the other hand, feedback from the control phase often identifies the need for new plans or at least adjustments to existing one."[16]

As Gannon suggests, you cannot have control without the planning. "Control is the monitoring of plans and the pinpointing of significant deviations from them. Hence planning and control are intimately related and, in fact, represent opposite sides of the same coin."[17] Most contemporary texts on management and organization theory include chapters on both planning and control.

Control is so much a part of managerial work that management and control sometimes are viewed as one and the same activity. They are not identical, however, because goal setting and planning also are essential to effective management. The overwhelming majority of control processes used in organizations are relatively simple. They are not real-time processes. Some very effective management control is the result of imagination and personal experience rather than formal knowledge about computerized control processes.

Designing a Management Control System

Designing a control system can be an expensive endeavor. Therefore, the anticipated benefits of such a system should exceed the costs. A simple project may require a very simple control system, with a few indicators to determine whether or not the project is progressing on schedule and if it is within the desired limits of cost and performance. Overdesigning a set of controls can restrict the flexibility that operating managers can use to make "seat of the pants" corrections which often are more timely and responsive than more elaborate control and reporting procedures.

Basic Conditions of a Control System

Regardless of their sophistication or complexity, all management control systems must meet the following basic conditions:

1. The system must be understood by those who use it and obtain data from it. In designing management controls, the needs of at least four groups must be taken into consideration:
   a. Top management, concerned with policy decisions and the relative effectiveness of particular projects;
   b. Planners and analysts, concerned with obtaining data by which to estimate costs and benefits;
   c. Operating managers, concerned with strategic effectiveness and administrative efficiency, including whether a project or program is on schedule;
   d. Groups outside the organization (for example, stockholders, governmental agencies, and the general public).
2. The system must relate to the structure and process of the project or program, since the control system and the organization are interdependent.

3. The system must have the capacity of reporting early deviations from scheduled plans on a timely basis so that corrective actions can be initiated before more serious deviations occur.
4. The system must have sufficient flexibility to remain compatible with changes in the organization's broader environment.
5. The system must be economical to be worth the additional expense of maintenance.
6. The nature of the corrective actions required to bring the project or program back into compatibility with the plan should be clearly indicated.
7. The system should be capable of being reduced to a visual display (words, pictures, graphs, and so forth) that is easy to read and comprehend.
8. The system should be developed with the active participation of all major executives and managers in the organization.

Establishing Standards

The design of a management control system should start with the very beginning of a project (see figure 9–2). The important function of identifying appropriate standards begins with the development of estimates of resource needs and the design of program schedules. Standards are based on input measures or the description of resources consumed. They also include performance criteria, measures of outputs and effectiveness, and work schedules. A work breakdown schedule (WBS) can be prepared to show the physical products, milestones, and technical performance goals or other indicators, the budget estimates required for each task, the starting and completion times for each task, and the assigned task responsibilities.[18]

Once the project or program is initiated, the tasks for which a formal control process is created and maintained should focus on specific inputs, performance criteria, and/or outputs. Performance and program measures can be developed after management has decided on which aspects to focus.

The establishment of a formal control process requires answers to such questions as: (1) From a technical standpoint, what information is feasible? (2) What are economic costs of obtaining this information? (3) What are the expected benefits associated with obtaining the information? (4) Does variation in the information impact the performance of each task in terms of goals or objectives? Since the design and implementation of a system for program monitoring and control can be relatively expensive, program managers should be involved in the identification of standards and measures.

Measuring Performance

A management information system includes the means for obtaining measurements of program achievements (that is, performance measures and measures of effectiveness). Such measurement may be through periodic inter-

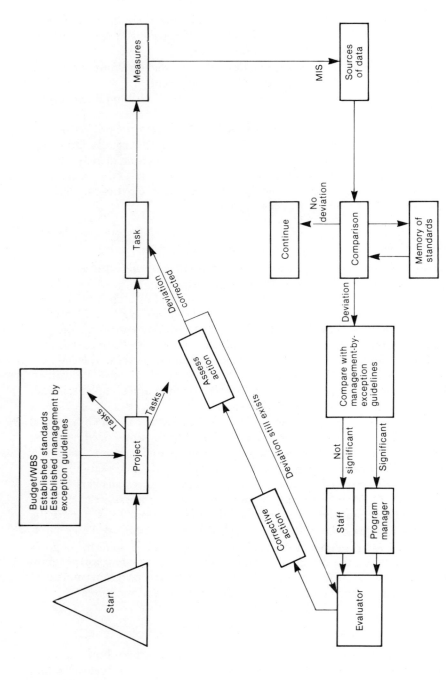

Source: Alan Walter Steiss, *Management Control in Government* (Lexington, Mass.: Lexington Books, 1982), p. 18. Reprinted by permission.

Figure 9–2. An Expanded Model for Management Control

vention in the ongoing management information system (that is, through management inquiries), or it may entail automated reporting procedures (monthly fiscal summaries, for example). Sometimes the measurement may actually be undertaken by the individuals or groups whose performance is to be controlled. Care must be exercised in this approach, however, because self-measurement sometimes results in a loss of meaningful control. Data may be concealed or distorted if it is thought that such data might be used as a basis for sanctions or to reduce the availability of rewards. To counter this inherent tendency, special organizational units often are created (for instance, internal auditors) to serve as sensors in the evaluation of certain activities of other organizational units.

The best information systems will not guarantee that a manager will stay out of trouble. However, improved information will help keep the manager from being surprised when trouble comes along. GIGO—"garbage in, garbage out"—has become a watchword in computer systems. A management information system is only as good as its inputs. A good information system should (1) identify the long-range objectives of projects or programs; (2) analyze available information in terms of its suitability to evaluate the process of specific programs, projects, and activities; (3) provide for the interfacing of information on specific programs or projects with the overall management information system of the organization; (4) establish a timetable for the development and implementation of additional information; and (5) accomplish this time plan within a framework that meets the needs of management. A management information system must be more than a collection of disjointed data designed to meet the unique needs of individual projects and programs.

Comparison and Evaluation

The comparison step indicates if deviations from the original plans have occurred in actual activities and result. And, if so, the magnitude of these deviations should be revealed. Questions to ask at this stage might include: (1) Where does the project stand in relation to cost schedules and expected performance characteristics? (2) What is the interrelationship between costs and performance characteristics such as output and effectiveness? (3) What is the evaluation of progress on the project? This comparison of actual versus planned is extremely important. Although basic information is provided, not all deviations from the plan are of equal significance. Therefore, judgments must be made to determine whether the deviations from the plan warrants corrective action.

Evaluation involves a diagnosis of the types, amount, and possible causes of reported deviations. The control system detects and reports exceptions. It must also identify those deviations that, taken together, hold the greatest threat to the successful achievement of program objectives. The manager must be able to evaluate those deviations in actual performance that significantly impact the consumption of scarce resources or affect the timely completion of scheduled activities.

Effective management control is more than merely "putting out fires." If each deviation is seen as a crisis, the energies of management can quickly be dissipated, with little or no positive results in bringing the program activities back on track. Managers must decide which events are significant and which deviations must be corrected. In some cases, it may be appropriate to amplify such deviations, as they may represent positive consequences of program activities.

Corrective Action

Unless corrective action is taken when standards are not met, the control process amounts to little more than historical record-keeping. The causes of the problem should be investigated as soon as a significant deviation from established standards is identified. It may be discovered that the cause of the deviation is an unrealistic plan, and a revision in the original objectives may be required. All too often, plans are assumed to be fixed points rather than dynamic guidelines that may have to be altered to meet changing conditions.

Sometimes the gap between actual performance and the plan reflects a lack of effort. Sometimes the gap in performance is the consequence of a simple misunderstanding or a failure to communicate expectations (goals and objectives). Before setting in motion corrective actions directed at the apparent source of the problem, managers should ask themselves: "Have I clearly identified and communicated what I expected will be achieved in terms of this program or activity?" At times, it also must be recognized that a reduction in productivity may be the result of events outside the immediate control of management.

Finally, management must make a systematic assessment of the effects of correction actions. Did the corrective action actually close the gap between planned and actual performance? If the answer is yes, then the various tasks can continue to be implemented and monitored. However, if the answer is no, then it is necessary to reevaluate the possible causes of the deviation and examine more closely the alternative courses of remedial action.

Implementing a Management Control System

It is always easier to implement a new management control system when operations are expanding and budgets are increasing. Whether warranted or not, operating managers will associate such control measures as the consequence of growth—a necessary evil that accompanies boom times. It is much more difficult to implement new controls in periods of program contraction and funding reduction. Under such circumstances, the system is likely to be associated with a "tightening of the screws." Unfortunately, all too often more systematic management controls are not deemed necessary in periods of growth and only are called on in periods of tight fiscal resources.

The concept of *responsibility centers* should be emphasized in the development and implementation of management control systems. A responsibility center is that subunit of the larger organization where the resource inputs required to carry out clearly defined objectives are under the direct control of the center's management. Operating managers should be held accountable for program performance only to the extent that the wherewithal has been provided to carry out agreed-upon objectives. In the absence of such a clear delineation of responsibility, the management control system will be viewed, at best, as merely a mechanism for reporting performance to top management. And, at worst, it will be seen as unjustified and unwarranted spying.

The Information Base

Management control is predicated on the notion that some measure of output is better than none. At the same time, however, the limitations of existing output measures should be recognized. A continuous search must be made for more valid measures. Only output measures that are actually used in the control system should be collected. Since many people dislike the idea of accountability, the collection of output measures that have no foreseeable application only further aggravates this basis for resistance to further management control.

It is important to ensure information continuity, in terms of both the existing data base and other data users. Often a new control system may be implemented in one segment of an organization on a trial basis. Or the system may be designed to serve the specific needs of a particular functional area within the organization (for example, to provide further accountability for contracts and grants or other forms of external funding). In such instances, explicit provision must be made to cross walk the data from the new system's format to other established formats within the organization. It also may be necessary to develop crosswalks for other organizations that may have grown accustomed to receiving information in a certain format.

The crosswalking process requires that information in management control records (for example, accounts) be reclassified into the file formats required by other units outside the system. In some cases, this reclassification can be exact. Detailed data exist in such a form that they can be rearranged in the prescribed format. More often, however, the reclassification can only be approximate, some records must be subdivided, combined, and/or reclassified, more or less arbitrarily, to obtain the summaries required. To the extent possible, however, every effort should be made to hold such crosswalks to a minimum. From the standpoint of the organization, this is a relatively nonproductive activity.

In designing a new system, it is necessary to determine what features of the existing system, if any, should be retained. It also is important to determine how the transition from the old to the new system should be accomplished. It usually is neither feasible nor desirable to abandon entirely the old system. Operating managers will have much to learn about the new system. The new system will seem less strange to them to the extent that it incorporates familiar practices, particularly familiar terminology, from the existing system. Running the new system in parallel with the existing system until the bugs have been worked out has obvious advantages. This approach avoids the possibility that bugs in the new system will result in the permanent loss of vital data.

It is important, however, that top management use information from the new system as soon as it becomes available. Operating managers are not likely to take the plunge in using the new format until top management breaks the ice. The utilization by top management is particularly important when a dual system is in place. If the new and old system are run in parallel, the old system should be discarded slightly before managers become completely comfortable with the new system. Thus holdouts will have no choice but to use the new system when the old data are no longer available.

Notes

1. Henri Fayol, *General and Industrial Management* (New York: Pitman Corporation, 1949), p. 107.

2. Robert J. Mockler, *The Management Control Process* (New York: Appleton-Century-Crofts, 1972), p. 2.

3. Robert N. Anthony and Glenn A. Welsch, *Fundamentals of Management Accounting* (Homewood, Ill.: Richard D. Irwin, 1977), p. 445.

4. Mockler, *Management Control Process,* pp. 17–18.

5. Fremont E. Kast and James E. Rosenzweig, *Organization and Management* (New York: McGraw-Hill, 1979).

6. Robert Albanese, *Management: Toward Accountability for Performance* (Homewood, Ill.: Richard D. Irwin, 1975).

7. Martin J. Gannon, *Management: An Organizational Perspective* (Boston, Mass.: Little, Brown, 1977).

8. C.J. Slaybough, "Pareto's Law and Modern Management," *Price Waterhouse Review* 2 (Winter 1966):27.

9. Peter F. Drucker, *Managing for Results* (New York: Harper, 1964), pp. 78–84.

10. Richard A. Johnson, Fremont E. Kast, and James E. Rosenzweig, *The Theory and Management of Systems* (New York: McGraw-Hill, 1973), pp. 82–86.

11. Alan J. Rowe, Richard O. Mason, and Karl Dickel, *Strategic Management and Business Policy: A Methodological Approach* (Reading, Mass.: Addison-Wesley, 1982), p. 265.

12. Herbert G. Hicks and C. Ray Gullett, *The Management of Organizations* (New York: McGraw-Hill, 1976), pp. 499–501.

13. Rowe, Mason, and Dickel, *Strategic Management and Business Policy,* p. 266.

14. Drucker, "What Results Should You Expect? A Users' Guide to MBO," *Public Administration Review* 36 (January-February 1976), p. 19.

15. Donald F. Harvey, *Business Policy and Strategic Management* (Columbus, Ohio: Charles E. Merrill, 1982), p. 329.

16. Kast and Rosenzweig, *Organization and Management,* p. 443.

17. Gannon, *Management,* p. 140.

18. Alan Walter Steiss, *Management Control in Government* (Lexington, Mass.: Lexington Books, 1982), pp. 275–300.

10
Managerial Accounting

Managerial accounting provides information useful in making decisions about the development of resources and the exploitation of program opportunities.[1] Financial accounting focuses on the accurate and objective recording of fiscal transactions and the preparation of reports on the fiscal affairs of an organization for external users. Managerial accounting is involved in the formulation of financial estimates of future performance (the planning and budgetary processes) and, subsequently, in the analysis of actual performance in relation to these estimates (program evaluation and performance auditing). Managerial accounting develops information for internal users; its emphasis is on future decisions.

Objectives of Managerial Accounting

The same basic accounting system can be used to compile data for both financial and managerial accounting. Often an organization must accommodate to an accounting system developed in response to externally imposed legal requirements, rather than to its own management needs. There are no generally accepted principles to guide (or inhibit) managerial accounting. From a management point of view, any accounting system or method is desirable as long as it produces incremental benefits in excess of its incremental costs.

Underlying Assumptions

The objective of managerial accounting is to improve the effectiveness of both the planning and control functions. This approach is predicated on two basic assumptions. First, plans should be built on the same information base as the mechanisms of control. Management does not require some grandiose master plan drawn in the abstract. Rather, it needs the fundamental ability to know what is being spent where and for what purposes. Planning depends on the same reporting and control mechanisms that make central oversight possible and decentralized management feasible.[2] Building the mechanism of control on one data base (financial accounting) and the planning process on another (program analysis) places too great a stress on the management system as the intermediary.

The second assumption underlying managerial accounting is that the success of a decentralized management system is dependent on an understanding at the department level of the rules of the game, as well as the incentives and expectations, governing planning and budgeting. An important task of managerial accounting, then, is to enlarge the circle of those familiar with the process of planning and budgeting. This is accomplished through the communication of pertinent management information as well as financial data.

The significant features of managerial accounting can be summarized as follows:

1. Greater emphasis on the generation of information for planning and programming purposes, seeking to establish a balance with the control function of accounting;
2. Performance standards (workload and unit cost data) added to traditional control mechanisms based on legal compliance and fiscal accountability;
3. Experimentation and innovation in the types of information supplied to management at various levels;
4. Greater cost consciousness generated among operation units through the identification of cost and responsibility centers and the use of performance standards;
5. The linkage between management control, program budgeting, and performance auditing facilitated by the cost analyses.

Managerial accounting focuses on segments of the total organization, that is, on individual activities, operations, programs, or other responsibility centers. Managerial accounting includes estimates and plans for the future of these centers, as well as information about the past. Although managerial accounting reports contain financial data, much of the information in these reports is nonmonetary, for example, data on number of employees, number of hours worked, quantities of materials used, and purpose of travel.

Timely Information Requirements

Managers need information on a real-time basis (that is, as problems occur and opportunities arise). Often they are willing to sacrifice some precision to gain in the currency of data. Thus, in managerial accounting, approximations often are as useful as—or even more useful than—numbers calculated to the last penny. In spite of the mystique that often surrounds its data, financial accounting cannot be absolutely precise. Therefore, the difference is one of degree.

The informational boundaries of managerial accounting are not rigid. There is little point in collecting any data unless its value to management exceeds the cost of data collection.[3] Managerial accounting provides a basis for financial interpretations that assist in the formulation of policies and decisions and in the control of current and future operations. Such internal reporting to management often requires the collection and presentation of financial information in a completely different format than followed for external reporting.[4]

Managerial accounting will not supersede financial accounting. However, new processes for the collection and application of both cost data and statistical data can be devised under an optimal system. With the adoption of such standards, there also must be recognized sanctions. Some performance and cost configurations will be highly satisfactory; others will be painfully inadequate. Work unit performance and cost standards must be revised periodically to keep pace with changes in operations. Ultimately, they must have the concurrence of those persons impacted by these management expectations.

Functions of Managerial Accounting

Managerial accounting is concerned primarily with four basic functions: planning, cost determination, cost control, and performance evaluation. Component costs must be determined before decisions can be made regarding the commitment of resources in support of particular objectives or programs. Costs must be evaluated, both in the more immediate future and in the long run, and must be weighed against anticipated benefits. Once commitments are made, costs must be monitored and controlled to ensure that they are appropriate and reasonable for the activities performed. And the overall performance of a program, activity, or subunit must be evaluated to improve future decisions and resource allocations. The primary focus of this discussion will be on the functions of cost determination and cost control.

Basic Concepts of Cost

Cost can be defined as a release of value required to accomplish some goal, objective, or purpose.[5] Costs should be incurred only if they can be expected to lead to the accomplishment of some predetermined end or serve as a means to an end. Costs are incurred by some organizations for the purpose of generating revenues in excess of the resources consumed. This profit motive is not applicable, however, for most public organizations, where costs are incurred in the provision of some public service. The test as to whether the cost is appropriate and reasonable is still the same: Did the commitment of resources advance the organization or program toward some agreed-upon goal or objective?

Cost is not a unidimensional concept, however. One of the primary objectives of managerial accounting is to further define and categorize the basic components of cost that must be incurred in the implementation of the plans and programs of any organization.

Costs can be defined by how they change in relation to fluctuations in the quality of some selected activity, for example, number of hours of labor required to complete some task, the dollar volume of sales, the number of orders processed, or some other index of volume. Some costs do not change in total as the volume of activity increases but become progressively smaller on a per unit basis. These are known as *fixed costs.* Other costs are more or less uniform per unit, but their total fluctuates in direct proportion to the total volume of activity. These are known as *variable costs.*Note that the variable or fixed character of a cost relates to its total dollar amount and not to its per unit amount.

The acquisition of equipment illustrates a fixed cost. As the volume of activity increases, the total cost of the equipment is spread over an increasing number of units. Therefore, the cost per unit becomes less and less. Personnel, on the other hand, illustrate variable costs. Each employee carrying out similar tasks is paid approximately the same amount, but as the number of tasks increase, the number of employees must also increase (assuming some level of productivity or efficiency is to be maintained).

Costs also may be *semifixed,* described as a step-function, or *semivariable,* whereby both fixed and variable components are included in the related costs. Supervisory salaries might be described as semifixed costs. At some level of increased activity, additional supervisory personnel may be required. Maintenance costs often exhibit the characteristic of semivariable costs. A fixed level of cost is required initially, after which maintenance costs increase with the level of activity. Since costs usually are classified as either fixed or variable, the incremental character of these mixed categories often is a determining factor. If the increments between levels of change are large, the costs may be identified as fixed; if the increments are relatively small, the costs usually are defined as variable.

Five basic cost components are involved in any activity, operation, project, or program: (1) labor or personal services (that is, salaries and wages and related employee benefits); (2) materials and supplies (or consumables); (3) equipment expenses (sometimes categorized as part of fixed asset expenses); (4) contractual services (that is, "packages" of services purchased from outside sources); and (5) overhead.

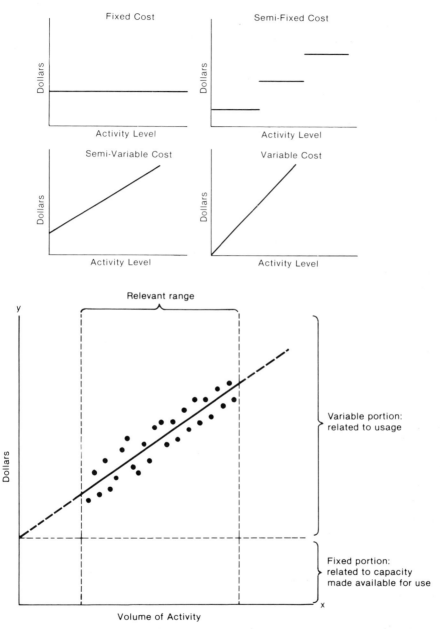

Source: Alan Walter Steiss, *Management Control in Government* (Lexington, Mass.: Lexington Books, 1982), p. 59. Reprinted by permission.

Figure 10–1. Graphic Illustration of Cost Concepts

Overhead has a fairly specific meaning when applied in the private sector. It usually is defined as all costs other than direct labor and materials that are associated with the production process. Used in this context, overhead may involve variable costs (for example, power, supplies, contractual services, and most indirect labor) or fixed costs (for instance, supervisory salaries, property taxes, rent, insurance, and depreciation). In the jargon of cost accounting, various direct cost components, such as direct labor and materials, are reclassified as *prime costs,* whereas indirect labor and overhead are reclassified as *conversion costs.*

Decisions must be made in cost accounting as to the distribution of direct and indirect costs. A *direct cost* represents a cost incurred for a specific purpose which is uniquely associated with that purpose. The salary of a manager of a day care center, for example, would be considered a direct cost of the center. If the center were divided into departments according to different age groups of children, with a part of the manager's salary allocated to each department, then the salary would be an indirect cost of each department. An *indirect cost* is a cost associated with more than one activity or program that cannot be traced directly to any of the individual activities. In the public sector, the terms *indirect cost* and *overhead* often are used interchangeably.

In theory, all costs are controllable by someone within an organization, given a long enough time. For purposes of managerial accounting, however, *controllable costs* are defined as those costs subject to the influence of a given manager of a given program or organizational unit for a given time. The supervisor of an emergency room in a hospital, for example, might exercise significant control over the costs of supplies, maintenance, assigned nursing staff, and so forth. However, he or she may have little or no control over the cost of doctors working in the emergency room or insurance costs allocated to this aspect of the hospital's operations.

Noncontrollable costs include all costs that do not meet this test of significant influence by a given manager. Thus, costs assigned to the manager of any department may contain both controllable and noncontrollable elements. Although clear distinctions often are difficult to make, every effort must be made to separate these cost components for the purposes of performance evaluation.

Other cost categories often encountered in managerial accounting are described below:

1. *Engineered costs* can be predicted with a reasonable degree of accuracy, given some level of activity; both direct labor and direct material costs fall into this category.
2. *Discretionary costs* usually are established for some short period of time, based on the judgment of management and are subject to variation at the discretion of the manager (also called managed costs).

3. *Committed costs* typically result from long-term decisions related to activities or programs (that is, depreciation).
4. *Products costs* initially are identified as part of the inventory on hand and become expenses only when the inventory is sold.
5. *Period costs* are deducted as expenses during a given fiscal period without having been previously classified as product costs (for example, administrative expenses).
6. *Out-of-pocket costs* involve current or upcoming outlays of funds for some decisions that have been made.
7. *Sunk costs* have already been incurred and therefore, are irrelevant to the current decision-making process; allocation of cost expirations based on depreciation and amortization schedules are examples of sunk costs.
8. *Marginal costs* represent the cost of providing one additional unit of service (or product) over some previous level of activity.
9. *Differential costs* represents the difference in total costs between alternative approaches to providing some product or service.
10. *Opportunity costs* involve the maximum return that might have been expected if a resource had been committed to an alternative; that is, the impact of having to give up one opportunity to select another.
11. *Associated costs* are any cost involved in utilizing project services in the process of converting them into a form suitable for use or sale at the stage when benefits are evaluated; associated costs are incurred by the beneficiaries of programs and services.
12. *Investment costs* vary primarily with the size of a particular program or project but not with its duration.
13. *Recurring costs* are operating and maintenance costs that vary with both the size and the duration of the program; recurring costs may include salaries and wages, equipment maintenance and repair, and materials and supplies, and so forth.
14. *Life-cycle costs* are incurred over the useful life of a facility or duration of a program, including investment costs, research and development costs, operating costs, and maintenance and repair costs.

Many of these cost categories operate in pairs, for example, product and period costs, investment and recurring costs, and out-of-pocket and sunk costs.

Cost Approximation Methods

The first step in the classification of costs is to determine how the costs in question react under various conditions. This process, frequently called *cost approximation* or *cost estimation,* involves an attempt to find predictable relationships between a dependent variable (cost) and an independent variable (some relevant activity), so that costs can be estimated over time based on the behavior of the independent variable.

This cost function often is represented by the basic formula

$$y = a + bx$$

where y is the dependent variable (cost), x is the independent variable, and a and b are approximations of true (but unknown) parameters. In practice, such cost approximations typically are based on three major assumptions: (1) linear cost functions can be used to approximate nonlinear situations; (2) all costs can be categorized as either fixed or variable within a relevant range; and (3) the true cost behavior can be sufficiently explained by one independent variable instead of more than one variable. Problems of changing price levels, productivity, and technological changes also are assumed away under this approach.

The analytical task in choosing among possible cost functions is to approximate an appropriate slope coefficient b, defined as the amount of increase in y for each unit increase in x, and a constant or intercept a, defined as the value of y when x is 0. The analyst may use goodness-of-fit tests, ranging from simple scatter diagrams to full-fledged regression analysis, to ensure that the cost function is plausible and that the relationship is credible. When possible, the best evidence of a credible relationship is provided by physical observations.

Four major types of cost functions are suggested by this discussion of fixed and variable costs:

1. A fixed cost does not fluctuate in total as x changes within the relevant range; that is, $y = a$, because $b = 0$.
2. A proportionately variable cost fluctuates in direct proportion to changes in x; that is, $y = bx$, because $a = 0$.
3. A step-function (or semifixed) cost is nonlinear because of breaks in its behavior pattern; that is, $y' = a'$, $y'' = a''$, $y''' = a'''$, and so forth.
4. A mixed or semivariable cost is a combination of fixed and variable elements; that is, its total fluctuates as x changes within the relevant range, but not in direct proportion, that is, $y = a + bx$.

The first three of these cost functions are relatively straightforward and simple to resolve. The mixed-cost situation is the more common, however, and the more problematic.

The fixed portion of a mixed cost typically is the result of providing some initial capacity. The variable portion is the result of using the capacity, given its availability. A photocopying machine, for example, often has a fixed monthly rental cost plus a variable cost based on the number of copies produced.

Ideally, there should be no accounts for mixed costs. All such costs should be subdivided into two accounts, one for the variable portion and the other for the fixed portion. In practice, however, such distinctions seldom are made because of the difficulty of analyzing day-to-day cost data into variable and fixed categories. Even if such distinctions were possible, the advantages might not be worth the additional clerical effort and costs.

Several basic methods are available for approximating cost functions. These methods are not mutually exclusive and frequently are used in tandem to provide cross-checks on assumptions. The five most commonly applied methods are described below:

1. *Analytic or industrial engineering methods* entail a systematic examination of labor, materials, supplies, support services, and facilities—sometimes using time-and-motion studies—to determine physically observable input-output relationships.
2. *Account analysis* involves a classification of all relevant accounts into variable or fixed cost categories by observing how total costs behave over several fiscal periods.
3. *High-low methods* call for estimations of total costs at two different activity levels, usually at a low point and at a high point within the relevant range. The difference of the dependent variable is divided by the difference of the independent variable to estimate the slope of the line represented by b.
4. *Visual fit methods* are applied by drawing a straight line through the cost points on a scatter diagram, which consists of a plot of various costs experienced at various levels of activities.
5. *Regression methods* refer to the measurement of the average amount of change in one variable that is associated with unit increases in the amounts of one or more other variables.

Whatever method is used to formulate cost approximations, it is important in managerial accounting to have reasonably accurate and reliable predictions of costs. Such cost estimates usually have an important bearing on a number of operational decisions and can be used for planning, budgeting, and control purposes. The division of costs into fixed and variable components (and into engineered, discretionary, and committed categories) highlights major factors that influence cost incurrence. Although cost functions usually represent simplifications of underlying true relationships, the use of these methods depends on how sensitive the manager's decisions are to the errors that may be introduced by these simplifications. In some situations, additional accuracy may make little difference in the decision. In others, it may be very significant. Selection of a cost function often is a decision as to the cost and value of information.[6]

Cost Accounting

To arrive at an accurate estimate of total cost, decisions must be made as to the distribution of direct and indirect costs in the operation of any class of accounts. Cost accounting is the process of assembling and recording all the elements of expense incurred to attain a purpose, to carry out an activity, operation, or program, to complete a unit of work or project, or to do a specific job. Cost accounting encompasses a body of concepts and techniques used in both financial accounting and managerial accounting. As a result, it is found to be useful in both areas.

Cost accounting systems can be found in both product- and service-oriented entities and in both profit- and nonprofit organizations. Firms providing a service or a product for sale must have a system for accumulating and determining the necessary costs of the service or product. Cost allocation methods, at best, are only as good as the cost data used to provide information for inventory valuation or other purposes. The expense of obtaining cost data, however, must be maintained at a reasonable level, and the distribution of costs should not go beyond the point of practical use. The procedural steps for summarizing and posting data to cost accounts are shown in figure 10–2.[7]

Classes of Cost Accounts

For the purposes of managerial accounting, several approaches may be relevant in measuring costs. *Absorption* or *full costing* considers all the fixed and variable costs associated with the provision of the goods or services in question. Unless an accrual accounting system has been adopted, however, several problems may be encountered.

Unit costs often are determined simply by dividing the current budget allocation for a given activity by the number of performance units. This approach may produce rather misleading results, however. Budgetary appro-

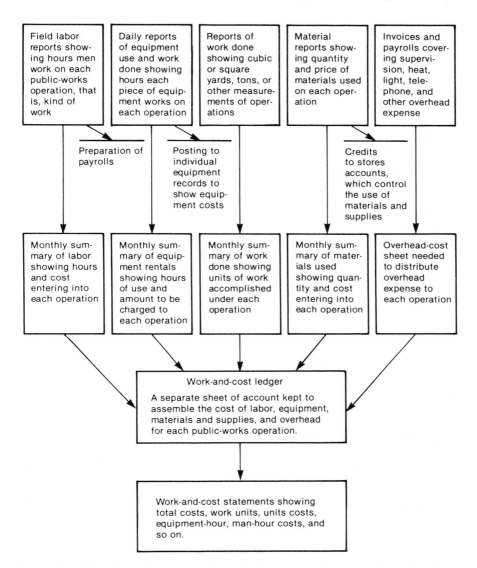

Source: Alan Walter Steiss, *Management Control in Government* (Lexington, Mass.: Lexington Books, 1982), p. 68. Reprinted by permission.

Figure 10–2. Procedural Steps for Posting Data to Cost Accounts

priations may not be a good measure of current expenses, since encumbrances for items not yet received may be included. At the same time, expenditures to cover outstanding encumbrances from the preceding fiscal period may be excluded. Even if costs are limited to expenditures, current unit costs may be overstated if (a) new capital equipment is included in the expenditures or (b) there is a large increase in inventories. On the other hand, unit costs may be understated in many organizations because of a failure to account for the drawing down of inventories or for depreciation (or user costs) of equipment.

The method for assigning overhead or indirect costs to operating departments is one of the more controversial aspects of the full-costing approach. Overhead includes the cost of various items that cannot conveniently be charged directly to those jobs or operations that are benefited. General administrative expenses are included in this concept of overhead. It can be argued, for example, that the cost of a personnel department, an accounting department, and other service or auxiliary units should be assigned in some fashion to the operating departments of an organization. These indirect costs often are distributed on a formula basis, as determined by labor hours, labor costs, or total direct costs of each job or operation.

Many of these indirect costs, however, are clearly beyond the control of the managers of operating departments. In recognition of this fact, *responsibility costing* assigns to an operating department only those costs that its managers can control or at least influence. Many argue that this approach is the only proper measure of the financial stewardship of an operating manager. Responsibility costing will be discussed further in a subsequent section of this chapter.

A useful approach to cost accounting is to consider only the variable or incremental costs of a particular operation. For example, a city manager might want to know how much extra it would cost to keep the public swimming pools open evenings, or how much it would cost to increase the frequency of trash collection from two to three times a week. The same questions might be raised by the management of any organization that delivers a service on some regularly scheduled basis. This approach is called *direct costing* and is relatively easy to associate with an organization's budget. Direct costing can be very helpful for incremental decision making.

Two approaches to cost accounting frequently used in the private sector are job order costing and process costing. As the name implies, job order costing is used by companies in which products are readily identifiable by individual units or batches. Industries that commonly use job order costing include construction, printing, furniture manufacturing, and machinery manufacturing. The essential feature of the job cost method is the attempt to apply cost to specific jobs, which may consist of a single physical unit (for example, a custom sofa) or a few like units in a distinct batch or job lot (for example, twelve end tables).

Process costing is most often found in such industries as chemicals, oil refining, meat packing, mining, glass, and cement. These industries are characterized by the mass production of like units, which usually pass in continuous fashion through a series of uniform production steps called operations or processes. Costs are accumulated by departments (often identified by operations or processes) with attention focused on the total department costs for a given period in relation to the units processes. Average unit costs may be determined by dividing accumulated department costs by the quantities produced during the period. Unit costs for various operations can then be multiplied by the number of units transferred to obtain total costs applicable to those units. This method cannot be used to determine cost differences in individual products, however.

Process costing creates relatively few accounting problems when applied to various types of service organizations, including public agencies. Unit costs can be calculated for many activities by simply dividing total program costs for a given period by the number of persons served (or tons of trash collected, number of inspections made, miles of road patrolled, or some other applicable measure of the volume of activity during some period). When it is important to determine costs in greater detail by individual projects or tasks, a job order costing approach is necessary.

Cost Allocation

Cost allocation (sometimes called *cost absorption*) is necessary whenever the full cost of a service or product must be determined. In cost allocation, the variable, fixed, direct, and indirect components of cost must be considered. Examples of this requirement in the public sector include the costing of governmental grants and contracts, the establishment of equitable public utility rates, the setting of user rates for internal services expected to operate on a breakeven basis (that is, recover full costs), and the determination of fees (for example, for inspections).

Variable costs directly associated with a given service or activity do not represent an allocation problem. Using methods outlined in the previous section, such costs usually can be measured and assigned to appropriate activities/programs with little difficulty.

A given organizational unit may also experience direct, fixed costs. Such costs should be allocated to specific services or projects. These direct costs do not vary with the activities being measured, however. Such costs might be allocated by assuming some level of operation (such as number of persons to be served), and then the total annual cost can be divided by the estimated level of activity to arrive at a unit rate. In other instances, direct fixed costs may have to be allocated on the basis of some arbitrary physical measure, such as floor space occupied. In either case, it is important that full accrued costs are allocated to avoid the problem of encumbrances.

For purposes of determining full unit costs, costs identified as direct to the total organization must be allocated to various departments or programs.

This represents a major allocation problem. The salaries of various adminis-trative and support personnel in a hospital, for example, are direct costs to the hospital as a whole. When allocated to various separate departments or service functions—such as the intensive care unit, nursery, surgery, cafeteria, laboratories, and other components of the hospital—these salaries become indirect costs to these units. Although often arbitrary, the basis for such allo-cations should be reasonable and should be based on services provided to these related units.

As previously noted, some overhead items can be identified directly with specific programs or departments (that is, they are direct costs of these orga-nizational units). Others have to be arbitrarily allocated because they cannot be traced directly to the individual organizational units (they are indirect costs). Therefore, overhead often is divided into two categories. Actual over-head costs incurred by an organizational unit typically are recorded by means of an overhead clearing account and some type of subsidiary record, such as a departmental expense analysis or overhead cost sheet. Allocated or applied overhead (indirect costs) is distributed through the use of predetermined rates.

One approach to the allocation of indirect costs involves the identifica-tion of a number of indirect cost pools. Each pool represents the full costs associated with some specific administrative or support function (which cannot be allocated directly to individual projects or activities), such as operation and maintenance of the physical plant (including utility costs); central stores, motor pool, computing center, or other internal service units; general building and equipment usage; and central administration. Note that with internal service units, some part of the operating costs can be assigned directly as organizational units access these services. Indirect costs often represent the fixed costs of these service units (the basic cost of having the ser-vices available).

Once these indirect cost pools are determined, they can be arrayed from the most general to the most specific with regards to the particular programs or activities for which indirect cost rates are to be established. Costs from the more general pools are allocated (or stepped down) to the more specific pools and finally, to the primary functions or activities of the organization. For example, central administrative functions incur space and utility costs, and these indirect costs must be allocated to this pool before it can be allocated, in turn, to other functions. The indirect cost rate is finally determined by divid-ing the total direct costs associated with a given program or activity into the total indirect costs allocated to that function. Through this approach, it is possible to determine the impacts on the full costs of individual programs, projects, or activities arising from changes in these indirect costs.

Underapplication or overapplication of overhead may develop when pre-determined rates are used, and significant differences might arise from month to month. However, if the cost-approximation methods have produced reliable estimates, these accumulated differences should become relatively insignificant by the end of the fiscal year.

Standard Costs and Variance Analysis

Standard costs relate the cost of production to some predetermined indexes of operational efficiency. If actual production costs vary from these standards, management must determine the reasons for the deviation and whether it is controllable or noncontrollable with respect to the responsible organizational unit. Misdirected efforts, inadequate equipment, defective materials, or any one of a number of other factors can be identified and eliminated through a standard cost system. In short, standard costs provide a means of cost control through the application of variance analysis.

Standard cost systems have received broad application in the private sector. Their use in government and in the not-for-profit area, however, has been very limited. Nevertheless, such standards have potential application in a number of organizational environments.

In setting up standards, optimal or desired (planned) unit costs and related workload measures are established for each job or activity. Workload measures usually focus on time-and-effort indexes, such as number of persons served per hour, yards of dirt moved per day, or more generally, volume of activity per unit of time. After these measures are established, total variances can be determined by comparing actual results with planned performance. Price, rate, or spending variances should then be determined for differences between standard and actual costs. Quantity or efficiency variances can be developed for measured differences between actual and standard usage. Knowledge of differences in terms of cost (price) and usage (efficiency) enables the manager to identify more clearly the cause and responsibility for significant deviations from planned performance.

Although there are no hard-and-fast methods for establishing cost standards, workload and unit cost data from previous years serve as a logical starting point. More detailed studies may be required to determine the quantity and cost of personal services, materials, equipment, and overhead associated with particular kinds of effort or volume of activity. Unit costs can be estimated for each of these cost elements by adjusting trend data for expected changes during the next fiscal period. Standards should be established for each of the cost elements entering into a given job or operation. These standards can then be combined to establish a unit cost standard for the particular type of work, activity category, or program element.

Standard costs should be systematically reviewed and revised when found to be out-of-line with prevailing cost conditions. Changes in these standards may be required when new methods are introduced, policies are changed, wage rates or material costs increase, or significant changes occur in the efficiency of operations. Furthermore, standard costs are local in their application; such standards often will differ from organization to organization, reflecting different labor conditions, wage rates, service delivery problems, and operation methods.

Responsibility Accounting and Performance Evaluation

The concept of responsibility accounting has emerged to accommodate the need for management information within an organization at a more specific level of detail than can be provided by procedures of financial accounting. Responsibility accounting recognizes various responsibility centers within an organization and reflects plans and actions of these centers by assigning pertinent costs and revenues to them.[8] Ideally, the design of an organizational structure and a management control system should be interdependent. In practice, however, the organizational structure usually is in place and taken as a given when control systems are developed or modified.

Responsibility and Cost Centers

Responsibility accounting attempts to report results (actual performance) so that (1) significant variances from planned performance can be identified; (2) reasons for the variances can be determined; (3) responsibility can be fixed; and (4) timely action can be taken to correct problems. This information is reported to managers who are directly responsible for an activity or operation, as well as to the next higher level of management. Under this approach, departments, programs, and functions are referred to as responsibility centers. In municipal government, for example, the chief of police might receive separate reports on the cost of operations of the traffic control division, the vice squad, the detective division, the forensic laboratory, and so forth so that each unit can be held accountable for its respective area of responsibility.

In the private sector, responsibility centers may take several forms: (1) a *cost center* is the smallest segment of activity or area of responsibility for which costs are accumulated; (2) a *profit center* is a segment of a business, often called a division, that is responsible for both revenue and expenses, and (3) an *investment center,* like a profit center, is responsible both for revenue and expenses but also for related investments of capital. Outside of relatively large corporations, the cost center is the most common building block for responsibility accounting. In fact, in many applications the terms cost center and responsibility center often are used interchangeably.

Costs charged to responsibility centers should be separated between direct and indirect costs. Not all direct costs are controllable at the responsibility center level. Therefore, direct expenses should be further broken down between those which are controllable and noncontrollable at the responsibility center level. A distinction sometimes is made between a cost center, as one that is fully burdened with indirect costs, and a *service center,* which may be assigned only the direct portion of overhead.

The ability to control cost is a matter of degree. A controllable cost has been defined as any cost that is subject to the influence of a given manager for a given period of time. Responsibility accounting focuses on human responsibility, placing emphasis on the work of specific in relation to well-defined areas of responsibility. Managers often inherit the effects of their predecessors' decisions. The long-term effects of costs such as depreciation, long-term lease arrangements, and the like seldom qualify as controllable costs on the performance report of a specific responsibility center manager.

To illustrate this point, consider the costs of nursing services in a hospital. The extent to which these costs are controllable at the responsibility or cost center level depends on the policies of top management regarding intensive care, the lead time available for planning the number of nurses in relation to patient load, the availability of short-term or part-time help, and so on. Some nursing managers may have relatively little control over such cost-influencing factors. These factors must be taken into account when judging performance. Clearly, an item such as depreciation on the hospital building is outside the realm of controllable costs at the responsibility center level.

Performance Reports

Most performance measurement models in the private sector are tied to profits, for example, profit percentage (profit divided by sales), return on investment (profit divided by initial investment), or residual income (profit minus deduction for capital costs). At the cost center level, however, profits are not a viable measure. Rather, performance most often is measured by comparing actual costs against a budget. Thus a *variance* can be defined as the difference between the amount budgeted for a particular activity (during a given period) and the actual cost of carrying out that activity. Variances may be positive (under budget) or negative (over budget).

Performance reports usually are aggregated from the bottom up. An array of detailed expenditure categories may be monitored within a given cost center (for example, as various objects of expenditure or line items). These categories may be aggregated (and reported to the next level in the management hierarchy) into a single comparison. Such comparisons often are made in terms of the actual costs of personal services (salaries, wages, and employee benefits) and of operations (all other direct costs) versus the amounts budgeted for these broad categories. Specific items might be broken out from operations (for example, travel, computing, and rental charges), depending on the nature of the cost center's activities (and the needs of management). This aggregation/selective reporting supports the concept of management by exception; at each level in the organizational hierarchy, the manager's attention can be concentrated on the variance from the budget items deemed to be most important.

An alternative reporting format would be to group the data according to predetermined program elements. This approach is particularly applicable where a program budget format has been adopted. The aggregation of data would then proceed by subprograms and programs. Yet another approach is to report costs by level of service (particularly applicable where a zero base budget format has been adopted). The costs associated with providing a minimum level of service during a given period and with increments of service above this minimum can provide important management insights for future planning.

Performance reporting can be undertaken without a full-blown responsibility accounting system supported by designated cost centers. Performance data can be developed for management purposes independent of the budget and control accounts. In fact, this kind of performance reporting has been used in many organizations for some time, particularly in the justification of budget requests. It also has been used as a management control mechanism for assessing cost and work progress where activities are fairly routine and repetitive.

Under this approach, units of work are identified and changes in quantity (and, on occasion, quality) of such units are measured as a basis for analyzing financial requirements. The impacts of various levels of service can be tested, and an assessment can be made of changes in the size of the client groups to be served. This approach is built on the assumption that certain fixed costs remain fairly constant regardless of the level of service provided and that certain variable costs change with the level of service or the size of the clientele served. Marginal costs for each additional increment of service provided can be determined through such an approach. With the application of appropriate budgetary guidelines, these costs then can be converted into total cost estimates.

Responsibility Accounting and MBO

The emphasis on controllable costs and budgeted results in responsibility accounting makes it a good supporting companion to the procedures of management by objectives. MBO involves the joint formulation of goals and objectives by a manager and his or her superior.[9] Plans for achieving these objectives within some identified time period also are set forth.

MBO plans often take a form that is amenable to responsibility accounting in that they include a budget with supplementary objectives, such as levels of safety and staff development, that may not be incorporated in the budget. The performance of the manager is then evaluated through these budgeted objectives. An MBO budget is negotiated between a particular manager and his or her superiors for a particular period with a particular set of expected internal and external influences in mind. Thus, managers are not held responsible for costs that are beyond their control and, consequently, may be willing to accept assignments that evidence more than the usual management challenges.

Responsibility versus Blame

Variances, budgeted results, and other techniques of responsibility accounting are relatively neutral devices. When viewed positively, they can provide managers with significant means of improving future decisions. They also can assist in the delegation of decision responsibility to lower levels within an organization. These techniques, however, frequently are misused as negative management tools—as means of finding fault or placing blame. This negative use stems, in large part, from a misunderstanding of the rationale of responsibility accounting.

Responsibility accounting seeks to assign accountability to those individuals who have the greatest potential influence, on a day-to-day basis, over the costs in question. It seeks to determine which individuals in an organization are in the best position to explain why a specific outcome has occurred. It is the reporting responsibility of these individuals to explain the outcome regardless of the degree of their control or influence over the results.[10]

It is easy to criticize the concept of controllability. Nearly every cost is affected by more than one factor. Energy prices, for example, are influenced by various external forces, and energy usage is influenced by more than one manager within an organization. By the same token, a purchasing manager may have some influence over unit prices but relatively little influence over the use of the materials purchases. In some cases, however, the purchasing manager may influence the results of material usage, particularly if he purchased inferior quality materials or was locked into a bidding process that resulted in the acquisition of materials that only met minimum specifications.

Passing the buck is an all-too-pervasive tendency in any large organization. When responsibility is firmly fixed, however, this tendency is supposedly minimized. Nevertheless, a delicate balance must be maintained between the careful delineation of responsibility on the one hand and a too-rigid separation of responsibility on the other. When responsibility is overly prescribed, many activities may fall between the cracks. This problem is particularly evident when two or more activities are interdependent. Under such circumstances, responsibility cannot be delegated too low in the organization but must be maintained at a level that will ensure cooperation among the units that must interact if the activities are to be carried out successfully.

Summary: Future-Oriented Accounting Information

A basic tenet in strategic management is that costs should be incurred only if by so doing the organization can be expected to move toward the achievement of predetermined goals and objectives. The primary concern of financial accounting is the accurate and objective recording of past events (financial transactions). What is needed is an approach that will provide information for improved decisions in the context of strategic management which is future-oriented. This is the basic objective of managerial accounting.

This chapter has focused on two basic functions of managerial accounting—cost determination and cost control—and on the more specific techniques of cost accounting and responsibility accounting, which support these basic functions. The first step in controlling costs is to determine how costs function under various conditions. This process is called *cost approximation* or *cost estimation*. It involves an attempt to find predictable relationships (cost functions) between a dependent variable (cost) and one or more independent variables (organizational activities). Several methods for approximating cost functions were discussed in this chapter, the regression methods being the most reliable.

Whenever the full cost of a service or product must be determined, costs must be allocated according to their variable, fixed, direct, and indirect components. Various accounting mechanisms must be maintained to ensure the proper recording of cost flow. These mechanisms, for the most part, are embodied in the procedures of cost accounting.

Responsibility accounting seeks to assign accountability to those sectors of an organization where day-to-day influence can be exercised over the costs in question. The concept of controllable costs, that is, any cost that can be influenced by a given cost center manager for a given period, is a key to responsibility accounting. The emphasis on controllable costs and budgeted results makes responsibility accounting a good supporting component of strategic management.

Notes

1. Robert G. May, Gerhard G. Muller, and Thomas H. Williams, *A Brief Introduction to the Managerial and Social Uses of Accounting* (Englewood Cliffs, N.J.: Prentice-Hall, 1975), pp. 1–2; Robert J. Mockler, *The Management Control Process* (New York: Appleton-Century-Crofts, 1972), pp. 95–96; Charles T. Horn-

gren, *Introduction to Management Accounting* (Englewood Cliffs, N.J.: Prentice-Hall, 1978), p. 4; Robert N. Anthony, *Management Accounting Principles* (Homewood, Ill.: Richard D. Irwin, 1965), pp. 185–187.

2. Robert Zemsky, Randall Porter, and Laura P. Oedel, "Decentralized Planning: To Share Responsibility," *Educational Record* 59 (Summer 1978):244.

3. Robert N. Anthony and James S. Reese, *Management Accounting: Text and Cases* (Homewood, Ill.: Richard D. Irwin, 1975), p. 422.

4. James H. Rossell and William W. Frasure, *Managerial Accounting* (Columbus, Ohio: Charles E. Merrill, 1972), p. 4.

5. Leo Herbert, Larry N. Killough, and Alan Walter Steiss, *Governmental Accounting and Control* (Belmont, Calif.: Brooks/Cole, 1984), p. 212.

6. Horngren, *Introduction to Management Accounting,* p. 225.

7. For a further discussion of these procedures, see Alan Walter Steiss, *Management Control in Government* (Lexington, Mass.: Lexington Books, 1982), pp. 67–71.

8. Horngren, *Introduction to Management Accounting,* p. 246.

9. For further discussion of this point, see Steiss, *Management Control in Government,* chapter 7.

10. Horngren, *Introduction to Management Accounting,* p. 252.

11
Implementation of Strategic Management

T he implementation of any new management system can be a trau-
matic experience. At a minimum, changes in management procedures will impact the ways in which plans are made, programs are
developed, and performance is evaluated within the organization. New
patterns of communications will emerge, and new information—presumably
better information—will be available to assist managers in carrying out their
decision-making and administrative responsibilities. Efforts to improve the
management system may also uncover the need for changes in the established
structure and functional interfaces within the organization. And these organizational changes may be even more unsettling than the procedural changes
necessary to implement the newly adopted management system.

Planning, Budgeting, Control, and Evaluation

Any organization can gain several significant benefits from the implementation of a strategic management system: (a) more comprehensive plans, based
on more thorough analyses of the relevant costs and benefits of alternative
courses of action; (b) more appropriate budgets to ensure the most effective
allocation of organizational resources to achieve its goals and objectives; and
(c) better management control, that is, greater assurance that activities will be
carried out as efficiently and effectively as possible in accomplishing organizational objectives. Strategic management provides a basis on which to measure performance of individuals and of the organization as a whole. Feedback
from such evaluations can be used to determine appropriate modifications in
resource allocations and organizational structure to meet environmental
demands. Planning, budgeting, control, and evaluation are complementary
responsibilities of management; one cannot operate effectively without the
others (see figure 11–1). These management functions are interdependent
and essential to the overall well-being, and sometimes the survival, of any
complex organization.

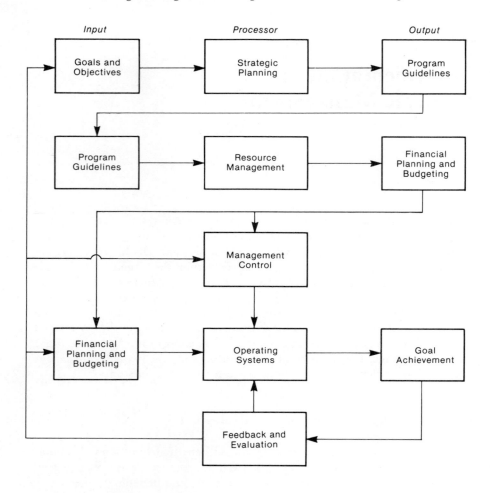

Figure 11–1. The Strategic Management Process

If the implementation of strategic management is successful, the organization will be managed in a different way; after all, this is the basic objective of such a system. This success, however, may present the most significant challenge because of the human elements involved—attitudes, perceptions, misconceptions, and biases regarding the manifest and latent intents of strategic management.

Implementation of strategic management may be more difficult in some organizations because system changes are likely to represent greater departures from current practices. Many of the basic concepts of strategic management are taken for granted in the private sector—accrual accounting procedures, cost and responsibility centers, financial ratio and cost-benefit analyses, program budgeting, the relationship between individual assignments and performance results, and so forth. In many profit-oriented organizations, a formal strategic management system may be viewed as a refinement of existing concepts and procedures and not the introduction of a fundamentally new process.

Public organizations often do not have even the rudiments of satisfactory management planning or control procedures, however. At the same time, the climate essential for the functioning of such a system may not be readily available. Thus, the introduction of strategic management can represent substantial change in the established way of doing business, which can be viewed with considerable alarm (and generate signficant resistance) by those within the organization.

Commitment of Top Management

Anthony and Herzlinger have suggested that "the driving force behind a new system must come from top management, . . . it is unlikely that a majority of operating managers will voluntarily embrace a new system in advance of its installation, let alone be enthusiastic advocates of it."[1] The support of top management means more than mere acquiescence to the system as a necessary evil. Responsible managers in the organization must be willing to devote sufficient time and effort to fully understand the general concepts and objectives of strategic management. They must explain to principal subordinates how these procedures will help them and the organization as a whole. If problems arise during the design and implementation of these procedures, top management must listen to opposing viewpoints and then make decisions that will resolve such problems and remove any impediments. The organization's leadership may also have to battle outside interest groups, which might otherwise seek to prevent the adoption of such systems. Management often uses the excuse that it has no choice but to implement certain procedures to meet externally imposed requirements. In so doing, however, the basis has been laid for less-than-enthusiastic support (and perhaps organized resistance) from within the organization.

Top management must set the example in terms of the importance of the system design effort by their willingness to take time away from other pressing problems to clearly articulate goals and objectives and to discuss management information needs and expectations. Top management's participation in these efforts will help to convince organizational personnel at the various operating levels to devote the necessary and appropriate time and effort to the task.

Education through Participation

Advocates of strategic management "should understand that the installation of a new system is a political process. It involves pressure, persuasion, and compromise in proper proportions as is the case with any important political action." Efforts to involve organizational personnel in the development of the strategic management system can help to reduce negative attitudes. Operating managers will be more likely to support the strategic management system if they are convinced that, on balance, it will benefit them in carrying out their assigned responsibilities. The new system should provide operating managers with better information about the activities and performance of those staff members for whom they are responsible. With this information the operating managers should have a better basis for directing and controlling the efforts of subordinates. On the other hand, uncertainty about the manager's performance is also likely to be reduced, and depending on personal interpretations of how such information will be received by "higher ups," an operating manager may resist the system.

The preparation of manuals of procedures and other explanatory materials is a necessary part of the educational process. These materials are not the most important part of the process, however. Management at all levels within the organization must be convinced that the new system, in fact, is going to be used and that it will help them do a better job. The best way to implement new systems is to have managers discuss the new system with their subordinates, who then carry the message to their staff, and so on. Since the teachers must themselves become more fully indoctrinated, this process aids in the education of all those involved.

The president of a major northeastern university, for example, initiated a new management information system by installing computer terminals in the offices of all the vice presidents, substituting electronic mail messages for the more traditional written memoranda. The vice presidents quickly adapted to this system (as a matter of survival) and began communicating with academic deans and other administrators through the same process. Once a system goes into operations, even on a trial basis, the use of the management information that it generates is the best educational device available.

It may not be feasible to install a strategic management system across the whole organization all at one time. Initial efforts may be concentrated on those segments of the organization where the results of such improvement will be most visible. Demonstrated success in one area often can lead to more general acceptance of the system throughout the organization.

It is difficult to be specific about an appropriate period required to successfully design and implement a strategic management system. In a large, complex organization, two to three years may elapse from the time the decision is made to initiate systems development and the date that the system is fully implemented. The time available is never quite enough. There always will be worthwhile refinements that could be made. However, if enough time were allowed for all the fine-tuning efforts, the system might never go into operation.

A Final Caveat

It is important not to oversell the potential of the new system, however. Aaron Wildavsky offers a number of rules applicable to the implementation of any new management system.[3] The *rule of skepticism* suggests that, when presented with the initial concept of an improved management system, organizational officials should exercise a good deal of skepticism. The *rule of delay* cautions officials to give the system adequate time to develop and to be prepared to face periodic setbacks in its implementation. As Wildavsky observes, "If it works at all, it won't work soon." The *rule of anticipated anguish* is a restatement of Murphy's Law—"most of the things that can go wrong, will." Wildavsky suggests that management must be prepared to invest personnel, time, and money to overcome breakdowns in the system as they occur. And the *rule of discounting* asserts that anticipated benefits to be derived from the new management system should significantly outweigh the estimated costs of mounting the system. The costs involved in developing an improved management system must be incurred before the benefits are achieved. Therefore, the tendency is to inflate future benefits, to oversell the system, to compensate for the increased commitment of present resources.

Even with the best strategic management system, data must still be analyzed and interpreted by managers, and based on this information, judgment must be exercised in decision making. Allowance must be made for the inadequacies or unavailability of data. Although the system can provide certain decision parameters, it cannot make decisions. Managers must continue to exercise judgment regarding the exceptions that prove the rules. Such caveats must be emphasized during the educational processes. Otherwise, managers who are skeptical or are aware of such limitations will regard the whole effort as the work of impractical theorists.

The notion of Maxwell's demon was introduced in chapter 2 as an allegory for anything that contributes organization to a disorganized or chaotic situation. In this context, the term *demon* refers to a positive genius, designed to address a host of problems within an organization. The objective is to reduce management costs as a percentage of total organizational costs and to satisfy the "increasingly voracious appetite for decision-influencing management information."[4] On the other hand, Maxwell's demon can become a resource-demanding devil, an organizational black hole that can absorb considerable energy with little apparent payoff. The careful design and implementation of a strategic management system, to include the elements outlined in this book, can contribute significantly toward the demon-genius—or at least help avoid the demon-devil.

Notes

1. Robert N. Anthony and Regina Herzlinger, *Management Control in Non-profit Organizations* (Homewood, Ill.: Richard D. Irwin, 1975), p. 316.

2. Ibid., p. 323.

3. Aaron Wildavsky, "Review of *Politicians, Bureaucrats and the Consultant,*" *Science* 28 (December 1973):1335–1338.

4. Robert C. Heterick, "Administrative Support Services," *Cause/Effect* 4 (November 1981):29.

Indexes

Subject Index

Author Index

About the Author

Alan Walter Steiss is associate provost for research and director of sponsored programs at Virginia Polytechnic Institute and State University. He received his A.B. in psychology and sociology from Bucknell University and his M.A. and Ph.D. in urban and regional planning from the University of Wisconsin. Dr. Steiss has served at Virginia Tech as director of the Center for Urban and Regional Studies, chairman of the Urban and Regional Planning Program and Urban Affairs Program, chairman of the Division of Environmental and Urban Systems, and associate dean for research and graduate studies of the College of Architecture and Urban Studies. He was formerly the head of statewide planning for the state of New Jersey and has served as consultant to the states of Wisconsin, New Jersey, Maryland, Virginia, South Carolina, New York, Alaska, and Hawaii, the Trust Territory of the Pacific, and the Federal-State Land Use Planning Commission for Alaska. Dr. Steiss is the author of several books, including *Systemic Planning: Theory and Application* (with Anthony J. Catanese); *Public Budgeting and Management; Models for the Analysis and Planning of Urban Systems; Urban Systems Dynamics; Dynamic Change and the Urban Ghetto* (with Michael Harvey, John Dickey, and Bruce Phelps); *Local Government Finance: Capital Facilities Planning and Debt Administration; Performance Administration* (with Gregory A. Daneke); *Governmental Accounting and Control* (with Leo Herbert and Larry N. Killough); and *Management Control in Government.* He has contributed to numerous professional journals in the United States and abroad.